"Marukobune", the traditional sailing boats in the Lake Biwa region, Japan.

Kumi Makino

Kamakura Women's University

YUZANKAKU, Inc.

Tokyo

Kumi Makino is Professor in the Department of Education, Kamakura Women's University, Japan. Her research theme is comparative study of lake environments and cultures. She is co-editor of and a contributor to Report on the Construction of a Maruko-bune Boat, the Traditional Wooden Boat Formerly Used for Transport on Lake Biwa, which appeared as Research Report of the Lake Biwa Museum, no. 13 (1999) (in Japanese), Kodaiko no Kouko-gaku [Archaeology of World Lakes] (2000) (in Japanese), and author of Biwako no Dento-teki Mokuzosen no Henyou ["Marukobune", the Traditional Sailing Boats in the Lake Biwa Region, Japan](2008) (in Japanese).

"Marukobune", the traditional sailing boats in the Lake Biwa region, Japan.
Copyright ©2013 Kumi Makino
Text ©2008 Kumi Makino『琵琶湖の伝統的木造船の変容―丸子船を中心に―』

Published by YUZANKAKU, Inc.
6-9 Fujimi 1-chome, Chiyoda-ku, Tokyo 102-0071
URL   http://www.yuzankaku.co.jp
E-mail   info@yuzankaku.co.jp

ISBN978-4-639-02262-6 C3021 Printed in Japan
First edition, Feb 2013

All rights reserved. No part of this book may be reproduced in any form or by any means without the prior written consent of the publisher.

Contents

Preface   05
List of Figures, Photos, and Tables   15
Glossary   23

Chapter I Introduction
(1) Geographical Background of Boat Use in the Lake Biwa Region   30
(2) General History of the Lake Biwa Region and its Water Transportation   42

Chapter II Building the Marukobune Replica and Related Researches
(1) Marukobune Reconstruction Project   68
(2) Carpenter's Tools for Traditional Boats in the Lake Biwa Region   89
(3) The Marukobune Tankentai   96

Chapter III The Rise and Fall of Traditional Boats on Lake Biwa
(1) The Rise and Fall of the Traditional Boats as seen through the Life of a Shipwright   106
(2) Number and Usage of Marukobune   113
(3) Number and Use of the Farming Boat, or Tabune   128
(4) Statistical Data of Traditional Boat Use in Each County in the Early 20th Century   140

Chapter IV The Hull Structure and Evolution of Marukobune: A Hypothesis
(1) Shiki-Expanded Structure   176
(2) Function of Omogi   187
(3) Transition of Marukobune's Role Reflected in its Bow Shape   195
(4) Another Element of the Bow, Heita   207

Summary   213

Reference   216
Index   233

Preface

The earthquakes which struck, Kobe in January 1995, and Tohoku in March 2011 were a psychic, as well as a physical shock for Japan. In a society that was considered both civilized and highly developed, these calamitous events created, beyond the visible damage, sudden changes in basic infrastructure, such as power outages, shortages of food, loss of sanitation and more. Most of the conveniences of modern life were suddenly compromised. People's lives were severely impaired.

Often forgotten is the fact that it was only a few decades ago that Japan adopted such modern infrastructure and technology on a wide scale. These earthquakes were reminders of how rapidly people have lost the ability to confront natural events. Our relationship with nature has been sacrificed, in exchange for the rapid growth of the economy.

We call this process acculturation, referring to the loss of traditional culture in the face of rapid development and the adoption of new information from foreign countries. One of such changes happened in Japan during the first half of the 20th century, a period that was in many ways a turning point for Japanese culture. Rapid modernization and education replaced the wisdom, techniques and values that are now considered traditionally Japanese. The culture of traditional boats underwent unprecedented changes. Boats and ships had been an important component of Japanese daily life, as Japan is composed of a large number of islands surrounded by the sea. However, they were also very important around the lakes and rivers. An enormously rich and varied maritime culture existed; one that is now largely forgotten.

Traditional wooden boats, especially marukobune (Fig. 1), of Lake Biwa, reflect these cultural changes, and the main purpose of this book is to provide an example to readers of an exploration of our natural environment through the context of traditional boats. Historically, the local people's relationship to Lake Biwa was shaped by these boats, and hopefully this study can teach us

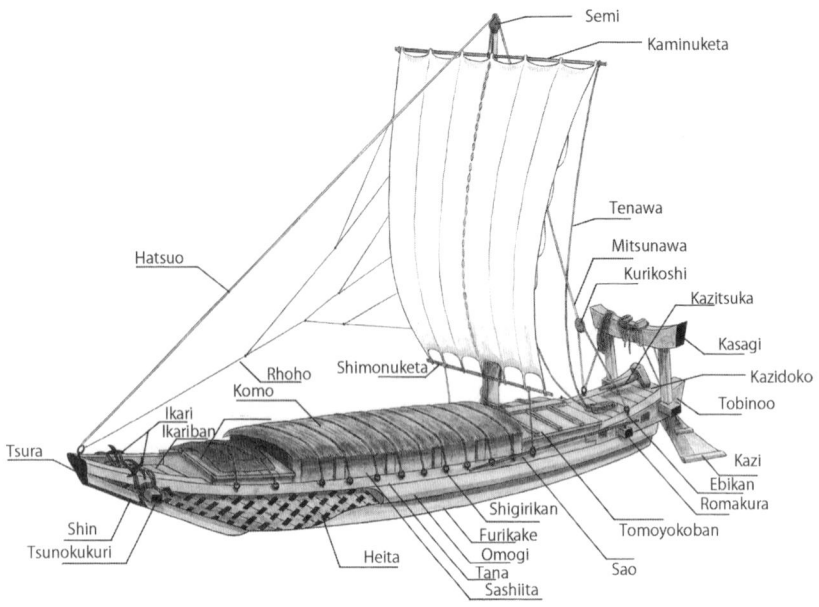

Fig. 1 Marukobune.

something about how we understand our modern environment, as well as our future.

The idea of writing this book was inspired when a shipwright named Sanshiro Matsui unexpectedly passed away. Not only was he a good friend to the author, but he was also an important source of information about the traditional boats in the Lake Biwa region (Photo. 1). One day, after a normal workday in his boatyard, he returned home in the evening, took a bath, abruptly fell, and passed away at the age of 92. Mr. Matsui lived through the period when people had an intimate relationship with nature. His death was a stark reminder of the depth of traditional knowledge of his generation and, as the last shipwright of Lake Biwa, it was also the end of a craft culture in the region.

From the historian's perspective, Mr. Matsui's passing was also emblematic of the fragility of the type of intimate knowledge he possessed. Much of what he and his contemporaries knew about traditional techniques and ways

Photo. 1 A shipwright, Mr. Sanshiro Matsui.

of life were never recorded, but part of a long oral tradition. Unfortunately the rapid changes in contemporary society have effectively erased much of this wisdom. The marukobune reconstruction project was an attempt to preserve as much of this information as possible.

Until the first half of the last century, there were many types of wooden boats sailing on Lake Biwa. The lake was regarded as an important route in the ancient period for connecting the northern, southern, eastern and western regions of Japan, a kind of transportation hub, to use a modern term. Lake Biwa was also an important source of food, both directly from fishing and in irrigating croplands of the region. Both these elements have faded with time, as urbanization of the lakeshore brought new transportation systems and farmland was squeezed out.

The wooden boats sailing on Lake Biwa were roughly classified into marubune and hiratabune. Maru means round in Japanese, so marukobune get their name from the cross section of the hull, which is roughly circular (Fig. 2). Hirata, which means square in Japanese (Fig. 3), describes fishing boats and farming boats (the latter called tabune), which have rectangular

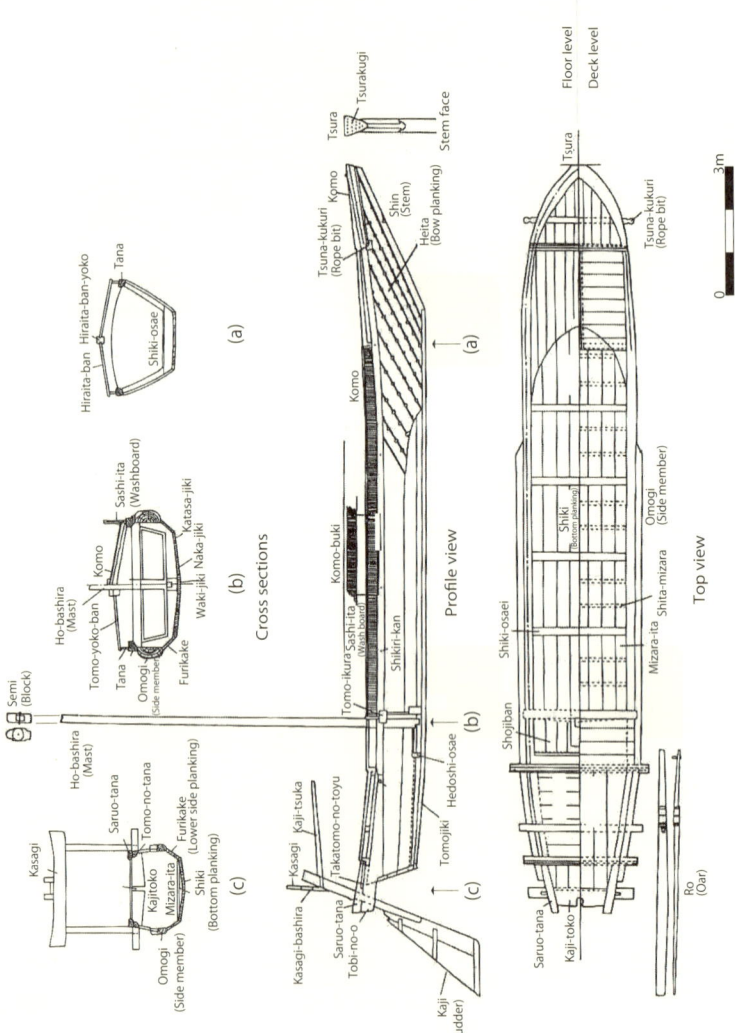

Fig. 2 Marukobune (100koku).

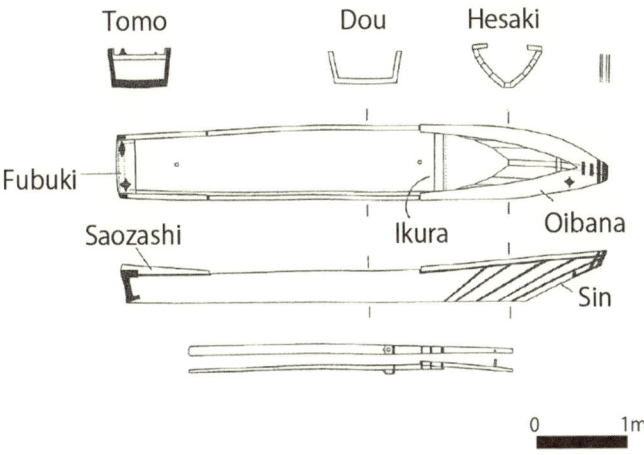

Fig. 3 Hiratabune.

cross sections.

"Boat" and "ship" can be expressed by one of two Chinese characters: 舟 or 船. Both characters are read as "fune" or "sen" in Japanese. 舟 usually means a simpler boat, while 船 usually denotes a ship. There is no distinctive form between singular or plural. A type of boat or ship is qualified by a word or words prefixed to fune or sen, sometimes with the change of the pronunciation of the first syllable. For example taraibune, and not taraifune (literally "tub boat") for the barrel-type boats found on Sado Island in the Sea of Japan.

The marukobune was a cargo boat particular to Lake Biwa. It had a leading role in trade until the 18th century, when it was supplanted first by railroads and then automobiles. Traditional marukobune also changed with the introduction of marine engines. In boatbuilding, a transition in materials - from wood to steel and fiberglass - ultimately also affected the smaller fishing and farming boats. Over time, the number of wooden boats decreased. The goal of this study is to shed light on the process of acculturation through an examination of the traditional wooden boats of Lake Biwa.

Material culture is the study of people's relationship with the natural environment, particularly through the production and use of objects in their social environment. The traditional wooden boats of Lake Biwa are an important subject, because the end of the era of wooden boats on the lake is within living memory of many people. Furthermore, there is a wealth of written information, such as historical and administrative documents. Fortunately, the author was able to conduct several research projects as a research scientist at the Lake Biwa Museum from 1991 to 2007. The core of the folklore data presented here was collected during the marukobune reconstruction project undertaken by the Lake Biwa Museum from 1992 through 1995 (see Chapter. II). It was about half a century after the last marukobune was built. The purpose of the project was to create a core exhibit for the museum, and to observe and record the actual marukobune building process.

   Another key goal was to collect information on how these boats were used in the past. The information was gathered and recorded through interviews with shipwrights and other local residents.

   Another project involved restoring the last marukobune (see Chapter. II), which dated from before the Second World War and had been converted to a powered vessel from its original sailing configuration. It was the last working marukobune on Lake Biwa. In 2003, the boat was purchased privately. The owner planned to modify the boat for tourism and asked Mr. Matsui to restore the vessel. This project provided a rare opportunity to see how marukobune were repaired, and to further understand how the shipwright worked.

   Many traditional customs are well preserved in Shiga Prefecture. Some local residents still remember marukobune and the period when marukobune were used. Through the marukobune reconstruction project the public was able to provide diverse information concerning the traditional boats of Lake Biwa in the middle of the 20th century (Photo. 2). The most valuable

Photo. 2   Reconstructed marukobune.

information collected concerned how traditional boats were used, as well as the history of their decline and disappearance.

A large number of government records were also used for this study. Fortunately, much documentation survived the Second World War, as Shiga Prefecture is adjacent to Kyoto, and was spared the bombing. These records include nearly all of the government records from the end of 19th century. The prefectural administration had historically kept many government records related to the lake and boats, given their importance to the region.

Unfortunately, no experimentation was conducted, documenting the sailing characteristics of the replica marukobune, as the main purpose of the project was to produce an exhibit for the museum. It was decided that a sailing study might result in damage to the boat. After the original Japanese edition of this book was published, the sailing performance was analyzed, using model boats, in a joint research project of the author and the Department of Maritime Technology at Osaka University. These results are included in this English edition in Chapter IV.

The traditional wooden boats of Lake Biwa provide an important key to understanding one aspect of the tide of modernization. It is hoped that this book will provide more understanding, and allow future generations to reflect on traditional ways of living with nature.

This book would not have been possible without the dedicated work of my research fellows. I wish to thank former Director Hiroya Kawanabe, Dr. Masaharu Yoda, Mr. Michinori Hashimoto, and the entire staff of the Lake Biwa Museum, for giving me the unique opportunity to work with the late Mr. Sanshiro Matsui, the last marukobune shipwright. Mr. Matsui's unparalleled knowledge of the region's boating culture, and his skills as a traditional shipwright were invaluable and provided the basis for this book. I would also like to thank marukobune explorers and other local people in the Lake Biwa region to work with me, also to Professor Emeritus Masashi Chikamori, Professor Yoshito Abe of Keio University, to Professor Emeritus Shuzo Koyama and Professor Emeritus Tomoya Akimichi of the National Museum of Ethnology, also to members of the Sailing Yacht Research Association of Japan especially to Professor Yutaka Masuyama of Kanazawa Institute of Technology, Professor Emeritus Satoshi Matsuki of Kobe University of Mercantile Marine, Professor Naoya Umeda of Osaka University, to Professor Takeshi Kinoshita of the Tokyo University, and all other colleagues for providing important assistance from a variety of academic fields.

    I was very fortunate to find several people to help me in the preparation of this English version. In particular, Mr. Nobuo Tani's patient and diligent work in translating my manuscript, and guiding it through the editing process. I also want to thank my editors, Mr. Douglas Brooks and

Mr. Patrick Utley, whose familiarity with sailing and traditional Japanese boatbuilding helped to make this text clearer for non-Japanese readers. I am also grateful to the Japan Society for the Promotion of Science for their financial help, Grant-in-Aid for Publication of Scientific Research Results. Without this funding, and the support of many friends and colleagues, this book would not have been possible.

Finally, I wish to thank my family, especially my daughter Yumi, for spending so much time with me in the fields while doing this research.

Kumi Makino
February 28th, 2012.

List of Figures, Photos, and Tables

<Figures>

Preface-Fig. 1 Marukobune. (Otsu City Mueum of History (ed.), 1993, p. 64.)

Preface-Fig. 2 Marukobune (100koku). (Makino 1995.)

Preface-Fig. 3 Hiratabune.

I-Fig. 1 Location of the Lake Biwa.

I-Fig. 2 Lake use information.

I-Fig. 3 Lake formation origin.

I-Fig. 4 Lakes used for passenger and cargo transportation.

I-Fig. 5 Tectonic lake use information.

I-Fig. 6 Glacier lake use information.

I-Fig. 7 Artificial lake use information.

I-Fig. 8 Faults and major roads in the Lake Biwa region. (Based on the data of The Headquarters for Earthquake Research Promotion, Japan.)

I-Fig. 9 Major rivers in the Lake Biwa region. (South, east, and west). (Drawing by M. Ota, LBM)

I-Fig. 10 Names of winds in different directions.

I-Fig. 11 The pattern of the circling currents and the currents in the Lake Biwa. (Okamoto 1974, pp. 59-61.)

I-Fig. 12 The currents and their names in regions. (Hashimoto 1999, p. 95.)

I-Fig. 13 Major sites in the Lake Biwa region where dugouts were excavated. (Otsu City Museum of History(ed.) 1993, p. 12.)

I-Fig. 14 A dugout excavated from Matsubaranaiko site, Late Jomon period. (Otsu City Museum of History (ed.) 1993, Fig. 1.)

I-Fig. 15 Site distribution in the Jomon period and the Yaoi period. (Kimura 1987, p. 56 & 68.)

I-Fig. 16 Traditional fishing methods on the Lake Biwa. (Shiga Prefectural Fisheries Experiment Station (ed.) 1910.)

I-Fig. 17 Boat figures drawn on Dotaku and pottery in Yayoi period. (Based on Sahara & Harunari 1997 p. 18, Photo. 21(1) & p. 19, Photo. 22(2).)
I-Fig. 18 Sailing routes from China and Korean Peninsula to Japan.
I-Fig. 19 Distribution of the Kofun period sites. (Kimura 1987, p. 80.)
I-Fig. 20 A boat model excavated from Irienaiko site, Kofun period. (Maihara Town Board of Education (ed.) 1988, pl. 58.)
I-Fig. 21 Sites where wooden model boats were excavated. (Otsu City Museum of History (ed.) 1993, p. 14.)
I-Fig. 22 A part of a semi-planked boat excavated at Irienaiko site. (Maihara Town Board of Education (ed.) 1988, pl. 71.)
I-Fig. 23 Location of the ancient capitals and timber supply. (Kimura 1987, p. 93.)
I-Fig. 24 Routes in the ancient period. (Kimura 1987, p. 113 and Otsu City Museum of History (ed.), 1993, p. 17.)
I-Fig. 25 Routes in the Medieval period. (Kimura 1987, p. 133.)
I-Fig. 26 Routes in the Azuchi-Momoyama period. (Kimura 1987, p. 176.)
I-Fig. 27 Shore protection structure in the 15th to 17th century from Sekinotsu site. (Based on Shiga Board of Education (ed.) 2004.)
I-Fig. 28 Opening of the westward sailing route.
II-Fig. 1 Metate method in Edo period, around the middle of 17th century. (Based on Yoshida 1977 (revised edition), Figs in pp. 194-195.)
II-Fig. 2 Joinning two planks.
II-Fig. 3 Sail cloth binding and Matsuemon weaving.
II-Fig. 4 Marukobune paper craft. (http://www.lbm.go.jp/kumi/maru_pc.pdf)
II-Fig. 5 Data base of traditional wooden boats in the Lake Biwa region. (http://www.lbm.go.jp/kumi/kenbun/maruko_top.html)
III-Fig. 1 The life history of a shipwright. (Makino 1999b, p. 16, Fig. 5.)
III-Fig. 2 The process of making lumber materials for boats. (Makino 1999c, p. 171, Fig. 16.)
III-Fig. 3 Changes of the boat lumber professionals. (Makino 1999c, p. 171,

Fig. 16.)

III-Fig. 4 Rise and fall of the traditional boats on the Lake Biwa region.

III-Fig. 5 Variation of sizes of marukobune, marubune, and kokaisen. (Makino 1999c, p. 164, Fig. 4.)

III-Fig. 6 The shoreline in 1869 (left) and the current shoreline (right).

III-Fig. 7 Washing space example(Kawaya) in Tomie family dwelling in Honjo Ward, Hikone. (Based on Y. Kada & A. Furukawa (eds.), 2000, p. 276, Fig. 4 & p. 279, Fig. 7.)

III-Fig. 8 Number of boats in each village in the Meiji period.

III-Fig. 9 Summary of boat statistics based on "Shigaken bussan-shi". (滋賀県物産誌)

III-Fig. 10 Use of boats in each county.

III-Fig. 11 Shiga County.

III-Fig. 12 Fishing boat in Katata region. (prepared by Human History Division, LBM.)

III-Fig. 13 Sosuibune. (prepared by Human History Division, LBM.)

III-Fig. 14 Kurita County.

III-Fig. 15 Shijimikakibune. (prepared by Human History Division, LBM.)

III-Fig. 16 Amiuchibune. (prepared by Human History Division, LBM.)

III-Fig. 17 Tsuribune. (prepared by Human History Division, LBM.)

III-Fig. 18 Yakatabune. (taken by M. Yoda, LBM.)

III-Fig. 19 Boat in Yamada region. (prepared by Human History Division, LBM.)

III-Fig. 20 Boat in Akanoi and Oroshimo region. (prepared by Human History Division, LBM.)

III-Fig. 21 Boat in Yamaga region. (taken by M. Yoda, LBM.)

III-Fig. 22 Yasu County.

III-Fig. 23 Tabune in Imahama region. (prepared by Human History Division, LBM.)

III-Fig. 24 Ushibune.

III-Fig. 25 Fishing boat in Ayame region. (prepared by Human History Division, LBM.)

III-Fig. 26 Tabune in Konohama region. (prepared by Human History Division, LBM.)

III-Fig. 27 Koga County.

III-Fig. 28 Gamo County.

III-Fig. 29 Tabune in the region between Omagari and Hachimanbori. (prepared by Human History Division, LBM.)

III-Fig. 30 Fishing boat in Okinoshima. (prepared by Human History Division, LBM.)

III-Fig. 31 Tabune in Okinoshima. (prepared by Human History Division, LBM.)

III-Fig. 32 Fishing boat in Chomeiji. (prepared by Human History Division, LBM.)

III-Fig. 33 Tabune in Notogawa region. (prepared by Human History Division, LBM.)

III-Fig. 34 Kanzaki County.

III-Fig. 35 Tabune in Notogawa region. (prepared by Human History Division, LBM.)

III-Fig. 36 Echi County.

III-Fig. 37 Inukami County.

III-Fig. 38 Fishing boat in Mitsuya region. (prepared by Human History Division, LBM.)

III-Fig. 39 Sakata County.

III-Fig. 40 Higashiazai County.

III-Fig. 41 Ika County.

III-Fig. 42 Nishiazai County.

III-Fig. 43 Takashima County.

III-Fig. 44 Tabune in Imazu region. (prepared by Human History Division, LBM.)

III-Fig. 45 Fishing boat in Kitafunaki. (prepared by Human History Division, LBM.)

III-Fig. 46 Ikadakumibune (raft assembly boat).

III-Fig. 47 Ikadahakobibune (raft towing boat).

IV-Fig. 1 Evolution phases of boat.

IV-Fig. 2 Classification of dugout's cross section according to the development of shiki and tana. (Deguchi 2001, p. 6.)

IV-Fig. 3 The restored shape of the semi-planked boat excavated from the Shimonaga site. (Yokota 2004, p. 25, Fig. 3.)

IV-Fig. 4 Boat models of fork-shaped semi-planked boat (left) and semi-planked boat (right). (Matsusaka City & Matsusaka City, Board of Education (eds.) 2003.)

IV-Fig. 5 Distribution of Shiki-expanded dugout. (Deguchi 1987, p. 466, Fig. 9.)

IV-Fig. 6 Distribution of Tana-expanded dugout. (Deguchi 1987, p. 476, Fig. 17)

IV-Fig. 7 Elements of marukobune evolution.

IV-Fig. 8 Do-bune type vs. bocho type.

IV-Fig. 9 Cross section comparison of marukobune with different cargo capacity.

IV-Fig. 10 Distribution of raft. (Deguchi 1987, p. 458, Fig. 4.)

IV-Fig. 11 Evolution from semi-planked boat to planked boat. (Based on Ishii 1983, p. 47.)

IV-Fig. 12 Cross section comparison of marukobune in different period.

IV-Fig. 13 The restored shape of the semi-planked boat excavated from the Anap Pond, south Korea. (Kim 1997, p. 41, Fig. 3.)

IV-Fig. 14 The max preserved width of dugouts from the sites in Japan, Korea and China.

IV-Fig. 15 Marukobune with shin(stem) and without shin.

IV-Fig. 16 Sekibune. (Ishii 1983, p. 67, Fig. 86.)

List of Figures, Photos, and Tables

IV-Fig. 17 Kuruma hayabune (boat with wheel). (Shiga University Archival Museum (ed.), 1999, p. 12.)

IV-Fig. 18 Bow shapes. (Ishii,1983.)

IV-Fig. 19 Marukobune from the photo taken by E. S. Morce. (Drawing by K. Makino based on a photo from the E. S. Morse Collection, Peabody Museum of Salem.)

<Photos>

Pre-Photo. 1 A shipwright, Mr. Sanshiro Matsui.

Pre-Photo. 2 Reconstructed marukobune. (taken by M. Yoda, LBM.)

II-Photo. 1 A libation onto the root of the serected tree. Makino 1999c,p. 167, Fig. 7.

II-Photo. 2 Cutting and loading the timbers. (Makino 1999c,p. 167. Fig. 8.)

II-Photo. 3 Arrival of the logs at the boatyard. (Makino 1995, p. 2.)

II-Photo. 4 Cutting roughly into boards. (Makino 1995, p. 2.)

II-Photo. 5 Drying planks.

II-Photo. 6 Carpenter uses Sumitsubo to measurement marks on boards. (Makino 1999c,p. 168, Fig. 9.)

II-Photo. 7 Driving nails into boards. (Makino 1995, p. 3.)

II-Photo. 8 Shiki building.

II-Photo. 9 Nail holes on shiki.

II-Photo. 1 Preparing furikake.

II-Photo. 11 Furikake under omogi. (from restoration project.)

II-Photo. 12 Stem raising. (Makino 1999c,p. 168. Fig. 12.)

II-Photo. 13 Caulking between stem and shiki. (Makino 1995, p. 3.)

II-Photo. 14 Attaching omogi. (Makino 1999c, .168. Fig. 11.)

II-Photo. 15 Omogi on furikake (from restoration project.)

II-Photo. 16 Working with surinokogiri for caulking. (Makino 1995, p. 3.)

II-Photo. 17 Finishing the seams for caulking using surinokogiri.

II-Photo. 18 Rear view of marukobune with kasagi(mast gallows). (Makino

1995, p. 2.)

II-Photo. 19 Cabin/hold covered with kakiita(wash board) and komo(straw mat).

II-Photo. 20 Cabin roof framing mounted on the sheer strake.

II-Photo. 21 Inside of the cabin.

II-Photo. 22 Launching ceremony. (taken by M. Yoda, LBM.)

II-Photo. 23 Towing the marukobune. (taken by M. Yoda, LBM.)

II-Photo. 24 Pre-exhibition. (taken by M. Yoda, LBM.)

II-Photo. 25 Moving into the museum under the construction. (taken by M. Yoda, LBM.)

II-Photo. 26 Tools used for tree felling and rough cutting.

II-Photo. 27 Measurement tools.

II-Photo. 28 Tools for fine work.

II-Photo. 29 Nail driving tools.

II-Photo. 30 Tools for caulking process.

II-Photo. 31 Hashikake activity.

II-Photo. 32 Detail observations throughout marukobune while cleaning.

II-Photo. 33 Sail handling test by using a model of marukonbune.

II-Photo. 34 The museum activities with the paper craft boat kit.

II-Photo. 35 Boat models displayed with cargo.

IV-Photo. 1 Eguri bune in Oga peninsula, Akita prefecture.

IV-Photo. 2 Morotabune (right) in Miho shrine in Shimane Prefecture.

IV-Photo. 3 Sabani in a private collection of Mr. Y. Arashiro in Ishigaki island in Okinawa Prefecture.

IV-Photo. 4 The two different marukobune models for tank test.

<Tables>

III-Table. 1 Types and number of boats from 1904 through 1941.

III-Table. 2 Types and number of wrecked boats from 1904 through 1939. (Makino 1999a, p. 90, Table. 31.)

List of Figures, Photos, and Tables

III-Table. 3 Characteristics of agriculture in Shiga Prefecture. (Based on Shiga Prefecture, Agricultural Administration Division (ed.) 2003 p. 24.)

III-Table. 4 Variety of existing traditional boats. (Based on Naisuimen Gyoro Kenkyukai (ed.), 1999, p.4.)

III-Table. 5 Existing tabune. (Based on Naisuimen Gyoro Kenkyukai (ed.), 1999, p. 6, Table. 2.)

III-Table. 6 Events impacted the shoreline and the water level of the Lake Biwa.

III-Table. 7 The area(1) and the ratio(2) of the farm field improvement in FY 2002.

IV-Table. 1 Round haul netters in other regions. (Based on Ministry of Agriculture, Forestry and Fisheries (ed.), 1982, p.1188.)

IV-Table. 2 The size of modern fishing boats on Lake Biwa. (Based on Ministry of Agriculture, Forestry and Fisheries (ed.), 1982, p.1190.)

IV-Table. 3 The size of the traditional wooden fishing boats on Lake Biwa.

※ LBM・・・Lake Biwa Museum

Glossary

Akagi	Species Euphorbiaceae.
Amiuchibune	A boat for casting fishing nets.
Ashinaka	Half-soled straw sandals.
Atakebune	A large warship in the Age of Civil Wars.
Bokushodoki	Earthenware with letters or figures in black ink.
Boucho type	A term meaning shiki-expanded semi-planked boat.
Dambebune	A cargo boat used for lumber on Lake Biwa.
Do	Midship.
Domain (Han)	Japanese subnational jurisdictions before the Meiji period.
Doutaku	A bell-shaped bronze vessel of the Yayoi period.
Engishiki	A set of ancient Japanese governmental regulations
Enkaku-ji-ema	A votive picture of Enkakuji Temple.
Eri	A fishing weir (trap) made of bamboo.
Fubuki	Stern deck.
Fugyosen	A utility boat and/or fishing boat.
Funayakugin-nituki-Kitamura-Genjuro-kojogaki-an	A note on shipping duties by Mr. Genjuro Kitamura
Furikake	Planking at the turn of the bilge.
Goshu-kosui-shoura-fune-inzu-cho	A register of boats in Omi (Shiga Prefecture).
Goshu-kosui-shoura-marubune-hiratabune-nayose-goun-jocho	A register of boats in Omi (Shiga Prefecture).
Goshu-kosui-shoura-ryousen-hiratabune-no-cho	A register of boats in Omi (Shiga Prefecture).
Goshu-kosui-shoura-senin-sucho	A register of boats in Omi (Shiga Prefecture).
Goshu-shoura-funakazu-cho	a register of boats in Omi (Shiga Prefecture).
Gun (County/district)	A local administrative unit under prefecture in Japan.
Habune	A small-sized tabune
Hanzan	Foredeck beam
Hedoshioshi	Bottom beam
Heiankyo	The capital in Kyoto in the Heian period.

Glossary

Heita	Bow planking with narrow planks placed vertically.
Heitabune	A heita-bow boat.
Hesaki	Bow.
Hiraitaban	Foredeck.
Hiraitabanmune	Foredeck ridge beam.
Hobashira	Mast.
Hokkoku	The provinces along the Hokurikudo.
Hokkokubune	A large cargo boat used in the Sea of Japan coast from the late Middle Period to the middle of the Edo Period.
Hottatebashiratatemono	A building with its pillers sunk into the ground.
Hyakkokubune	A cargo boat with carrying capacity of 100 koku (hyakkoku).
Igushi	A sprig of the sacred tree.
Ikadabune	A raft-type boat.
Ikura	A beam between the side planks.
Ikuramotooshi	Bottom beam.
Isome-ke-monjo	Documents of the Isome family.
Jishimai-kechige-chusinjo	Rice tax report.
Jo	A unit of length. 1 jo is approximately 3 meters.
Kaisen	A cargo boat.
Kaji	Rudder.
Kajitsuka	Tiller.
Kajitoko	A rudder support.
Kajitokonoana	A rudder hole.
Kakiita	A plank attached on the sheer between the midship and the bow.
Kampaku	An advisor to the Emperor.
Kanda-jinja-monjo	Kanda shirine documents.
Kansei-ninen-inu-gounjo	A record of tax paid to the shogunate in 1790.
Kasagi	Mast gallows.
Kasagibashira	Gallows strut.
Kasugai	A large iron staple to join or hold two timbers.
Katasajiki	Outer bottom planking.
Kawarasueiwai	A bottom plank laying celebration.

Ken (Prefecture)	Japanese subnational jurisdictions and there are 47 prefectures.
Kenkatashiro	A sword used at a ritual ceremony.
Kensakibune	A cargo boat with a sharp bow.
Kitamura-Genjuro-ke-monjo	Genjuro Kitamura family's documents.
Kitamura-Genjuro-ke-yuishogaki	The history of Genjuro Kitamura family.
Kiwariho	A design method of tradiotional Japanese boatbuilders. Beam, depth and rig size are derived proportionately from the length of the bottom plank.
Kobiki	Lumberjack, Sawyer.
Kohayabune	A small speedy boat.
Kokaisen	A small cargo boat for short-hauls.
Koku	A unit of cargo capacity, 1 koku is 10 cubic shaku(0.28m^3) or 100kg.
Komo	A straw mat.
Komobuki	Straw mat roofing.
Komooshimune	Ridge.
Kosui-ezu-narabini-uraura-funakabu-oboe	Paintings of Lake Biwa and the record of the boat licenses.
Kotosanzan	The three old and renowned temples in the east side of Lake Biwa, namely Saimyoji Temple, Kongorinji Temple and Hyakusaiji Temple.
Koura-aratamegaki	A report of the Lake Biwa ports by an order of Naotaka Ii, the daimyuo of Hikone, including harbor data and wind conditions.
Kumibune	More than one boats tied together to form a katamaran-like craft.
Kurumahayabune	Hayabune with wooden wheels on the both sides of its bow.
Kyoto-oyakushomuki-taigai-oboegaki	A manual for the magistrates of Kyoto.
Maki	Wood species Podocarpus.
Makinawa	Oakum made from endodermis (inner skin) of podocarp tree.
Marukobune-sunpocho	A record of marukobune dimensions.
Matsu	Japanese red pine.
Mikuriya	Ancient institutions which control foods for the Imperial Court.
Mizaraita	Floor plates.
Mohon-Katada-keizu	A reprint of Katada scenary paintings.
Nakajiki	Center bottom planking.

Glossary

Nakasendo	One of the five major routes in the Edo Period.
Nidokosen	A boat hired by Ryohama-gumi for cargo transport.
Nuikugi	A edge nail used to join planks.
Oban	Afterdeck.
Oibana	V-shaped foredeck.
Omeshibune	A boat used by the Imperial Family.
Omi-meishozu	Drawings of Omi scenic places.
Ominokuni-Katata-Isome-ke-monjo	Documents of Isome family in Katata, Omi.
Omi-roku	A geographical description of Omi based on a survey in the late 17th or the early 18th century.
Omi-yochi-shiryaku	A geographical description of Omi based on a survey published in 1734.
Omogi	Side member cut out from a split log, its inner side is cut flat and the outer side is left round.
Omogi-zukuri	The hull construction using omogi as topside planking or bilge planking.
Oshikirihayabune	A small boat derived from hayabune.
Ringi	A simple boatbuilding jig made of timbers partially buried in the ground.
Ro	Oar.
Ryohamagumi	A partnership of Omi merchants.
Ryukyumatsu	Species of pine.
Saozashi	A holder for pole.
Sashiita	Washboard.
Sekibune	Originally a checkpoint boat. After the Age of Civil Wars it was referred to a primary warship.
Semi	Block.
Senkoyojutsu	A guide book of sailing and weather written in 1456.
Sewn Boat	Hougosen, shell built boat, or stitched plank boat.
Shigaken-bussanshi	Shiga Prefecture Product Report.
Shigaken-toukeisho	Shiga Prefecture Statistics Report.
Shijimikakibune	A fishing boat for raking shijimi clams.
Shiki	Bottom plank.

Shiki expanded semi-planked boat	A type of semi-planked boat in which cargo capacity is primarily increased by a transverse expansion (adding bottom planks).
Shikioshi	Frame, bottom member.
Shikioshitsuka	Frame, side member.
Shin	Stem.
Shinkurobune-namae-yuishogaki-tsuke	The history of shinkurobune.
Shitamizara	Floor beam.
Shoreline compexity	Shoreline complexity is the ratio of the length of the shoreline to the circumference of a circle of area equal to that of the lake.
Sosuibune	A cargo boat used in Lake Biwa canals.
Stem-rasing	Shintate, mounting the stem (shin) on the bottom plank.
Su	A net similar to a blind.
Tabune	A small cargo boat used for rice farming.
Takeita	Bow planking.
Tana	Top side plank, sheer strake.
Tana-expanded semi-planked boat	A type of semi-planked boat in which cargo capacity is primarily increased by vertical expansion (adding side planks).
Tanaitazukuri	Hull construction with a bottom member made of a hollowed out log and topsides with multiple planks.
Tani-Sumio-ke-monjo	Sumio Tani family document.
Tectonic lake	A lake formed by tectonis faults.
To	Hatch.
Tobinoo	Stern sheer plate.
Todaiji-fuko-syhoen-narabini-jiyocho	A journal of Todaiji Temple regarding its property.
Todate	Transom.
Tokaido	One of the Five Routes of Japan during the Edo period connecting Tokyo, then Edo, and Kyoto.
Tombi	Lumber surveyor.
Tomo	Stern.
Tomoikura	Quarter beam.
Tomoita	Transom.
Tomojiki	Stern bottom planking.
Tomonotana	Stern sheer strake.

Glossary

Tomooban	Quarter deck.
Tsura	Face.
Tsurakugi	Face nail.
Tsuribune	A small boat for line fishing.
Tsubanomi	A chisel used to make a hole needed to drive a Japanese nail (wakugi) into a piece of timber.
Tsunakukuri	Rope bitts, tips of the crossbeam in the bow protruding the side plankings.
Ushibune	A boat for carrying farm cattle.
Volume curve	Hypsometric curve, Hypsographic curve.
Wakan-sen-yo-shu	Historical records of Japanese and Chinese type ships.
Wakijiki	Middle bottom planking.
Wanzan	Foredeck beam.
Wasen	A historical Japanese wooden boat.
Yakatabune	A boat with a fixed roof used for pleasure/house boat.
Yama-bugyosho-kimo-cho	Ryukyu Dynasty's ordinace regarding the forest management and penal regulations.
Yamatonokuni-gangoji-ryo-echinosho	Echi manor of Gangozi Temple in Yamato Province.
Yatoku	A bamboo made wedge used for calking.
Yusen	A pleasure boat.

Chapter I
Introduction

(1) Geographical Background of Boat Use in the Lake Biwa Region.

Lake Biwa as a Tectonic Lake

Lake Biwa is the largest lake in Japan (Fig. 1). Located at 85.6 m above sea level, the surface area is 674 km^2, the volume is 27.3 km^3, and the average depth is 41 m. The maximum depth is 104 m near Chikubu Island in the north. The catchment area of the Lake Biwa basin is 3,174 km^2.

There are various kinds of lakes in the world, and not all of them are used for passenger and cargo transportation. The "Data Book of World Environments–A Survey of the State of World Lakes"[1] compiled by the International Lake Environment Committee (ILEC) surveys a total of 247 lakes: 61 in North America, 12 in South America, 64 in Asia, 4 in Oceania, 20 in Africa, and 56 in Europe. Each lake is represented by data containing location, water quality, vegetation, biota, surrounding land use, industrial usage, population density, and lake use statistics. Lake resources information includes major uses such as drinking water, fishing, tourism, recreation, and transportation. The data showing the ratio of the lakes used for passenger and cargo transportation to total usage was analyzed first.

Transportation data is divided into categories, transportation and navigation, with transportation indicating commercial cargo and navigation indicating passenger transport.[2] Out of all the lakes surveyed, 30% are used for passenger transportation, and 21% are used for cargo transportation (Fig. 2). Given that more than 50% of all lakes are used for drinking water, fishing, tourism and pleasure, about double that number of lakes are used for water transport.

The relationship between lakes used for passenger and cargo transportation, and their origin is presented below. Lakes and marshes are classified according to their origins (Fig. 3):

(1) Geographical Background of Boat Use in the Lake Biwa Region.

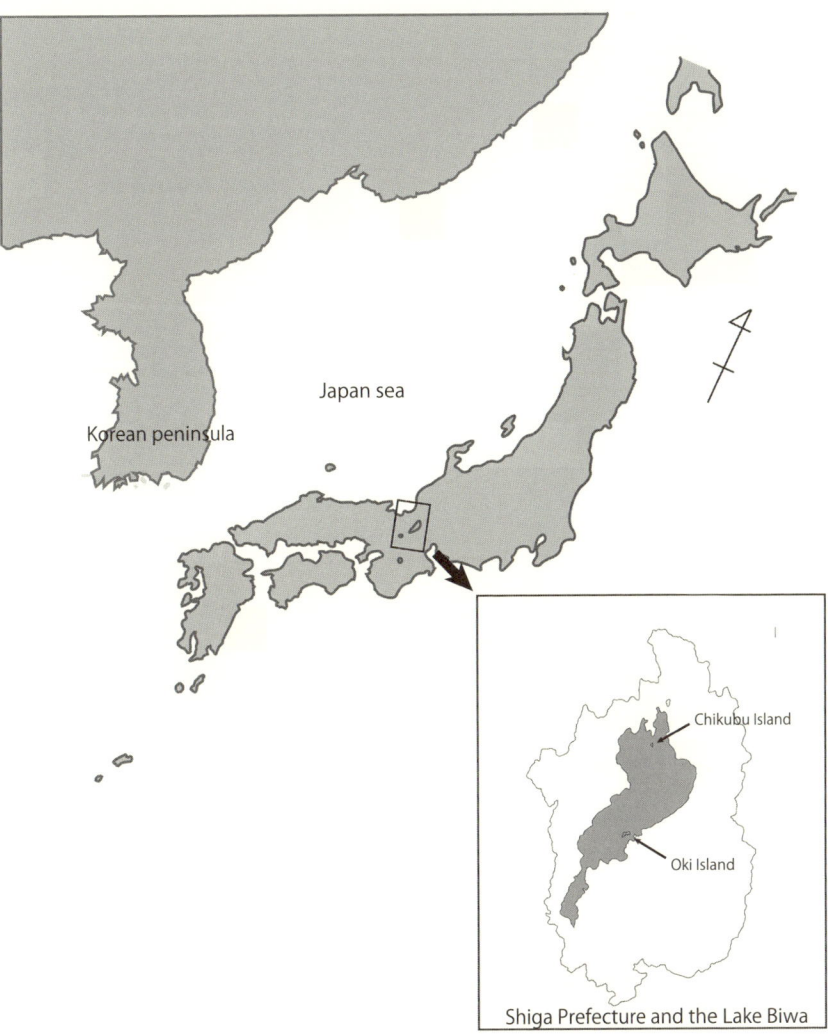

Fig. 1 Location of the Lake Biwa.

- Crater lakes-essentially pot shaped craters filled with water.
- Caldera lakes-sunken craters filled with water.
- Lagoons-inlets separated from the ocean by an accumulation of earth and sand at the mouth.

Chapter I Introduction

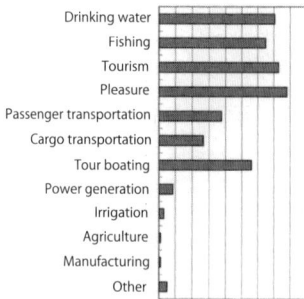

Fig. 2 Lake use information.

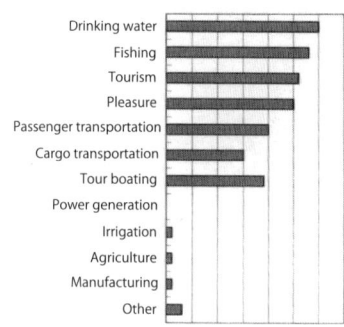

Fig. 5 Tectonic lake use information.

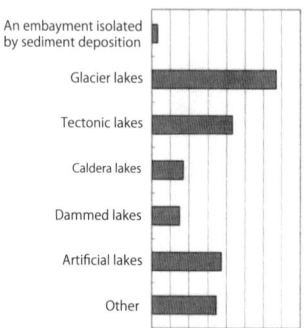

Fig. 3 Lake formation origin.

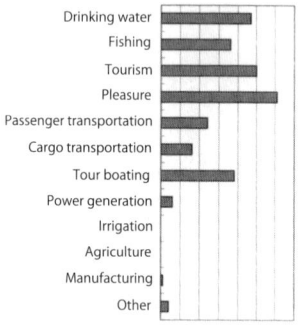

Fig. 6 Glacier lake use information.

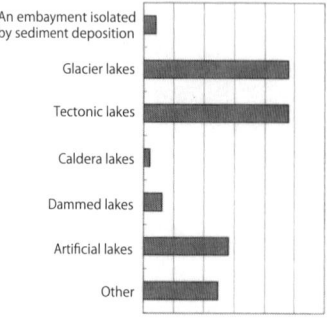

Fig. 4 Lakes used for passenger and cargo transportation.

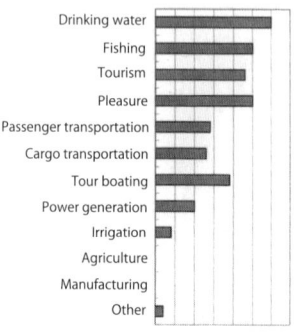

Fig. 7 Artificial lake use information.

32

- Tectonic lakes (fault lakes)-formed at sunken places caused by tectonic movements.
- Glacier lakes-hollows carved by a glacier, and then filled with water.
- Dammed lakes-made from a river dammed by fallen earth or sand.

About 62% of lakes used for transportation are tectonic lakes and glacier lakes, and about 18% are artificial lakes (Fig. 4-7). The ratio of tectonic lakes and glacier lakes are about the same. Since the number of the glacier lakes is larger, tectonic lakes are used most for transportation.

Rivers and Shorelines used as Routes.

Tectonic lakes are used widely for transportation for a reason. The undulating nature of the plain created along seismic faults (high and low land called, horst and graben), generally results in the formation of many rivers, which in turn lead to road development (Fig. 8). When such road transportation networks lie adjacent to lakes, waterborne transport develops as well.

Lake Biwa is a tectonic lake formed by seismic activity, and its origin dates back four million years. The geographical features of the surrounding region were suitable for roads, and routes to cultural centers ran through the region. This transportation network contributed primarily to the growth of lake transportation. The shoreline of the lake was shaped by tectonic movements and provided convenient geographical features for ports.[3] There existed several ports as early as the seventh century, such as Shiozu, Sugaura, and Oura in the north, and Katsuno, Hira, and Wani in the west. The Japanese names for these ports were minato, tomari, or ura. In the Medieval period (from about the middle of the 12th to the end of the 16th centuries), Sakamoto, and Katata prospered as ports. Initially the sailing routes from Sakamoto and Otsu were short, mainly to Shina, Yabase and Yamada across the lake, but later the routes were linked to distant ports such as Asazumatsukuma. The major ports in the Edo period (1603 to 1868) were Shiozu,

Chapter I Introduction

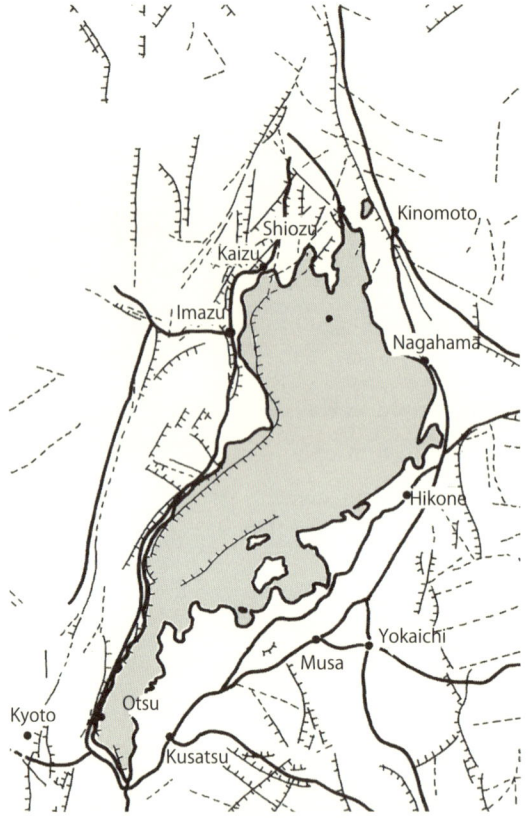

Fig. 8 Faults and major roads in the Lake Biwa Region.

Oura, and Kaitsu in the north, collectively called San-ura (three ports), and Imazu, Funaki, and Omizo in the west. To the east, major ports included Hachiman, along with Nagahama, Maibara, and Matsubara, collectively called Hikone-San-Minato (meaning, three ports of Hikone). Otsu was the major port in the south.

There is not much flatland in the west and north of Lake Biwa because mountains encroach on the shoreline. Major roads cross over these mountains to neighboring regions. Over 500 rivers flow into Lake Biwa, including small streams, and 125 of them are Class 1 rivers.[4] The Seta River[5] in the south is

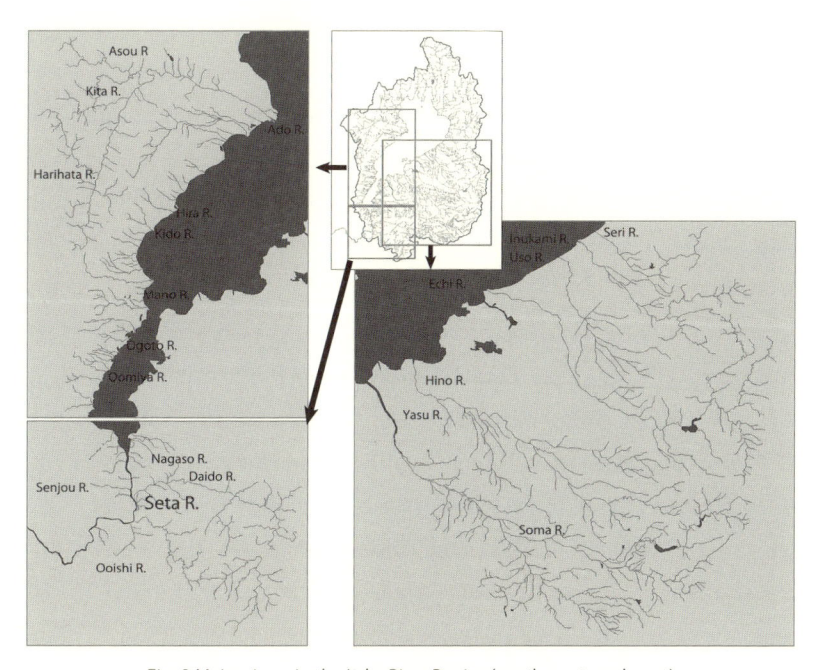

(1) Geographical Background of Boat Use in the Lake Biwa Region.

Fig. 9 Major rivers in the Lake Biwa Region(south, east, and west)

the only river flowing out from the lake (Fig. 9).

The Seta River has tributaries from east and west. The Seta River connects the Tanakami Mountains with ancient capitals via one of the tributaries in the east. The timber in the region's mountains was heavily cut to build these capitals. Due to deforestation, the rivers in the Lake Biwa basin have seen serious flooding, even in the modern era.

The Seta River was an important watercourse, not only to connect the region with its ancient capitals, but also to protect the capitals from the eastern region, which was perceived as wild and lawless. Several major roads were built along the river, and the routes were altered as the location of the capital was moved over time from Heijokyo, then Nagaokakyo, to Heiankyo. The road on the left bank from Setahashimoto to Oishi via Sekinotsu Village (Chapter. III-Fig. 14) was particularly important.

Chapter I Introduction

The lower reaches of the Seta River were fast-flowing and suitable only for raft transportation. The transportation route connecting Sekinotsu and Kurozu to Otsu in the upper reaches was used to transport goods like brushwood from the Tanakami area. In particular, Sekinotsu was a trading center and became an important port for boats in the Medieval period. Kurozu, where the Seta River and the Daido River merge, occupied a good location for transportation. In the north reaches of the Seta River, the Yasu River flows westward from its source at Mt. Gozaisho in the Suzuka Mountains. The length of the Yasu River is 65 km and its catchment area is 382 km^2. The Soma River, another tributary of the Seta River, was used to transport logs for building supplies, some of which were used in the construction of Todai-ji Temple during the Nara period (710 to 794).

On the east side of the lake, the Hino River flows east to west in the southern end from its source at Mt. Watamuki in the Suzuka Mountains. The flatland regions of the upper and middle reaches of the Hino River basin were known as Gamo, and are mentioned in ancient poetry.[6] Many archaeological sites that reveal the relationship with China and Korea have been found in the Sakura basin, a tributary of the Hino River. This indicates that people from China and Korea passed through this region on the way from Omi or Wakasa to Tamba, in ancient times.[7] The route to Ise ran in the valley of the Hino River. The Godaisankaido route, built in the Medieval period, connected the Tokaido and Nakasendo routes, from the Tsuchiyama-juku lodgings on the Tokaido to Obata near the Echigawajuku lodgings on the Nakasendo (Fig. 25). The distance was about 36 km and it was a primary route for merchants from Hino. To the north of the Hino River, the Echi River ran east to west. Its source is also in the Suzuka Mountains. In its upper reaches, there used to be many kijishi, craftsmen making wooden bowls and trays with lathes. The Happukaido route to Ise was built along the Echi River, and became popular after the Medieval period. To the north of the Echi River, the Seri River, the Inukami River, and the Uso River flow into Lake

Biwa forming an alluvial fan. There are several routes running north and south. In the Edo period travelers' stations were located at the intersection of the Inukami River and Nakasendo route. One of these stations, Tokoeki, was at the intersection of the Seri River and the old Tozando route.

Along the west side of the lake are the Hira Mountains (1,000 m elevation), the Katata Hills, and the Hiei Mountains (600-800 m). They form the border between Shiga Prefecture and Kyoto Prefecture. The Ado River is the largest river on the west side of the lake, and its source is in the Tamba highland. It flows north to the west of the Hira Mountains, through Kutsuki in Takashima City, and then east into Lake Biwa. The Ado River and its tributaries, the Harihata River, the Kita River, and the Aso River, were used to transport timber from the Hira Mountains in the Heian period.[8] Timber for boatbuilding was transported this way until the 1930s.

To the east of the Hira Mountains are the Yanamune, the Hira, the Otani, and the Kido Rivers, and in the east of the Katata hills run the Wani, the Mano, the Tenjin, and the Ogoto Rivers. To the east of the Hiei Mountains are the Yana River, the Omiya River, and the Sai River, all flowing into Lake Biwa. The distance between the Hira Mountains and Lake Biwa is relatively short and thus level land is limited. In the Kofun period (from the late 3rd to the beginning of the 8th century), a large number of tombs were built in the region along these rivers, indicating that people from China and Korea not only cultivated the narrow land, but also built ports.[9] Enryakuji Temple at Mt. Hiei controlled the transportation network in Omi and was a center of activity during the Medieval period. Goods were transported to Enryakuji Temple via Sakamoto, the nearest port on Lake Biwa.

Winds and Currents for Navigation in the Lake Biwa Region.

The valleys, mountains, and hills of the Lake Biwa region create a variety of wind[10] patterns suitable for sailing. Different winds flow on Lake Biwa depending upon the season, time of day, and location. Historically, it

Chapter I Introduction

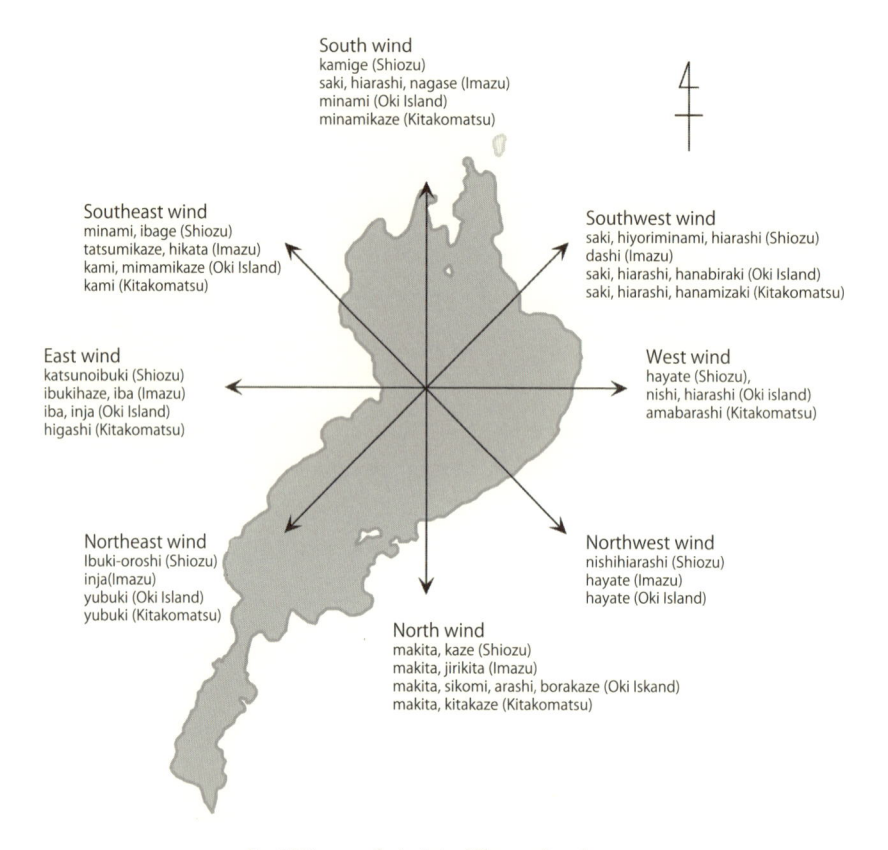

South wind
kamige (Shiozu)
saki, hiarashi, nagase (Imazu)
minami (Oki Island)
minamikaze (Kitakomatsu)

Southeast wind
minami, ibage (Shiozu)
tatsumikaze, hikata (Imazu)
kami, mimamikaze (Oki Island)
kami (Kitakomatsu)

Southwest wind
saki, hiyoriminami, hiarashi (Shiozu)
dashi (Imazu)
saki, hiarashi, hanabiraki (Oki Island)
saki, hiarashi, hanamizaki (Kitakomatsu)

East wind
katsunoibuki (Shiozu)
ibukihaze, iba (Imazu)
iba, inja (Oki Island)
higashi (Kitakomatsu)

West wind
hayate (Shiozu),
nishi, hiarashi (Oki island)
amabarashi (Kitakomatsu)

Northeast wind
Ibuki-oroshi (Shiozu)
inja(Imazu)
yubuki (Oki Island)
yubuki (Kitakomatsu)

Northwest wind
nishihiarashi (Shiozu)
hayate (Imazu)
hayate (Oki Island)

North wind
makita, kaze (Shiozu)
makita, jirikita (Imazu)
makita, sikomi, arashi, borakaze (Oki Iskand)
makita, kitakaze (Kitakomatsu)

Fig. 10 Names of winds in different directions.

was important for fishermen and boatmen to understand these patterns, no doubt they had a much deeper understanding of them than we do today (Fig. 10). Traditional types of weather forecasting included watching the sky above the lake in the morning. These predictions were called keshiki-mi or keshiki-wo-miru, meaning, weather forecasting signs. In winter, when it tends to become stormy, more than one person in a village would watch the sky and discuss whether or not to leave by boat. Forecasting the wind was particularly important, reflected in the wide variety of terms used to describe local winds:

38

- Makita-the north wind in winter.
- Shikomi-the wind starting to blow suddenly on a calm winter day.
- Borakaze-the wind blowing from the Mt. Hira.
- Yubuki-a typhoon in fall.
- Iba-the east wind blowing from the mouth of the river in Iba, in Notogawa Village, and in Kanzaki County.
- Injiya-the wind suitable for marukobune sailing which blows in spring when the weather is fine.
- Minami, Minami-kaze, or Tatsumi-kaze-the southeast and south winds, often used with a prefix indicating the direction. (ex: Chomeji-Minami)
- Saki, Kami, and Kami-kaze-the southwest wind blowing after the rainy season. Here, Kami means Otsu.
- Hiarashi, (a shortened form of Hiei-arashi meaning a Hiei storm)-the strong wind, which blows from the Hiei Mountains, i.e. from the Otsu region. In winter this wind causes the lake to be rough and prevents fishing.
- Hanabiraki-the wind that blows around March and April, and is a sign of continuing good weather and good fishing.
- Nishi-the strong west wind in winter also called, yukishimaki if accompanied by snow.
- Hayate-a northwest gust occurring in any season, but mainly in the early spring.
- Niwa-for the calm condition on the lake suitable for umi-kasegi,[11] meaning fishing in swamps.

People traditionally had an in-depth knowledge of the water currents as well. In the north basin of the lake there are three circling currents (Fig. 11, I-III). From the north, the first current circles counter-clockwise, the second current is clockwise, and the third is counter-clockwise. The first current exists continually from spring through fall, and is strongest in summer with a speed of about 20 cm/sec. These currents are called, shio or jio. People

Chapter I Introduction

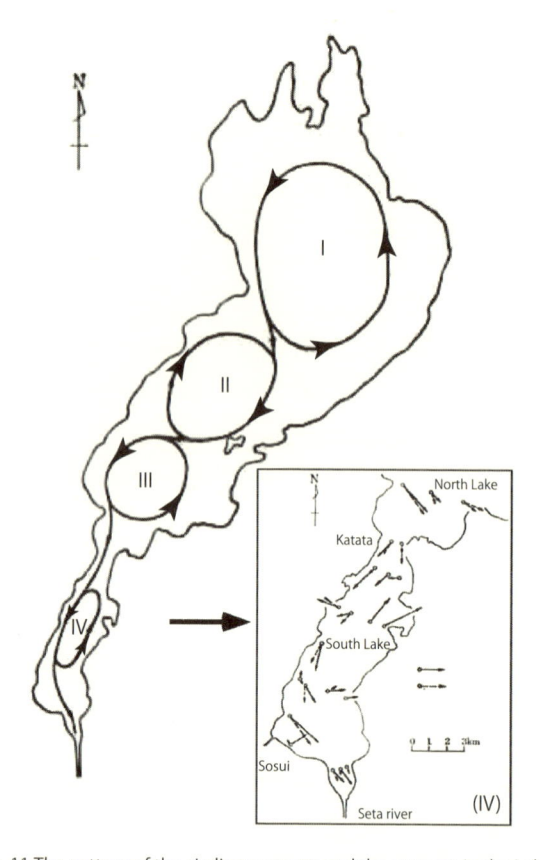

Fig. 11 The pattern of the circling currents and the currents in the Lake Biwa.

in the Minamihama region in the lower reaches of the Ane River on the north east side of the lake refer to the onshore current as okijio, the offshore current as kazashio, and the south-to-north current as minamijio. The fishermen on Oki Island call the current near the bottom sokoshio, the current in the middle as nakashio, and the surface current as kawashimo. The onshore current is called yosejio, the offshore current is dejio, and the current from Oki Island to the Otsu region is known as kudarijio. The current from Oki Island to the Nagahama region is called noborijio. (Fig. 12)

In addition to the circling currents, there are drift currents caused by winds,

(1) Geographical Background of Boat Use in the Lake Biwa Region.

	Minamihama (Biwa Town)	Kitakomatsu	The Oki Island
Offshore	ura-jio	haridashi	de-shio
Onshore	oki-jio	tsukiyose	yose-jio
Southbound	kasa-jio	noboru	nobori-shio
Northbound	minami-jio	kudaru	kudari-jio
Others			dekudari denobori yosekudari yosenobori

Fig. 12 The currents and their names in regions.

internal waves created by oscillations of the thermocline, seiches (temporary oscillations of the entire lake surface), density currents caused by a difference of water densities, inertial oscillations caused by the spin of the earth, and coastal jets which are very rapid currents developed near shore.[12] In the boundary region between the north and the south basin, the cooler water of the small and shallow south basin and the warmer waters of the large and deep north basin form a layer. The cold and heavy water of the south basin flows along the slanted bottom of the lake into the north basin, and it generates a density current from south to north. In the south basin, the south-southwest wind blows along the long axis of the lake throughout the year. This causes the current on the east side to flow north and the current on the west side to flow south in a counter-clockwise current. In protected regions like Shiozu Bay in the north basin, a circling current is occasionally observed.[13]

(2) General History of the Lake Biwa Region and its Water Transportation

Water Transportation in Ancient Times

Archaeological evidence for human habitation in the Lake Biwa region dates back about twenty thousand years. The first boat use dates to around 2500 B.C. to 1000 B.C., the late Jomon[14] period. The Jomon people were mainly hunters-gatherers. Boats were dugouts made of Japanese cedar logs hollowed out with stone axes and fire. A total of 24 dugouts of various sizes have been found (Fig. 13, 14), indicating these boats were commonly used in the region. An oar with a length of 1.49 m was found at the Motosuikei site in Omihachiman. Ten dugouts were excavated from the Matsubaranaiko site in Hikone City. One dugout had a beam of 0.55 m and a length of 5.15 m, and was found at the Onoehama site in Kohoku Town.[15] Another dugout with an overall length of 6.2 m, a maximum beam of 0.6 m, and the depth between the sheer and the bottom of 0.2 m, containing a hook and stone sinker, was found at the Chomeiji underwater site.

The Jomon period is followed by the Yayoi period from around the middle of 3rd century B.C. to the middle of 3rd century A.D.[16] In the Yayoi period, the intensive paddy field rice farming technique was introduced into Japan, probably from southern China via the Ryukyu Islands or Korean Peninsula. People in the Lake Biwa region started to settle near marshy land suitable for wet-rice farming (Fig. 15). In these regions, the black soil layer composed of rotting vegetation preserved wooden artifacts well. People also utilized various resources acquired from the lake and the mountains. At the Dainakanoko site, organic materials, shell mounds, and many wooden tools for farming were found. New fishing techniques used by the Yayoi resulted in a wider variety of catches. Fishing nets and tackle, such as eri, yana, yotsudeami and ue were particularly innovative (Fig. 16). The eri

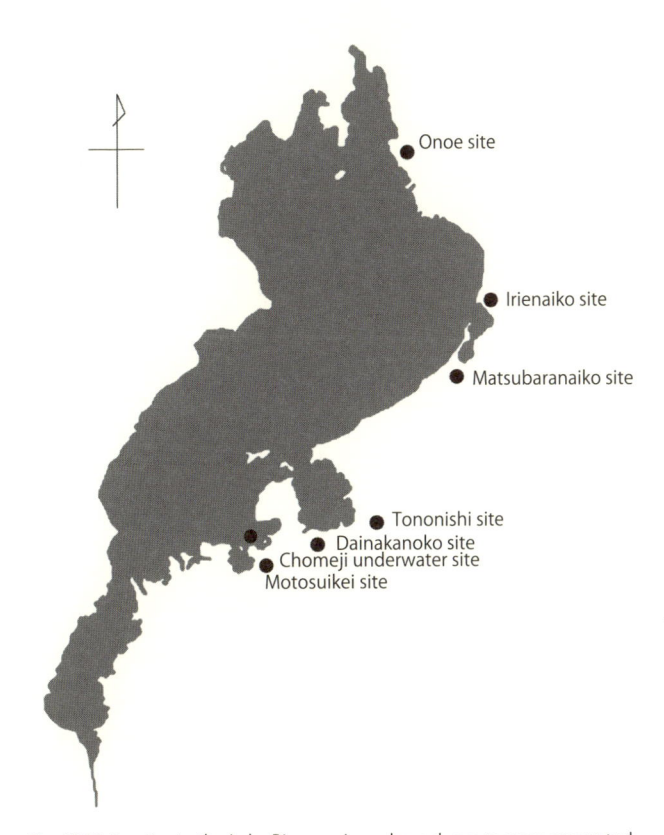

(2) General History of the Lake Biwa Region and its Water Transportation

Fig. 13 Major sites in the Lake Biwa region where dugouts were excavated.

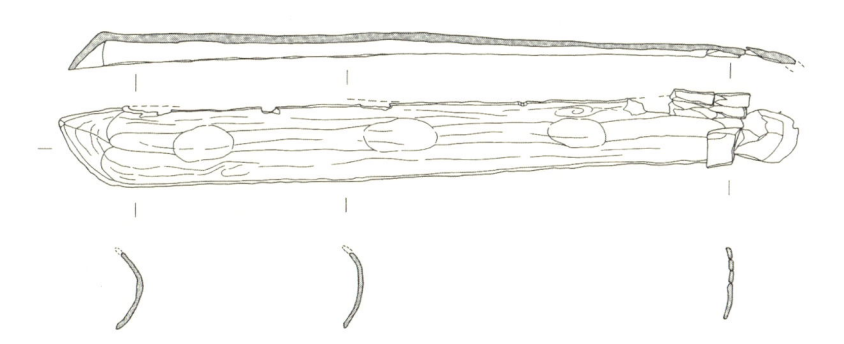

Fig. 14 A dugout excavated from Matsubaranaiko site, Late Jomon period.

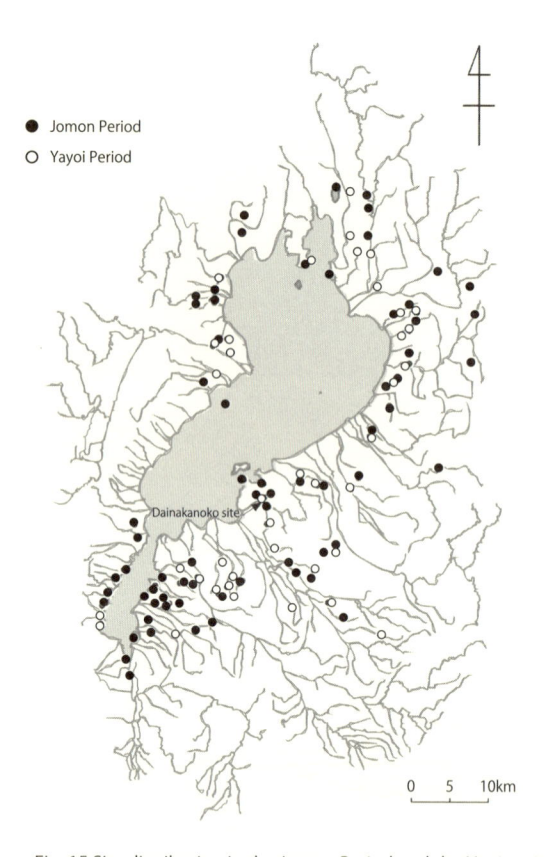

Fig. 15 Site distribution in the Jomon Period and the Yaoi period.

and yana are traps set up in the shallows that can catch fish while people are farming. Yotsudeami is four handed net. Ue is cylindrical fishing gear made of woven bamboo for catching mainly eel and crucian carp. They are commonly used even today.

Imported technologies of boatbuilding and iron metallurgy enabled the construction of semi-dugout boats. This hull type is comprised of a dugout hull to which side planks are added using fasteners. This technique is a more efficient use of timber. At this time other species of wood began to be used in boatbuilding, including podocarps, pines, and camphor, in addition to

(2) General History of the Lake Biwa Region and its Water Transportation

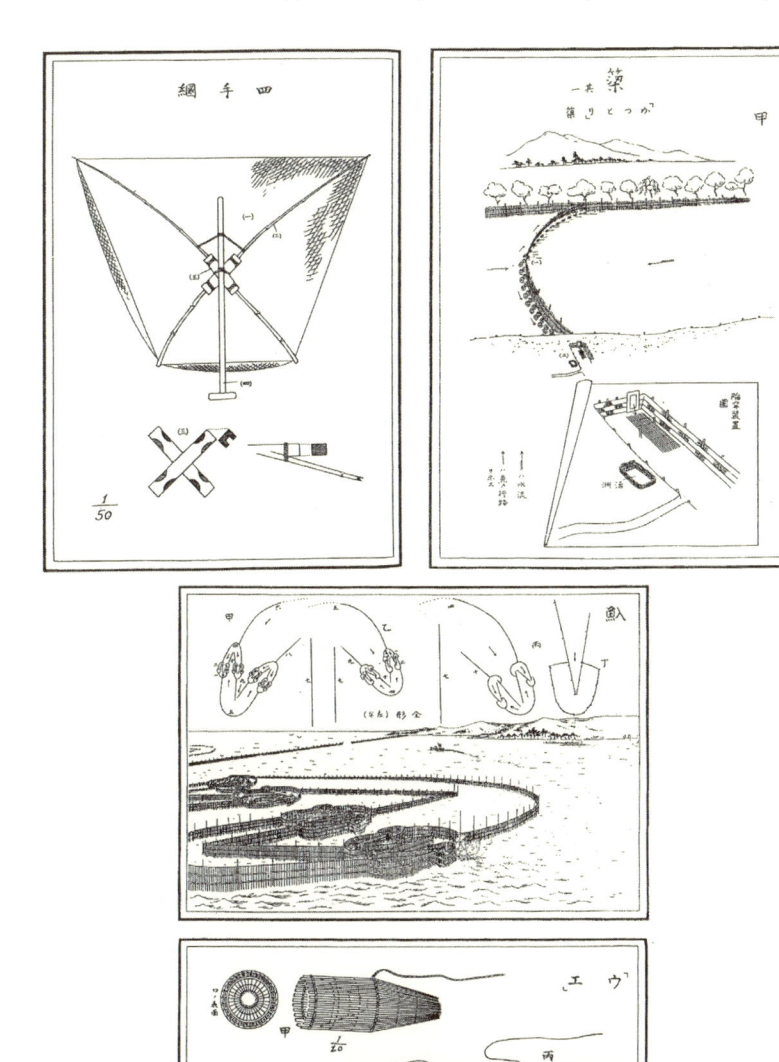

Fig. 16 Traditional fishing methods on the Lake Biwa.

45

Chapter I Introduction

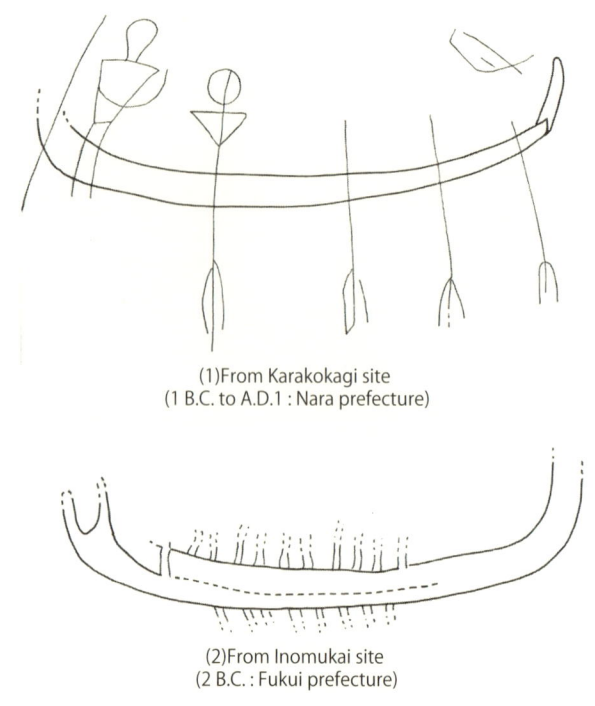

(1)From Karakokagi site
(1 B.C. to A.D.1 : Nara prefecture)

(2)From Inomukai site
(2 B.C. : Fukui prefecture)

Fig. 17 Boat figures drawn on Dotaku and pottery in Yayoi period.

cedar. Some bell-shaped bronze vessels of the period-called dotaku-and a drawing on pottery vessels bear a pattern displaying a large boat rowed with many oars (Fig. 17), but actual recovered artifacts are limited to dugouts and semi-planked boats.

The Development of Water Transportation

Following the Yayoi, in the Kofun period (around 300 to 600), some of the people from Korean Peninsula migrated and settled in the Lake Biwa region via Sea of Japan (Fig. 18). These people, including lords and landowners, formed a hierarchical society, and they built burial mounds Kofun, with various shapes in several places (Fig. 19). They built villages near rice paddy fields and surrounded them with moats to protect them. Boats were

46

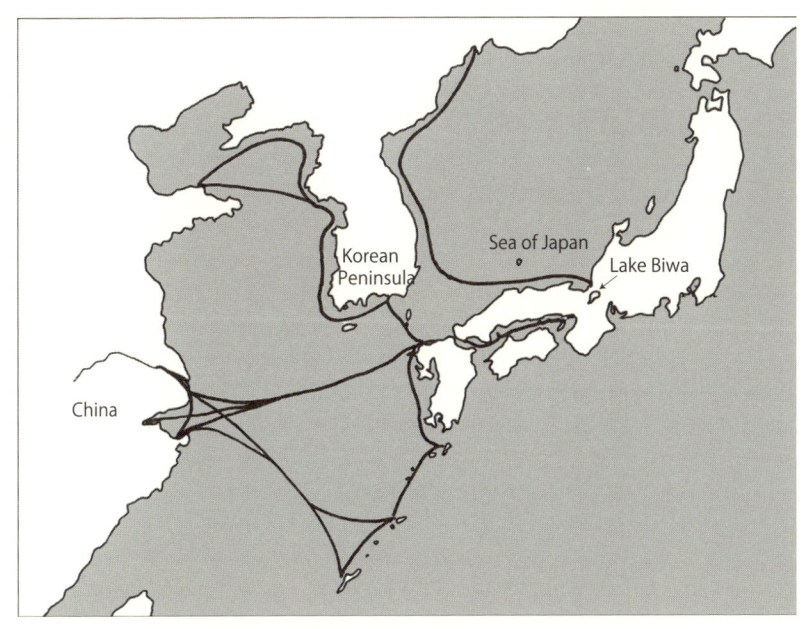

Fig. 18 Sailng routes from China and Korean Peninsula to Japan.

probably used in the moats and man-made canals, in addition to the lakes and the rivers. The lake resources fell under the control of these lords. Water transportation increased, and ports were improved.

More than 40 boat models (Fig. 20) were discovered in the region surrounding Lake Biwa (Fig. 21). At the Kurohashi site in Omihachiman City, an early Kofun settlement surrounded by moats, a model boat with a length of 32 cm and an oar with a length of 64 cm were found. The site is located near a river that flows into the western side of the lake. It is believed that the model boats were used to pray for the safety of those sailing on the lake. Similar boat-shaped wooden artifacts and a port facility were found at the Tononishi site in Sano Town of Higashiomi City. Various parts of what may have been semi-planked boats were excavated at several sites,[17] such as Shimonaga,[18] Akanoihama, Matsubaranaiko, and the Irienaiko site[19] (Fig. 22). At the Shimonaga site, a bow section with a length of 64.5

Chapter I Introduction

Fig. 19 Distribution of the Kofun period sites.

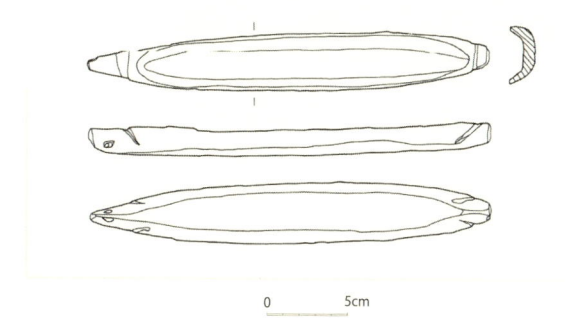

(2) General History of the Lake Biwa Region and its Water Transportation

Fig. 20 A boat model excavated from Irienaiko site, Kofun period.

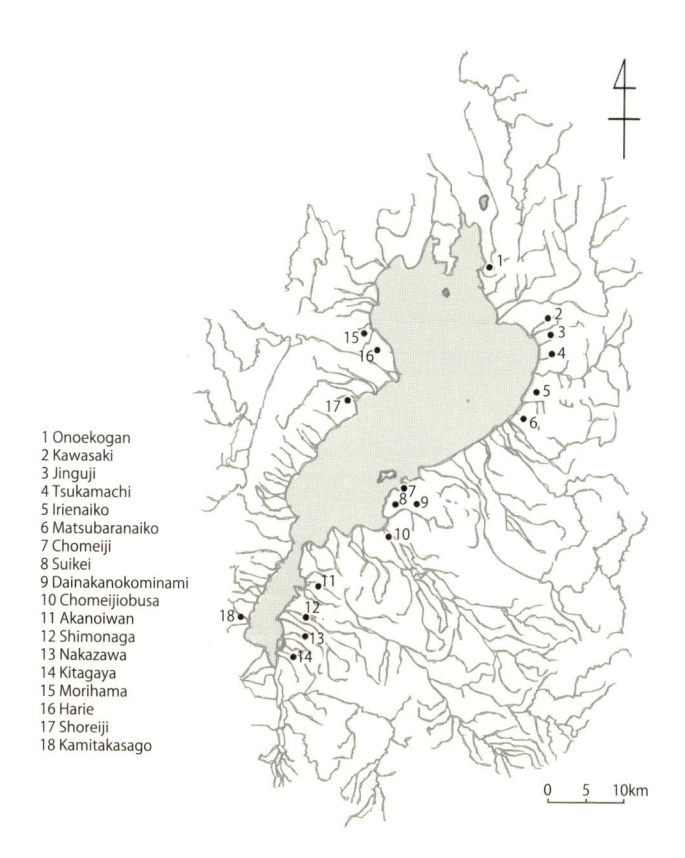

1 Onoekogan
2 Kawasaki
3 Jinguji
4 Tsukamachi
5 Irienaiko
6 Matsubaranaiko
7 Chomeiji
8 Suikei
9 Dainakanokominami
10 Chomeijiobusa
11 Akanoiwan
12 Shimonaga
13 Nakazawa
14 Kitagaya
15 Morihama
16 Harie
17 Shoreiji
18 Kamitakasago

Fig. 21 Sites where wooden model boats were excavated.

49

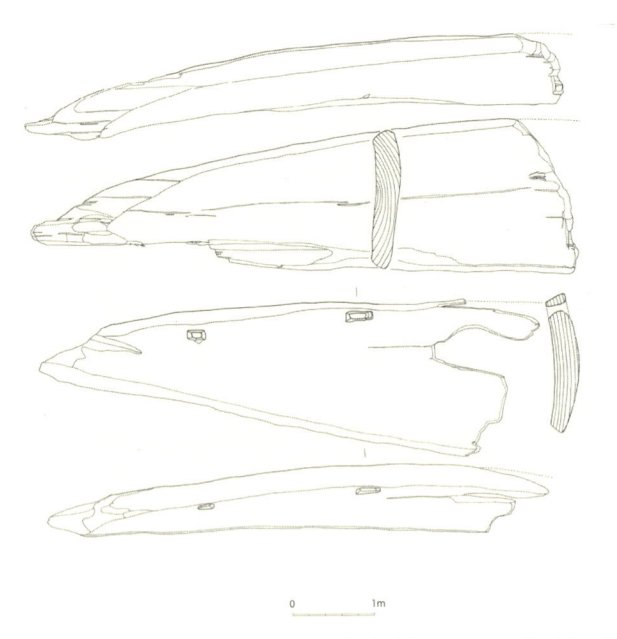

Fig. 22 A part of supposedly a semi-planked boat excavated at Irienaiko site.

cm and a width of 10.5 cm was found, along with two side planks, one with a length of 93.5 cm and a thickness of 3 cm, and the other with a length of 21.9 cm and a thickness of 3 cm. Japanese cedar was used in all cases and the bigger side plank was stitched to the bottom component with a lath made of thinned cherry bark. The lashing is tied through a mortise two to three times, and a wedge was driven into the mortise to prevent the lashing from loosening. Based on the components found, the overall length of the boat is estimated to have been relatively small, about 6 m. An oar made of cedar, with a length of 1.5 m and a maximum width of 10 cm, was also found nearby. The Shimonaga site is located about 3.5 km inland from Lake Biwa, and the rivers flowing into the lake changed their routes repeatedly. The variable watercourses suggest that the surrounding region was marshy during this period.

From the Shinkai 4th site[20] in Anyoji in Ritto City, many fragments of a clay model of a large boat from the middle Kofun period were excavated.[21] Its overall length is 114 cm, the maximum beam is 27 cm, and the height at the bow is 23 cm. Seven projecting beams for mounting oars are attached to both sides of the hull. It has a bulkhead, presumably to prevent the cargo from moving around. The bottom and bow are a single piece, and the model seems to represent a large boat, around 20 m long. Since horse-related artifacts from Korea were also excavated at this site, the model boat might represent a vessel used in the Sea of Japan for trade between the Lake Biwa region and Korean Peninsula or China.

After the Yamato Imperial Court was established, the Asuka period began (592-710). People migrated from China and Korea via the Lake Biwa region and settled in Nara, particularly in the Asuka region. The Yamato imperial Court took over control of the transportation on Lake Biwa, consolidating authority that previously had been held by local lords. The Imperial Court developed roads in the surrounding regions, established checkpoints, and imposed tolls. Because the court had ties with the eastern provinces of the Lake Biwa region, large amounts of timber and roofing tiles for building the capital were transported via the lake. The Court administered rice taxes as well. An inscription written on a small wooden plate found at the Nishigawara-Morinouchi site (Chuzu Town, Yasu County) includes a message written as evidence by Kuranoatai, a government official controlling the government's granary. It reads, "On order from Kuranoatai, I brought rice crops, but was unable to hire horses, thus returned without delivering them. You are asked to transport them by hiring boatmen. The crops are left at the house of Naniwanofuhito in Herunosato of Echinokori".[22] The message was an order addressed to residents ruled by the Urabe family. Clearly some sort of basic system of lake transportation had been established by that time.

At the beginning the Nara period (710-794), Lake Biwa was called Chikatsu-omi meaning "a fresh water lake (omi) near the capital (chikatsu)". Some

Chapter I Introduction

of the earliest written documents such as the Kojiki, Nihonshoki, and Manyoshu describe the importance of the Lake Biwa region. The Manyoshu includes many poems describing lake transportation and mentions 80 ports.[23] The ruins of one port were discovered at the Dainakanokominami site (Shimotoyoura, Azuchi Town). Various ritual utensils such as sacred spikes (igushi) were found at three sites of the period, dating from the latter half of the 7th century and the 8th century. These artifacts may suggest that ritual ceremonies involved praying for the safety of sailors were held at the port.

The most notable cargo in this period was logs for building materials used in the region (Fig. 23). Timber from the Koga Mountains to the southeast of Lake Biwa was brought to Mikumotsu via the Yasu River, assembled into rafts, and towed by boat to the port in Ishiyama. Then the logs were transported to the capital via the Seta River and the Uji River. In 753 they were used for building Todaiji Temple in Nara. Timber from Mt. Iga near Mt. Koga was transported to the port of Yagawa via the Soma River -a tributary of the Yasu River- fashioned into rafts, and transported by lake to the port of Ishiyama. Timber from Mt. Takashima in the northwest was brought to the port of Funakizaki via the Ado River, assembled into rafts, and also sent to the port of Ishiyama. Timber from Mt. Tanakami to the southeast of the lake was transported directly to Nara via the Uji River.

After the capital was moved to Kyoto in the Heian period (794-1185), the importance of the Lake Biwa region grew. Not only timber, but also various goods were transported to Kyoto through mikuriya (government offices).[24] Such goods included food, silk, paper, containers, leather goods, fruits, medicines, dyes, crops, dried fish, fermented food such as funazushi (the origin of sushi made from salted and fermented crucian carp), venison and wild boar meat, dairy products, and sesame oil (Fig. 24). Ajiro,[25] a type of wickerwork net, were set up in the Seta River, and became a source of fish for the Imperial Court.

At around the end of the Nara period, several land routes, such as

(2) General History of the Lake Biwa Region and its Water Transportation

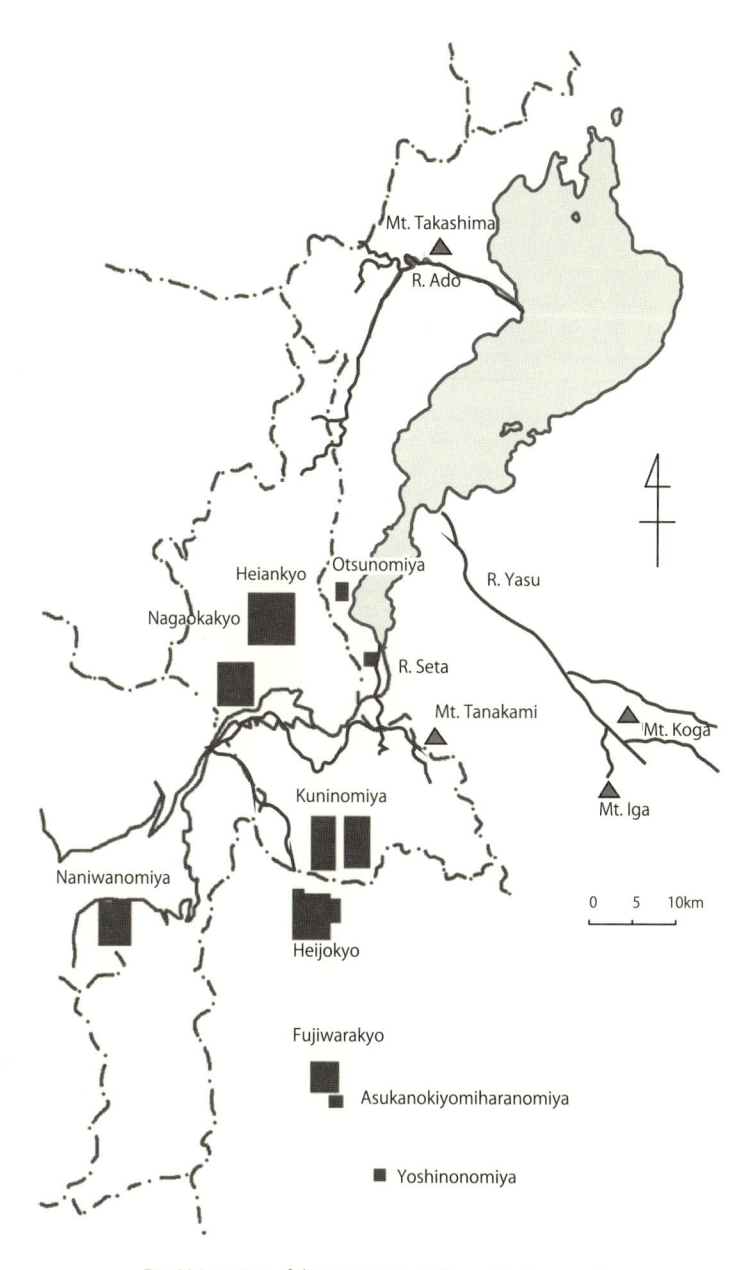

Fig. 23 Location of the ancient capitals and timber supply.

Chapter I Introduction

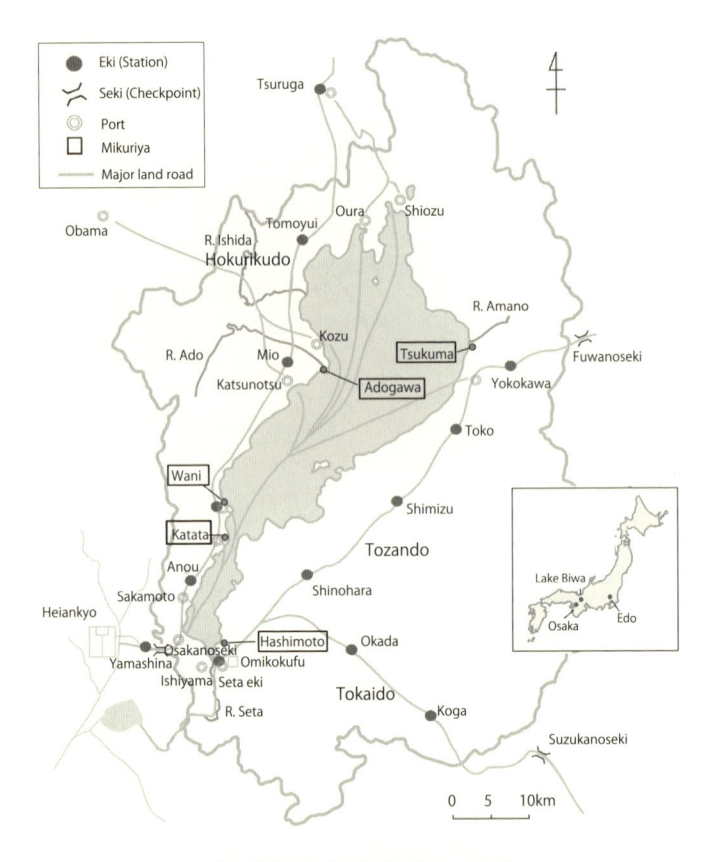

Fig. 24 Routes in the Ancient period.

Hokurikudo, Tozando and Tokaido became well developed, and post towns were established along these routes. The ruins of post towns along the Tozando, highway, were found at the Kitamachiya site (Kitamachiya, Gokasho, Higashiomi City), the Yamamoto site (Yamamoto Town, Gokasho, Higashiomi City), and the Amagonishi site (Amago, Kora Town, Inukami County). In the Amagonishi site, the main street was 12 m wide, the moats on the both sides were 1.5 m to 3 m wide and 72 m long, and the ruins of 42 buildings with posts sunk in the earth (hottatebashira) were found. These ruins were aligned along the Tozando road, which indicates the route and the village along the route were well developed. A group of storehouses were found at the Hirokawa site (Imazu Town, Takashima City) and at the Uchino site (Azuchi Town, Gamo County) presumably established to store various goods transported via these routes. In the Uchino site a group of 30 buildings with earthen posts were discovered. The largest building has a floor space of 36 m² and the average floor space was 20 m². The ruins of gates and roads were also found. The Ninoaze site (Yoshimi, Moriyama City) is adjacent to the Tozando road and the Yasu River, and near the Umajiiso Temple. From this site, the ruins of buildings standing in a row, and pottery shards with inscriptions in black ink were discovered. One of the inscriptions is "kawara" (川原), which might mean either a dry riverbed or a person's name. These finds show that the site was a well-managed central village for ferryboats serving the Yasu River.

In the year 810, a checkpoint was established in Osaka, only a few kilometers from Heiankyo, where the river flows out of Lake Biwa. A document from the late 11th century[26] includes a petition for a toll exemption at that checkpoint, because fresh fish were sent daily to the mikuriya at Kamomioya shrine in Kyoto. The most important port of this period was Otsu. Otsu was named by the Emperor Kanmu (737-806) when the capital was relocated to Kyoto.[27] The name comes from the region of Otsu-no-miya, one of the older capitals, close to Heiankyo.[28] A document of government regulations from the first half of the 10th century[29] has an account of rice crops from northern Japan that were shipped to Tsuruga, the north entrance of Lake Biwa, via the Sea of Japan. Crops were transported by land to Shiozu or Katsunotsu, from there to Otsu, landed there and transported to Kyoto. There is a report[30] that the transportation fee from the port of Asazuma to Otsu for 400 koku (60 t) of cargo from 100 families in Mino was 30% of the cargo.[31]

The route via Katsunotsu declined during the late Heian period, and the route via Kozu was used instead in the last period of the 11th century. Kozu is located between the Ado River and the Ishida River near the mouths, and played an important role in supplying timber from the mountains in the upper reaches since the mid-11th century.[32] Thus a change in the course of the Ado River caused the alteration of the route from Katsunotsu to Kozu.[33]

The route via Obama, Katsunotsu and Kozu was twice as long as the route via Tsuruga and Shiozu, but it was preferred for its flatness.

Water Transportation from the Medieval to the Modern Periods

During the Kamakura and the Muromachi periods (1185-1573) the lords of manors gained control of lake transportation. They developed ports and earned economic and military benefit from lake transport. Major checkpoints were established in Katata, Sakamoto, Hiyoshi, Funaki, and Okushima (Okinoshima)in addition to Osaka (Fig. 25). The importance of Katata on the west side of Lake Biwa increased because of the narrowness of the lake at this point.

Travelers had to pay a toll at checkpoints. One rice tax report written in 1050[34] recorded that 1 to and 5 sho (27 liters) of Japanese sake (liquor) were paid at the checkpoint in Katata.[35] Another document in 1303[36] recorded a tax of 1% of the cargo from Echizen, Hannan and Hongo was paid at Sakamoto, and more than 1% at Hiyoshi.[37] The checkpoints were controlled by people called sanmon, from the Enryakuji Temple in Mt. Hiei, and the tax was spent by the Enryakuji Temple. Sakamoto was located in an important place due to its proximity to the temple, and an additional seven checkpoints were established in the neighboring region.[38] Sakamoto is situated near the Hokkokudo route, which leads to Kyoto, and the cargo landed there was transported to Kyoto by horses via the Hiei Mountains.

The sailing routes used in the period can be seen in the historical records.[39] According to these documents, water transportation on Lake Biwa during this period was concentrated in the south basin, mostly between the east shore ports such as Otsu and Sakamoto, and the west shore ports of Yabase, Yamada,

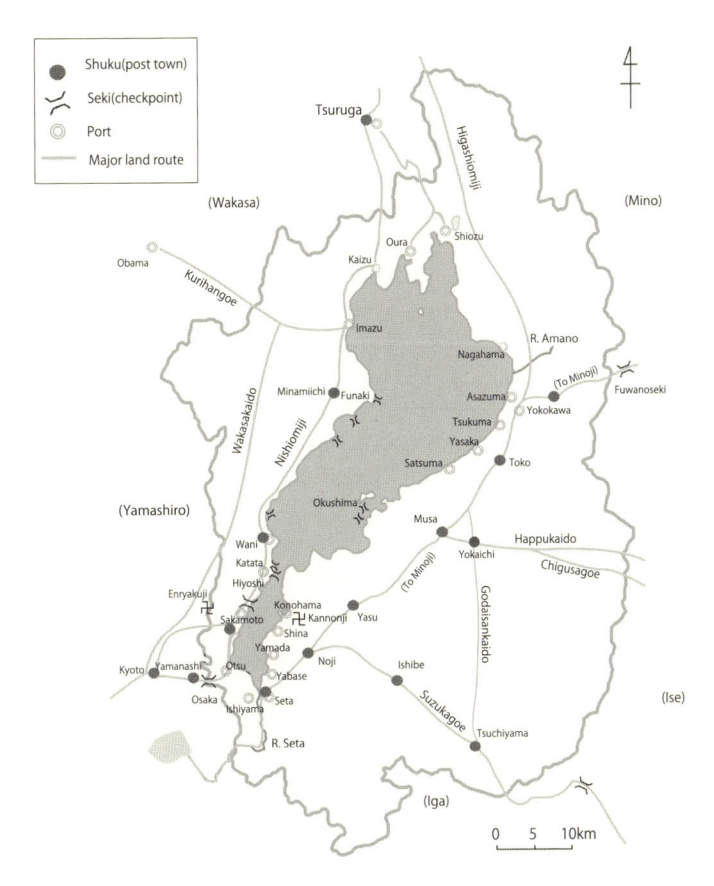

(2) General History of the Lake Biwa Region and its Water Transportation

Fig. 25 Routes in the Medieval period.

Shina, Yasaka, and Asazuma. These routes were connected to important highways such as the Tokaido, Tozando, and Hokurikudo. As mentioned earlier, Sakamoto was the port town closest to Enryakuji Temple, and the Hokurikudo route. The Yamanakagoe route, which connected Kyoto and the eastern region via Sakamoto, was the main route to Kyoto and the shortest as well. Yabase, Yamada and Shina were connected to Kusatsu, where there was a post town at the crossing of the two major highways, the Tozando and Tokaido.

The route from Kyoto to Moriyama on the Tozando via Sakamoto and Shina

57

was very convenient for travelers. Shina was particularly preferred because it was only 3.5 km from Sakamoto. However, the capture of Enryakuji Temple by Nobunaga Oda caused Sakamoto to decline, followed by Yamada and Shina. Only Yabase continued to be busy with travelers heading towards the Tokaido and Tozando. Meanwhile, Asazuma in the north prospered, as it was located at the mouth of the Amano River and adjacent to the Tozando. Rice and taxes from the eastern region were transported to Asazuma via the Tozando, then to Otsu on boats, and to Kyoto over land. The route via Kozu declined during the Kamakura period, while the route via Imazu expanded.

Water transportation in normal daily life is revealed in several archaeological sites, such as the Nishitai site in Yasu City,[41] the Yokoe site in Moriyama City, and the Myorakuji site in Hikone City. The Yokoe site and the Myorakuji site uncovered similar settlement patterns. Each had a Shinto shrine built in the middle of rice fields, with private houses built around it. There were public facilities such as water tanks, wells, bridges, and roads. Natural and man-made channels spread throughout the village, and it is assumed that small boats were used between the settlement and the rice fields, probably to carry rice crops and compost. In some cases, settlements were surrounded by moats, presumably for both protection and transportation.[42]

In the early Azuchi-Momoyama period (1568/1573-1600), Nobunaga Oda and Hideyoshi Toyotomi intended to take control of transportation on Lake Biwa, which was then under the control of manor lords. They built castles along the shore. The number of castles peaked at around 1,300, an exceptionally large amount compared to other parts of the country.[43]

Nobunaga planned to use Lake Biwa for military purposes. He constructed a residential castle in Azuchi, and used it as a base for expanding his power towards Kyoto. He also built a large boat with a length of 30 ken (54 m),[44] a beam of 7 ken (12.6 m), and 100 oars. However, it was sailed very little, and was later dismantled.[45]

(2) General History of the Lake Biwa Region and its Water Transportation

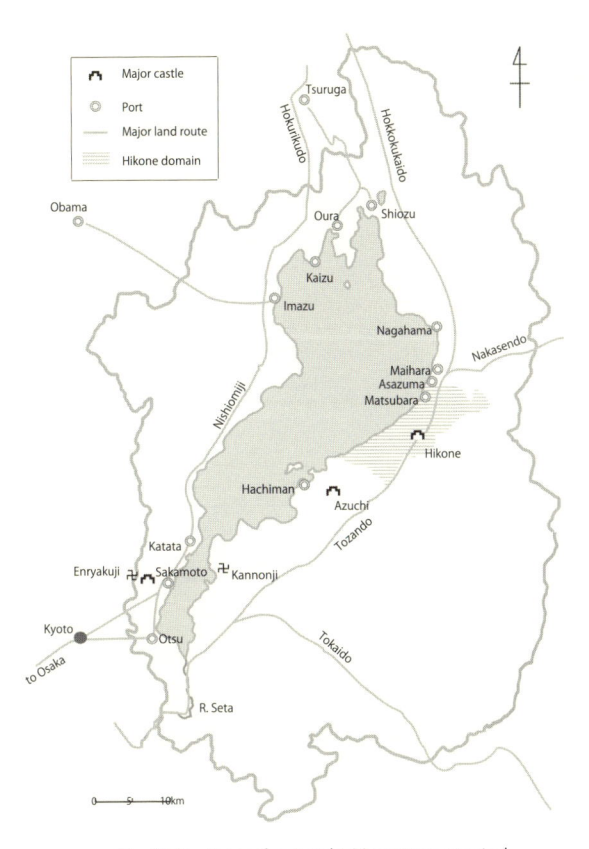

Fig. 26 Routes in the Azuchi-Momoyama period.

Following Nobunaga, Hideyoshi took over the Lake Biwa region, building a residential castle in Osaka in 1583. He established a water transportation route from the northern region to Otsu, and a land route from there to Fushimi and Osaka (Fig. 26). He gathered 100 boats from other ports to Otsu, boosting its importance, and he kept the boats under his control. Besides Otsu, Hideyoshi permitted sailing only to Katata and Hachiman. A magistrate was stationed at Kannonji temple, and Hideyoshi collected a portion of all cargoes as a tax. Thus Hideyoshi gained complete control over lake transportation. During this period Sakamoto city declined.

Chapter I Introduction

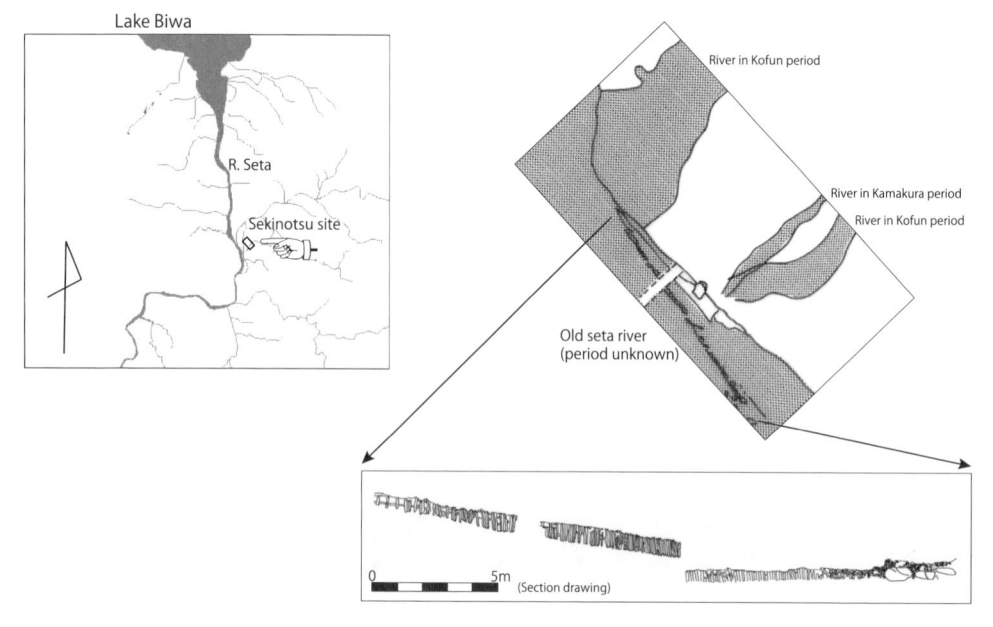

Fig. 27 Shore protection structure in the 15th to 17th century from Sekinotsu site.

An additional tax was imposed on boats from cities other than Otsu. Ports competed for transportation rights to the official ports. Shiozu, Kaitsu and Imazu in the north of the lake competed with Otsu, Katata and Hachiman. In particular, Nagahama, Maihara, and Matsubara in the north were competing under the protection of the Hikone domain.

Nagahama was the major port in the north of the lake. Maihara was established as a port in Asazuma in the Keicho period (1596-1614), and located at the gateway to the Nakasendo route. Matsubara was situated close to Hikone Castle. The Hikone domain government asked the three ports to monitor all cargo boats passing through its control, and tried to concentrate the boats in the three ports. The domain set up a collection and delivery facility in Otsu as well.

A rare example of a shore protection fort was discovered at the Sekinotsu site[46] along the Seta River in the south (Fig. 27). It dates back to between the

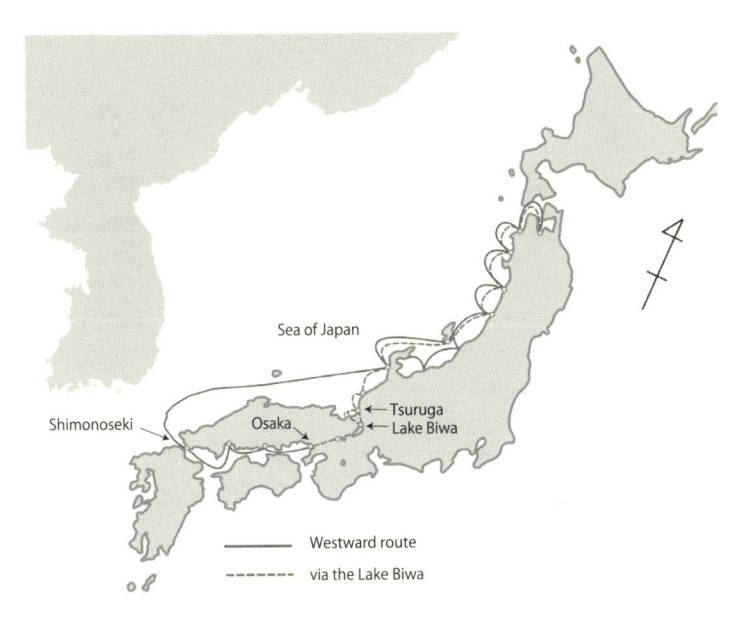

Fig. 28 Opening of the westward sailing route.

second half of the 15th century and the beginning of the 17th century, and is believed to be part of Sekinotsu port, used by the Zeze domain.

Water transportation on Lake Biwa reached its peak in the Edo period. According to historical records, the number of marukobune during the first half of the Edo period was 1,000 or more.[47]

This situation changed as the westward sailing route (Fig. 28) connecting the Sea of Japan and Osaka via Shimonoseki and the Seto Inland Sea was opened in 1672, and a new business center was established in Osaka. Cargo from northern Japan was not landed at Tsuruga or Obama, but transported directly to Osaka by sea. The result was the volume of boat cargo on Lake Biwa gradually declined, though it did not disappear entirely. The opening of the railroad in 1889 also diminished the lake's importance as a cargo route. After World War II marukobune were rarely seen.[48] Today, the role of boats on the lake has largely transitioned from transportation to tourism and pleasure.

Notes
1. Kira(ed.) 1995.
2. According to a personal communication with Dr. Kira.
3. Shoreline complexity is calculated to assess whether tectonic lakes have more complex shorelines than lakes of other origins. It is a value that indicates the degree of indentation of a shoreline, and Shoreline complexity (U) is the ratio of the length of the shoreline (L) to the circumference of a circle of area (A) equal to that of the lake. $U=L/2\sqrt{\pi A}$. Volume Curve, also known as Hypsometric Curve, is used to assess if a lake has a steep shore shape appropriate for a port. Hypsometric Curve shows the distribution of different depths in a lake. A curve is obtained when depths are laid out along the ordinate axis and the areas covered by the designated depths are laid out along the x-axis. Nishimura 1995, pp. 119-120.
4. They are designated by Minister of Land, Infrastructure and Transport.
5. The river reaches to the Uji River and then to the Yodo River, and flows into the Osaka Bay.
6. Manyoshu (『万葉集』), the oldest existing collection of Japanese poetry compiled during the Nara period.
7. Hayashi 2003, pp. 29-34.
8. The document of Shosoin recorded that the lumber was used for the Todaiji temple construction.
9. Ogasawara 2003, pp. 174-176.
10. See Yoshino 1985, pp. 81-82 for the local wind and geographic conditions.
11. A local expression for fishing in swamps. Hashimoto 1984, pp. 248-250.
12. Kitamura, S. et al. 1983, p. 60.
13. Okamoto 1974, p. 161.
14. Jomon means "cord-patterned" for the decorations that are seen on Jomon pottery.
15. Seguchi, S., Nakagawa, H. 2003, Nakagawa, M. 2003.
16. It is an Iron Age in Japan and named after the region (Yayoi township) of Tokyo where the first artifacts were discovered. A recent study used the accelerator mass spectrometry method to analyze carbonized remains on pottery and wooden stakes, and discovered that these were dated back to 900–800 B.C., 500 years earlier than previously believed.
17. Yokota 2004.
18. Found in the 7th excavation. Iwasaki, Shigeru 1997.
19. The excavation of the oar and the dugout, see Irienaiko site excavation report.
20. Shinkai 4th tomb (Anyoji, Ritto City).
21. It was restored by Ritto Museum of History and Folklore.

22 About the description on the wooden plate, see the excavation report of Nishigawara-Morinouchi site, pp. 8-17.
23 "I am rowing out the Omi Sea,and clearing around the shore rocks, cranes are crying in eighty harbors everywhere." (磯の先　漕ぎ廻み行けば近江の海　八十の湊に鵠多に鳴く).
24 Mikuriya were government offices to control the food resources in the Lake Biwa region, destined for the palace in the capital, and were established in Katata, Tsukuma, Adogawa, Wani, Awazu, Hashimoto, and Seta.
25 Ajiro was a government owned fishing facility to provide fishes to the Imperial Court. It was also set in the Uji River, and it used a type of yana, a bamboo trap set up between two wooden posts (see Chapter. I-Fig. 16).
26 Honpukuji-monjo (『本福寺文書』).
27 Kimura 1992, p. 229.
28 Nihon Giryaku, a history book written in the Heian period (『日本紀略』).
29 Engishiki (『延喜式』).
30 Todaiji-hodoshoen-hei-jiyocho (『東大寺封土荘園并寺用帳』): A journal of the Todaiji Temple.
31 "Journal of Todaiji Temple Manors" included in Collection of Historical Documents in the Heian Period　(東大寺封土荘園　寺用帳,『平安遺文』).
32 According to the excavation in Kozu, people started to settle in the middle of the 7th century, and colonnaded public buildings, which are supposedly related to the port, were found. Therefore, it is believed that Kozu had been used as a port even before supplying lumber. Mizuno 1994, p. 36.
33 Mizuno 1994.
34 "Jishimai-kechige-chusinjo, Echinosho, Omi" included in Collection of Historical Documents in the Heian period 『近江国愛智庄 地子米結解注進状』.
35 "Account Book of Echinosho, Omi" included in Collection of Historical Documents in the Heian Period (『近江国愛智庄結解 平安遺文』東南院文書).
36 Letter from Tokishige Kumon dated April 1st, 1303 in Yoshida Document (『吉田文書』).
37 Kimura 1992, p. 224.
38 Sakamoto seven checkpoints (Hiyoshi seven checkpoints): Honseki, Dobuseki, Kodoseki, Yokawanoseki, Chudoseki, Goseki, and Saitoseki.
39 Kimura 1992, 1995. The original documents are as follows.: "The troops of the Heike family rowed from Sakamoto to Yamada, Yabase, Shina and Konohama, and went north on land." (1183 Genpeiseisuiki (『源平盛衰記』)), "The troops sailed to Shina, Yamada and Yabase from Sakamoto in three days, and joined the troops of Emperor Godaigo." (1336 Baishoron (『梅松論』)), "Yoshihisa Ashikaga built a military base in Sakamoto as a preparation for a battle against Rokkaku Takase's troops. They attacked Shina by boats and defeated." (1487

Oninkoki (『応仁広記』)), "When priest Eison of Saidaiji Temple in Nara traveled to Kamakura, he sailed from Shiganoura, Shinomiya, and Bamba to Yamada, went on land via Moriyama, lodging one night, and reached Kagamiyado." (1262 Collected Biography of Eison of Saidaiji Temple (『西大寺叡尊伝記集成』)), "Kaneyoshi Ichijo, the former chief advisor to the emperor, traveled from Nara to Sakamoto, stayed there one night, sailed in the morning to Asazuma via Katata, and headed for Mino on land." (1493 Record of a round trip to Kanto (『関東往来記』)), "A messenger of Kofukuji Temple went to Musa from Sakamoto by boat, and paid tax of 32 mon." (1411 Record of a round trip to Kanto (『関東往来記』)), "Sonkai, a priest of Ninnaji Temple, crossed over Mt. Osaka, sailed from Sakamoto to Chikuma then to Asazuma, and took a rest at the Oki Island on the way." (1533 Record of Azuma Road Trip (『あずまの道の記』)), "Tokitsugu Yamashina left Sakamoto on board a boat for Shina, went south to Ise via Minoji and Happukaido, returned to Omi via Minoji again, and sailed back to Sakamoto from Asazuma." (1533 Diary of Tokitsugu (『言継卿記』)), "I (Tokitsugu Yamashina) went to Shina from Sakamoto by boat, and headed to Ise via Chigusakaido. On the way back I returned to Omi via Suzukaji, and sailed again from Shina to Sakamoto." (1556 Diary of Tokitsugu (『言継卿記』)), "I (Tokitsugu Yamashina) went to Asazuma from Sakamoto by boat, in November of the same year sailed from Sakamoto to Shina on the way to Mino. In 1571 I sailed from Awazu to Yabase, and left for Mino again." (July 1569 Diary of Tokitsugu (『言継卿記』).

40 Noji post town was located near Kusatsu post town, and supposedly the ruins of Noji post town were found at the Nojiokada site (Noji Town, Kusatsu City). Merchants' houses were built along the route, an unpaved road called Umamichi with a width of 5 m to 6 m running east and west, and leading to Yabase on its west.
41 Hanada 1993.
42 Kido 1992.
43 Nakai 1997.
44 ken=1.8 m, A unit of length used in Japan until the middle of 20th century.
45 Nobunaga Diary (『信長公記』).
46 An onsite briefing note dated August 1st, 2004. The remains indicate a sturdy structure. The foundation was built with posts and beams, twigs of pine tree and cherry tree were laid to protect the slope, then rocks were overlaid. The posts have a diameter of 10 cm and a length of around 1 m, and were driven in parallel to the stream of the time for 21 m. They were made of pine tree or Japanese cypress, formed 1 row or 2 rows, and more than 300 posts were found. The construction method is called, 'shikisoda' and is used to prevent the bank from washing away.
47 Studied by Kitamura 1946, Miyahata 1978, Hashimoto 1979, and Wada 1993 based on the documents such as Goshu-kosui-shoura-ryosen-hirata-bune-no-cho (『江州湖水諸浦猟船艜船之帳』),1601, Goshu-shoura-funakazu-cho (『江州諸浦船数

(2) General History of the Lake Biwa Region and its Water Transportation

帳』) 1649,Isome-ke-monjo (『居初家文書』),1655,Goshu-kosui-shoura-senin-kazucho (『江州湖水諸浦船員数帳』), 1677, Omi-roku (『淡海録』), 1690, Goshu-kosui-shoura-marubune-hiratabune-nayose-onhakobiage-cho (江州湖水諸浦丸船艜船名寄御運上帳), 1696, Kyoto-oyakushomuki-taigai-oboegaki (京都御役所向大概覚書), 1714, Omi-yochi-shiryaku (近江輿地志略), 1734, Kansei-ninen-inu-onhakobiage (寛政二年戌御運上), 1790.

48 Miyahata 1978, Hashimoto 1979, Makino 1999c.

65

Chapter II
Building the Marukobune Replica and Related Researches

(1) Marukobune Reconstruction Project

General Plan

Marukobune are a type of wooden sailing boat found only on Lake Biwa. Their origin is still unknown. The name probably comes from maru, meaning round, and most likely reflects the cross-section shape of marukobune hull. This is in contrast to other traditional boats on the lake, which have hard chine hulls composed of flat sections of planking (Preface-Fig. 2). The round shape is accentuated by two very unique components called omogi and heita. Omogi, form enormous rubrails on the sides of marukobune, and are composed of two halves of a cedar log split lengthwise. Tradition states that this odd construction provides stability. Heita refers to the bow planking of the boat, built of podocarpus planks running longitudinally, fastened to each other by edge nails. This type of construction, also not found elsewhere in Japan, forms a round bow and allows greater cargo volume without enlarging the boat itself.

The marukobune reconstruction project was carried out by the Lake Biwa Museum under the direction of Masaharu Yoda, the author's colleague, and the author from 1992 to 1995[1]. The marukobune built for the project was the first of its type built on Lake Biwa in 50 years.

The project's primary objective was to create an exhibit, as well as record and document the boatbuilding techniques. The mission of the Lake Biwa Museum is to educate visitors about the relationship between Lake Biwa and its people, and thus a marukobune was replicated for an exhibit on the historic culture of the lake. Building techniques of marukobune have been little studied. Despite the fact that these vessels survived until the early 1930s, there had been few studies documenting how they were built. As a result, the researches resolved to employ as many traditional techniques as possible in the boat's construction.

The project started with a search for a qualified shipwright. The last marukobune had been built before World War II. The museum hoped to find a shipwright with hands-on experience building marukobune. The final goal was to find a shipwright with an apprentice who could inherit the techniques via this project. Mr. Sanshiro Matsui (Preface-Photo. 1), 80 years old at the time, was running a boatbuilding business in Katata on the southwest shore of Lake Biwa. He was the only shipwright in the Lake Biwa region who met these requirements. His son Mitsuo joined the project as well. Mitsuo was running the shipyard and was a licensed builder of steel boats. This project, however was his first experience building a wooden boat. The participants in the reconstruction project felt fortunate that, not only could the building techniques of marukobune be documented, but also that an apprentice of a younger generation would be trained.

A marukobune with a cargo capacity of 100 koku was constructed. The overall length is 17 m (19 m when the rudder is lowered), beam 2.4 m, and the depth is 1 m. A mast is mounted slightly aft of the center of the hull and its height is 12 m. The entire project, from the felling of the trees to the final completion of the vessel, took two and a half years. The vessel was launched in March, 1995.

Marukobune are classified into two types according to their shape. One is the southern lake type, which is represented by the museum's replica, and the other is the northern lake type. Since Matsui was trained in the southern region, the research represented here is limited to the southern lake type. Despite this limitation, the boatbuilding process itself did not seem to differ between the southern lake type and the northern lake type, because the shape and the structure of the two boats are similar.

The main building process is illustrated through the following series of photographs. Some photographs show Matsui working on the repair of an old marukobune.[2]

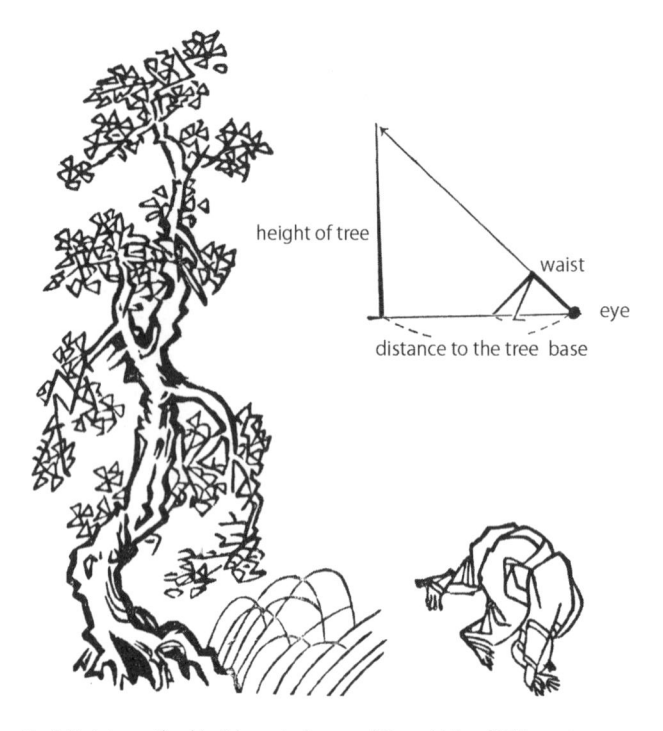

Fig.1 Metate method in Edo period, around the middle of 17th century.

Selection of the Timber (Photo. 1)

It is preferable to cut trees during the fall, when they have dried out after the rainy season. However, because of this project's schedule, the trees were felled in winter. Most of the timber came from Momoi, Kyoto Prefecture.

For marukobune construction, podocarp was used for the bow planking (heita), lower side planking (furikake), stern sheer planking (tobinoo), transom (tomoita), and for side planks (kakiita). Japanese cedar was used for bottom planking (shiki) and the half-logs that form the gunwale (omogi). Japanese cypress was used for the mast and components above the deck, including the sheer strakes (tana). In general, podocarp wood was used for below-the-waterline components because of its high oil content, though its strength is lower than cedar.

Photo. 1 A libation onto the root of the serected tree.

Cedar is stronger and more resilient than podocarp, and was used in areas of high load or impact. Cypress was used for deck components that require detail woodwork.

The timber was measured for size using a traditional method called "metate" (Fig. 1). The volume of the tree is calculated by measuring the girth of the tree at an eye level. Before cutting, the shipwright poured a small amount of sake (rice wine) onto the roots of the tree as a token of gratitude to the god of mountains (yamanokami).

Cutting and Loading the Timber (Photo. 2)

Ibaritori, a type of axe, was used when felling the trees. It was also used like a mallet to drive wedges (ya) into the cut. After a wedge-shaped cut was made on the side of the trunk near the root, wedges were driven into the opposite side. After several wedges were driven with the ibaritori, they forced the tree to fall. Chainsaws were also used in some parts of the process to save time. The cut timbers were loaded onto a truck. In the past, after waiting for the spring thaw, logs were thrown into rivers while the water level was high, and transported downstream (see Chapter. III-(1)). Because of time constraints however, the project's logs were transported to the boatyard by truck right after felling. This work was done by the shipwright, two apprentices, and three porters.

Chapter II Building the Marukobune Replica and Related Research

Photo. 2 Cutting and loading the timbers.

Arrival of the Logs at the Boatyard and Milling (Photo. 3, 4)

The logs were transported to Matsui's boatyard in Honkatata on the west shore. They were transported by truck most of the way, but the truck was unable to make a turn near the yard. As a result, the logs were thrown into a canal adjacent to the yard, and they were brought into the boatyard from the lake.

The logs were left untouched for a few months to dry. Then they were milled into rough-sawn boards. The milling was all done using modern equipment to save time. After milling, the material was stacked and left to dry further (Photo. 5).

Lofting (photo. 6)

Secrecy was endemic to the craft of boatbuilding; therefore builders rarely had design plans or diagrams of their boats on paper. Instead, craftsmen memorized crucial dimensions. However, some boatbuilders drew "plank drawings" (itazu) on a piece of wood. Mr. Matsui had recorded only the angle of the furikake (the lower side plank between the bottom and the side planking) on a plank. He kindly created comprehensive drawings of the boat for the museum.

Mr. Matsui's measurement tools were those familiar to the traditional carpentry, such as the square (sashigane or kanazashi), marking gauge

(1) Marukobune Reconstruction Project

Photo. 3 Arrival of the logs at the boatyard.

Photo. 4 Cutting roughly into boards.

Photo. 5 Drying planks.

Photo. 6 Carpenter uses Sumitsubo to measurement marks on boards.

(keibiki), and kusegane (bevel gauge).

He used an inkline and pot (similar to a chalk line in the West) called a sumitsubo. Sumitsubo are filled with cotton saturated in black ink, with a string passing through the pot. The string is pulled out from the pot and held against the work, stretched tight, then snapped to mark a line on the wood. All the layout on the timbers was done with these basic tools.

Driving Nails (Photo. 7)

The planking of marukobune is edge-nailed together. Small mortises are cut near the edges of adjacent planks and nails are driven through the mortises and into adjoining planks. The nail head rests in the mortises, which are plugged or covered so that no nail heads are visible in the finished work. All the mortises are on the outside of the hull. In this way any water that seeps into the seam cannot leak into the boat via the mortise.

The special nails used in boatbuilding are hand-forged and called nuikugi, literally "sewing nail" (Fig. 2). The nails are somewhat similar in function to doweling, a common technique used to edge-fasten boards in the West.

Mr. Matsui soaked his nails in salt water before using. He believed the rusty surface increased the friction of the nails, and improved their holding power. New nails are perfectly straight, and the builder must curve them

(1) Marukobune Reconstruction Project

Photo. 7 Driving nails into boards.

Nail driving direction

Boat nail (Sewing nail)

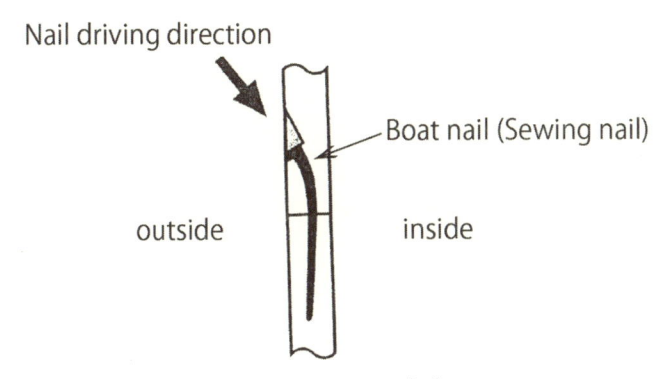

outside   inside

Fig. 2 Joinning two planks.

with a hammer before edge nailing planks.   The shipwright judges how deep to set the nail by listening to the sound of the hammer on the nail set.

Boatbuilders employ a special set of chisels called tsubanomi for making nail holes.   Mr. Matsui had three types of tsubanomi: sugutsuba are straight chisels, used for piloting more conventional nails; tamaritsuba are curved chisels, used for joining planks edge-to-edge; and koguchitsuba are chisels with a flat head, used when a nail is driven into end grain.   A full set of chisels includes different sizes to match different nail lengths.   Matsui believed the length of the nail should be three to three and a half times of the thickness of the lumber.

Shiki (bottom) Building (Photo. 8)

The first step in building the marukobune is constructing the bottom, or shiki. First, cedar planks are placed side by side and temporarily fastened using large iron staples called kasugai.

Then the boatbuilder runs a handsaw, called surinoko, down the seam between the planks (see also "Caulking" below in this section). This technique is called suriawase, and surinoko comes from the verb to rub (suru) plus a shortened version of the name for a handsaw (nokogiri).

By sawing between the planks, the edges gain a better fit. Japanese boatbuilders use this technique throughout the boat when fitting parts tightly.

In a marukobune with a cargo capacity of 100 koku, the bottom panels consist of a naka-jiki or center plank, and 6 (aft) to 7 (fore) longitudinal planks called waki-jiki (or katasa-jiki) on the sides. Waki-jiki are numbered 1st, 2nd and 3rd plank from the naka-jiki on both port and starboard. After the bottom planks are fitted, they are edge-nailed together into a single panel (Photo. 9). When assembling the shiki, the shipwright carefully inspects the cross section of each plank so that when joined they form a smooth curve. The curved shape is created by joining together tapered planks like the gores in clothing.

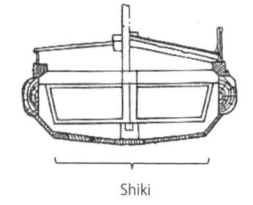

Photo. 8 Shiki building.

Building the Sides (Photos. 10 & 11)

The lower side of the marukobune is called the furikake. Made of maki, (podocarp), it forms the part of the hull between the bottom and the log rubrails. The mounting angle of the furikake is critical to the total balance of a boat. Mr. Matsui had kept the critical angles recorded on a plank for over 50 years.

Raising the Stem (Photos. 12 & 13)

After the bottom planks and furikake were joined, the stem (shin) was mounted at the front end. An auspicious day in the calendar was chosen for this work, and the owner of the boat was invited. When the stem-raising was finished safely, sake was poured on the stem and the stern, while praying for continued safe work.

Photo. 9 Nail holes on Shiki.

Bending and Attaching Omogi (Photos. 14 &15)

The most distinctive feature of marukobune are the huge, half log omogi that form the upper sides of the hull. They function as rubrails as well. Their round shape is one reason for the marukobune's name. A typical marukobune with a cargo capacity of 100 koku will have omogi cut from a cedar log with the girth of more than 2.3 m at the butt end. Since the hull tapers at the bow and stern, these timbers must be bent. In the past the boatbuilder would rely on other neighbouring shipwrights to come and help bend the omogi. Instead, Mr. Matsui was forced to prop the omogi against the walls of his shop. No heat was used at all to bend the timbers.

Chapter II Building the Marukobune Replica and Related Research

Photo. 10 Preparing Furikake.

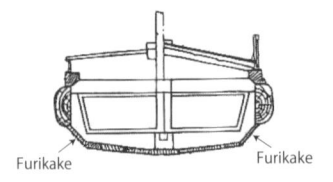

Photo. 11 Furikake under Omogi. (from restoration project.)

Building the Bow

The bow section of the hull is composed of planks that run longitudinally like the staves of a barrel. Called the heita, the bow is planked in maki. The distinctive curved shape of the marukobune bow may also contribute to the derivation of the name of these boats. Mr. Matsui had also retained all the information on the angles of the heita planking from the earliest days of his career.

Caulking (Photos. 16 & 17)

A saw was inserted between the timbers to shape and finish the gap for

(1) Marukobune Reconstruction Project

Photo. 12 Stem raising.

Photo. 13 Caulking between stem and shiki.

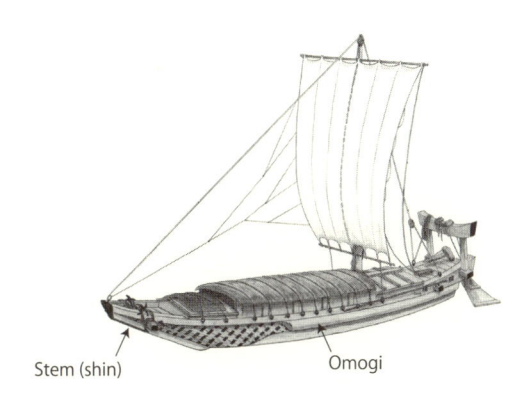

Stem (shin)   Omogi

Chapter II Building the Marukobune Replica and Related Research

Photo. 14 Attaching omogi.

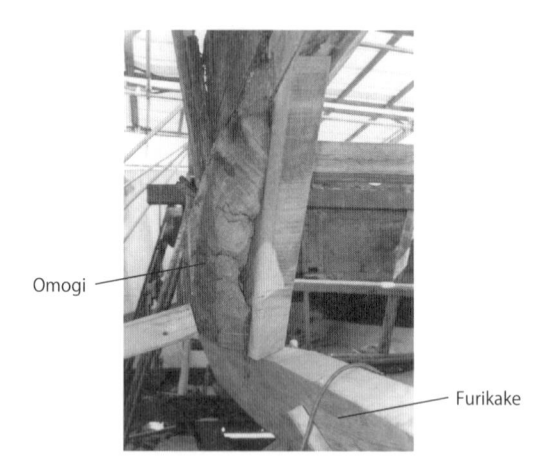

Omogi

Furikake

Photo. 15 Omogi on Furikake (from restoration project.)

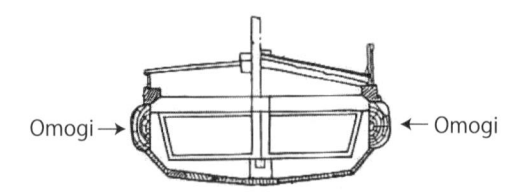

Omogi → ← Omogi

*The original omogi was a single piece half cut log, but a plank was installed under the sawed original omogi in photo. 15. Only the exterior part was retained during the restoration project.

caulking so the material would remain securely in place after being tamped into the seam. This was an essential tool in the development of such boats.

The material used to caulk the seams is made of the inner bark of the maki tree, and called either makinawa or makihada. The bark is softened before use by pounding the material with a wooden mallet, called a yokuzuchi. In the West, cotton caulking is driven into plank seams using a caulking iron (a blunt iron blade) and a mallet. Typically, Japanese boatbuilders do the same, but Mr. Matsui believed that makihada was too fragile, and needed to be worked with bamboo, rather than iron, tools. He called these tools yatoku, which he made himself. The first tool used for pushing the material in the seams was thin, followed by a thicker bamboo caulking tool to drive the material in tight. A final type of bamboo caulking tool he called sakiyari was used to pack in the caulking, and also to open tight seams in the planking. Matsui did have a conventional caulking iron as well, which he called a hokon-uchi

Another distinctive aesthetic feature of marukobune is the pattern of copper sheeting that covers the seams at the bow. Soft sheet copper, called akaita, is fastened with small nails. The copper is painted with a mixture of black ink and rapeseed oil to protect it from oxidation. The copper work is called datekasugai and has become an iconic symbol of Lake Biwa boats, such that even modern fiberglass and steel boats will have this pattern painted on their bows.

Mast, Sails, and Gallows (Photos. 18-21, Figures. 3 & 4)

The mast was made from Japanese cypress (hinoki). Its cross section is square with the corners rounded. The square cross section was chosen instead of a circular section to give the mast greater stiffness in strong winds. The mast gallows, called kasagi, was set up at the stern. The mast is stepped aft-of-center on the hull, but it could be lowered and rested on the mast gallows when not in use.

Chapter II Building the Marukobune Replica and Related Research

Photo. 16 Working with surinokogiri for caulking.

Photo. 17 Finishing the seams for caulking using surinokogiri.

The sail cloth for the replica was made using as traditional a process as possible. An example of historic sail cloth was found at the Marukobune Museum in Nishiazai. After studying this material and considering the replica's size, six sheets of plain fabric were made in a style called Matsuemon weaving (Fig. 3).[3] Matsuemon is unusual in that one yarn is woven in the warp while two yarns comprise the weft.

This weaving method was commonly used in the Edo period. A hemp rope was attached to the perimeter of each cloth, and the six sheets were loosely fastened to build the sail. Since the air flows through between the loosely fastened sheets, the sail is self-regulating in heavy winds, spilling air as the panels open up.

Ceremonies and other projects after the construction are as follows.

Launching Ceremony (Photo. 22)

The launching ceremony was held in keeping with traditional rites. A

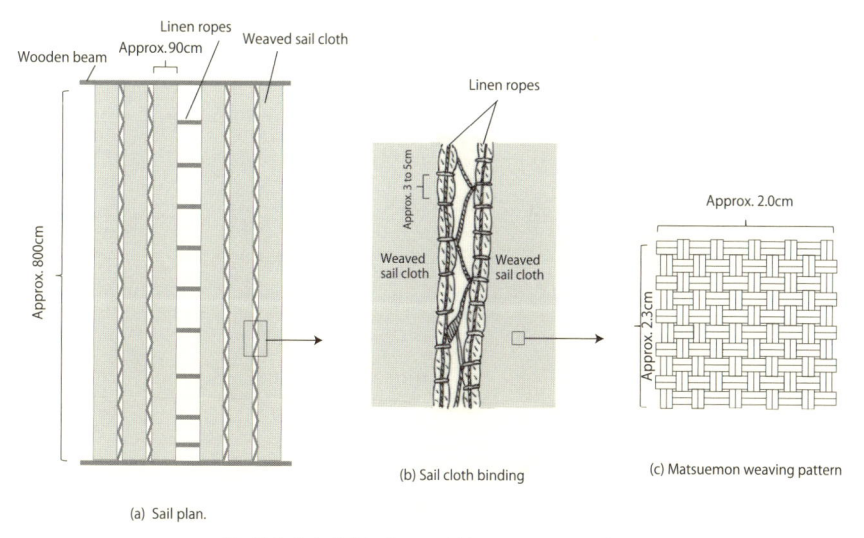

Fig. 3 Sail cloth binding and Matsuemon weaving.

launch song, with origins in Imakatata Town, Otsu City was sung. The lyrics read: "Oh, congratulations, congratulations. Today is the launch day for this family. The boat's hull is made of platinum, the oars are gold, the mast is gold and silver, and the sail of 8 m is hoisted by a three-strand iron rope. Seven fortune gods are on board, Ebisu-san and Daikoku-san (both are gods of wealth) are rowing and sailing before the winds of fortune. Oh, good fortune comes to this house."

Towing the Marukobune (Photo. 23)

The marukobune was towed by a power boat from Katata to the Lake Biwa Museum on the Karasuma Peninsula. At the time the museum was still under construction. Even though the crossing the marukobune would need to make was quite short, just 4 km, in order to minimize any risk to the replica, a fishing boat was used to tow the vessel. Only the shipwrights who built the boat went on board. The general public was invited to watch from a passenger vessel that accompanied the crossing.

Pre-Exhibition (photo. 24)

The marukobune was opened to the public after it arrived at Karasuma Peninsula. The shipwright was on site throughout the event, answering questions from visitors, and demonstrating bailing the bilge water and hoisting sail. The event produced an unexpected outcome; visitors began sharing their memories of marukobune.

Museum staff noticed that elderly visitors began making comments based on historical marukobune. These comments revealed many first person accounts, such as descriptions of sailing marukubune, seeing them under construction, and details of their features (see Chapter. III-(2)). Some visitors pointed out that sailors drank water straight from the lake, providing evidence of better water quality in the past. Museum staff recognized the value of such accounts, and realized that a tremendous body of knowledge existed unrecorded (see section (3) and note 10). The replica marukobune provided the touchstone for an outpouring of memories.

Moving into the Museum (Photo. 25)

After the public event, the boat was installed in a permanent exhibit at the Lake Biwa Museum. The hull was transported by truck to the back of the exhibition room, and hoisted by crane to the second floor where the exhibition room was located.

Chapter II Building the Marukobune Replica and Related Research

Photo. 18 Rear view of marukobune with kasagi(mast gallows).

Photo. 19 Cabin/hold covered with kakiita(wash board) and komo(straw mat).

(1) Marukobune Reconstruction Project

Photo. 20 Cabin roof framing mounted on the sheer strake.

Photo. 21 Inside of the cabin.

Photo. 22 Launching ceremony.

Chapter II Building the Marukobune Replica and Related Research

Photo. 23 Towing the marukobune.

Photo. 24 Pre-exhibition.

Photo. 25 Moving into the museum under the construction.

(2) Carpenter's Tools for Traditional Boats in the Lake Biwa Region

The traditional boatbuilding process relied on a variety of craftsmen, including loggers, sawyers, blacksmiths, and boatbuilders. All these trades developed over time, and the tools used evolved as well. The traditional boat building tools exhibited in the museum represent those used mainly in the 1930s. Several shipwrights, including Mr. Matsui, donated tools to the exhibit.[4]

Tools Used for Tree Felling and Rough Milling (Photo. 26)

Until the 1930s, logging was a task done by lumberjacks, and shipwrights were not involved (see Chapter. III-(1)). However, as sawmills expanded, and shipwrights did become more involved with choosing and cutting trees, they started to use tools such as ibaritori, ya and kigaeshi.

After felling, some of the larger tools used for the initial cutting and milling of timber included the kigaeshi and kandotatsubiki. Once cut to rough size, logs were thrown into rivers, assembled as rafts, and transported downstream to boat builders in various locations.

The craftsman who cut logs into planks (by hand) was called a kobiki, and his saws were known collectively as kobikinoko. The specific types of saws were the two-person yokobiki and one-man maebiki. The chonna (adze) and yoki (axe) were used for the finer cutting and rough shaping of round components.

Measurement Tools (Photo. 27)

The measurement tools include the sashigane or kanazashi (carpenters square), keibiki (marking gauge), and kusegane (bevel gauge). Older squares were made of thick brass and required periodic adjustment. Modern versions

Chapter II Building the Marukobune Replica and Related Research

Maebiki

Yokobiki

Kandotatsubiki

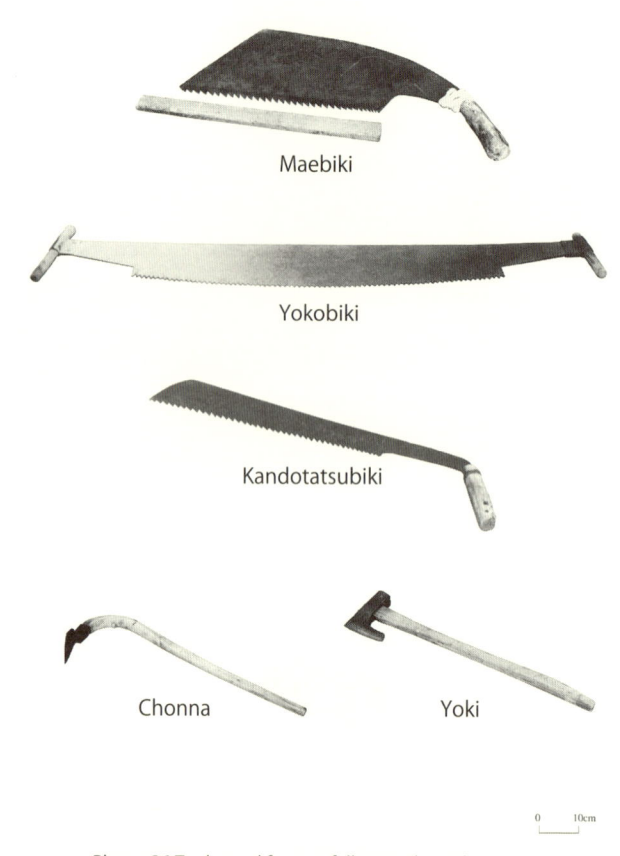

Chonna

Yoki

Photo. 26 Tools used for tree felling and rough cutting.

are made of stainless steel. Like its Western counterpart, the carpenter's square can be used to derive various shapes and angles.[5]

The sumitsubo is the inkline, indispensable to the boatbuilder and used to mark straight lines.

Tools for Fine Work (Photo. 28)

Various types of chisels and saws were used for fine woodwork. The tsukinomi is the largest Japanese chisel, a paring tool pushed by the user and never struck with a mallet. Marunomi are gouges. Obiro and kobiro refer

(2) Carpenter's Tools for Traditional Boats in the Lake Biwa Region

Sashigane

Oregane

Kusegane

Keibiki

Sumitsubo

Photo. 27 Measurement tools.

to conventional chisels with different blade widths. Their handles are fitted with iron rings and they are struck with a hammer.

The ryoba is a saw with teeth on the both sides; fine teeth on one side for crosscutting (across the grain), and large teeth on the other side for ripping (cutting with the grain). The tatebiki is a ripsaw, and the sakiboso (hikimawashi) is a narrow saw used for cutting circles. The kanzo is another narrow saw used for making holes. These saws require having their teeth set with saw files, which come in various sizes.

After sawing, timbers were further prepared using several types of planes.

91

Chapter II Building the Marukobune Replica and Related Research

Tsukinomi (5bu) Obiro Kobiro Marunomi (3bu)

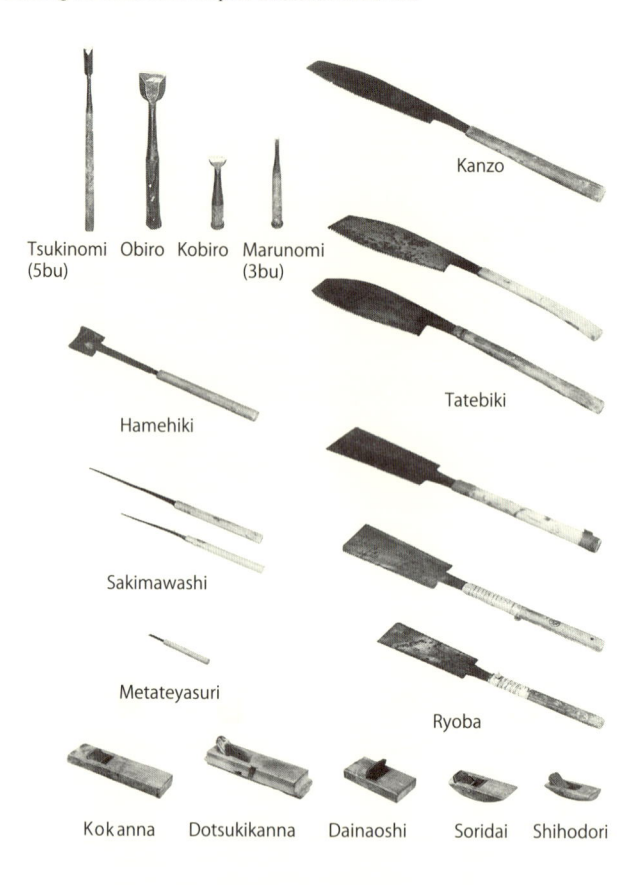

Kanzo

Hamehiki

Tatebiki

Sakimawashi

Metateyasuri

Ryoba

Kokanna Dotsukikanna Dainaoshi Soridai Shihodori

Photo. 28 Tools for fine work.

A boatbuilder would have a selection of planes, including a dotsukikanna (dotsuki plane), or rabbet plane. A sharply convex plane is called soridai (tenkozori), and a moderately convex plane is called hanzori. There is even a special plane, called a dainoshi, for tuning the bottoms of wooden plane bodies.

A special tool called a hamehiki was used to carve the hollow in which the copper plating was fastened. The thickness of akaita was normally 2 mm, and the hull surface was carved to that depth to accept the copper plate.

Kasugai

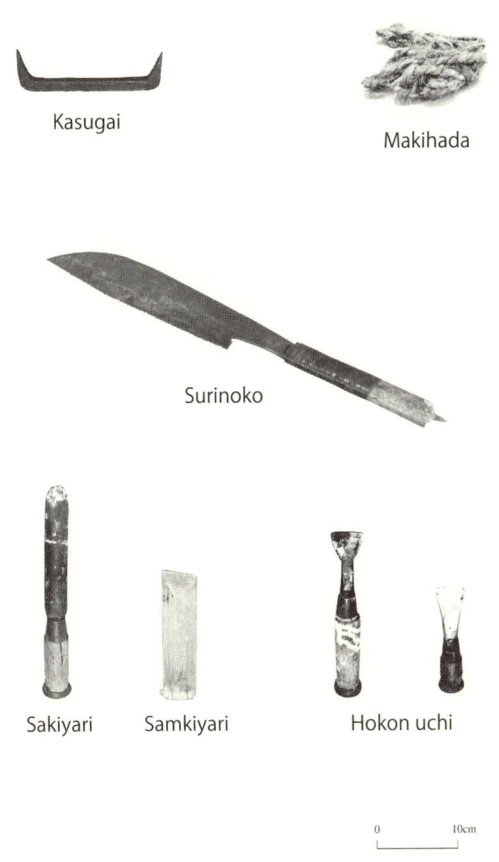

Makihada

Surinoko

Sakiyari   Samkiyari   Hokon uchi

0   10cm

Photo. 29 Nail driving tools.

Nail-Driving Tools (Photo. 29)

Nails of various lengths were used in the marukobune construction. They included 60 ami (9 cm), 50 ami (10.5-12 cm), 40 ami (13.5-15 cm), 30 ami (18-19.5 cm), and 20 ami (21-24 cm) boat nails.[6]

Mr. Matsui relied on both a wooden mallet and an iron hammer when driving nails. His tool chest also contained various punches, or nail sets, to aid in driving nails into the mortises that housed the nail heads. A copper nail set called a yogane also sometimes served as a caulking iron. Yogane wore down quickly through use.

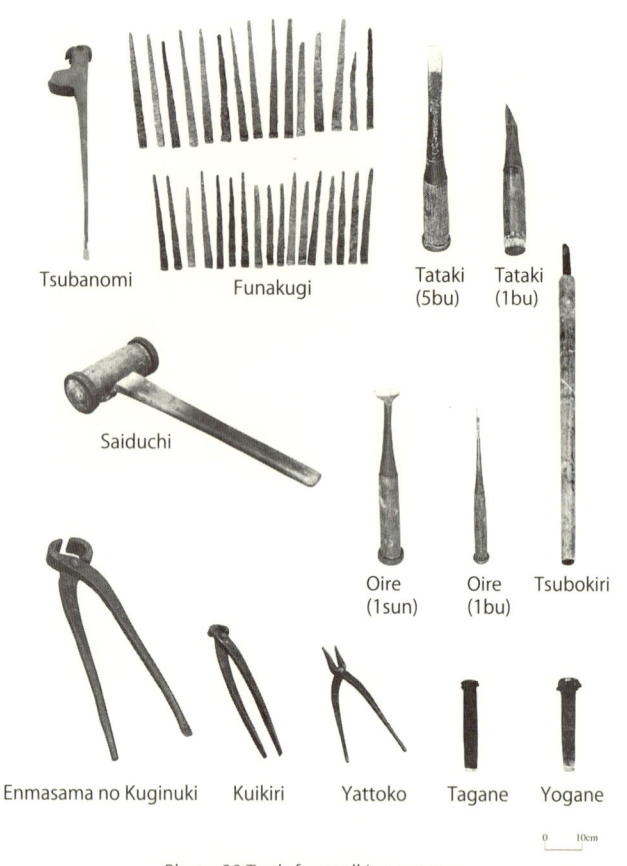

Chapter II Building the Marukobune Replica and Related Research

Photo. 30 Tools for caulking process.

The wooden mallet is the saizuchi, used both for driving caulking as well as nails. The ends of the mallet head are circled with iron bands like a chisel handle. The striking force of this mallet is less than an iron hammer, but Mr. Matsui preferred it because he felt this tool gave him a better feel for how hard the caulking or nail had been driven. Driving the largest nails (30 cm or more in length) required two men: one to hold the nail with a pair of pliers called yattoko while the other swung the mallet.

There were other nail sets in different sizes called tataki and oire, and they were used according to the size of the boat. Oire is thinner than tataki, and it was not hit hard. A nail set called kugijime is used for Western-style nails. A cold chisel called tagane is used for cutting nails when a boat nail is pulled out. The boatbuilder's iron hammer is long and balanced to be stable and less prone to miss. As mentioned above, the wooden mallet was used in nailing, but drove nails more slowly. While an iron hammer resulted in greater productivity, it was believed that using the mallet resulted in higher holding strength of the nail. The carpenter's nail puller was called the enma, meaning 'the king of the world of the dead' (in Buddhism), because its shape was similar to the tool that the enma used to pull out tongues of liars.

Tools for the Caulking Process (Photo. 30)

Mr. Matsui used primarily bamboo caulking tools in his work. After preparing the seams with handsaws, caulking material was pushed into the seams using spatula-type tools and a mallet.

(3) The Marukobune Tankentai

The Lake Biwa Museum, like many similar institutions, works with volunteers. The program here is referred to as the Hashikake System.[7] Hashikake means "bridging across," in reference to the museum's goal of utilizing volunteers as a bridge between the museum and visitors. As of 2004, there were 120 registered volunteers, and they participated in activities matching their interests. The primary mission of Hashikake System is to give the opportunity to local citizens to participate in research projects at the museum. The study of traditional culture was just one of several activities undertaken by volunteers, and the Marukobune Tankentai (Explorers) program was established in 2003 by the author (Photo. 31).

Around 30 people, most of them retirees, were gathered. They included weekend sailors, long-time workers of a shipbuilding company, and local residents interested in the local culture, among others.

Photo. 31 Hashikake activity.

(3) The Marukobune Tankentai

The primarily objective of the group was to research marukobune and other traditional boats of the Lake Biwa region, and to disseminate the results region-wide. The project was divided into the three specific subjects, (1) a study of marukobune's sailing performance, (2) reproducing scenes of the past containing traditional boats, and (3) exploring how traditional boats can be used in the future.[8]

For the first subject, detailed observations of the boat were made while simultaneously cleaning the marukobune and the fishing boat in the exhibition room (Photo. 32). In addition, sail handling was tested using a one third scale model of a marukobune with a cargo capacity of 100 koku (15 t) (Photo. 33). These were good opportunities to understand details of construction and the operation of the marukobune. The participants familiar with sailing were able to gain a basic idea of how its sail needed to be trimmed in ways specific to marukobune.

At the same time, members familiarized themselves with the construction of marukobune and designed a paper model (Fig. 4).[9] The model boat was assembled in a way that demonstrated the structure and the actual building process. Omogi, the side members of the hull and the most distinctive component of marukobune, are attached separately to emphasize their importance. The paper model boat kit was later printed and used in museum activities (Photo. 34).

A questionnaire on traditional boats was attached to the instruction manual of the model boat, and the data collected was added to the information on traditional boats of Lake Biwa kept at the marukobune communication desk.[10] This data was compiled in a database by the members of the Marukobune Tankentai (Fig. 5).

The core of the second topic, the reproduction of the scenes containing traditional boats, consisted of about 30 models of traditional boats owned by the Lake Biwa Museum. The use and function of the boats were hard to grasp completely by their shapes, but if the models are displayed with cargo

Chapter II Building the Marukobune Replica and Related Research

Photo. 32 Detail observations throughout marukobune while cleaning.

Photo. 33 Sail handling test by using a model of marukonbune.

in a realistic scene, they can be more clearly understood. Scenes were reproduced for each boat based upon data from interviews with shipwrights, and the pictorial materials of the Lake Biwa region (Photo. 35) in the mid-20th century.[11] It is worth noting that the volunteers who made the model cargo had personal experience either sailing marukobune or handling cargo. The process of making these reproductions in many cases spurred even more memories from the members of Marukobune Tankentai.

(3) The Marukobune Tankentai

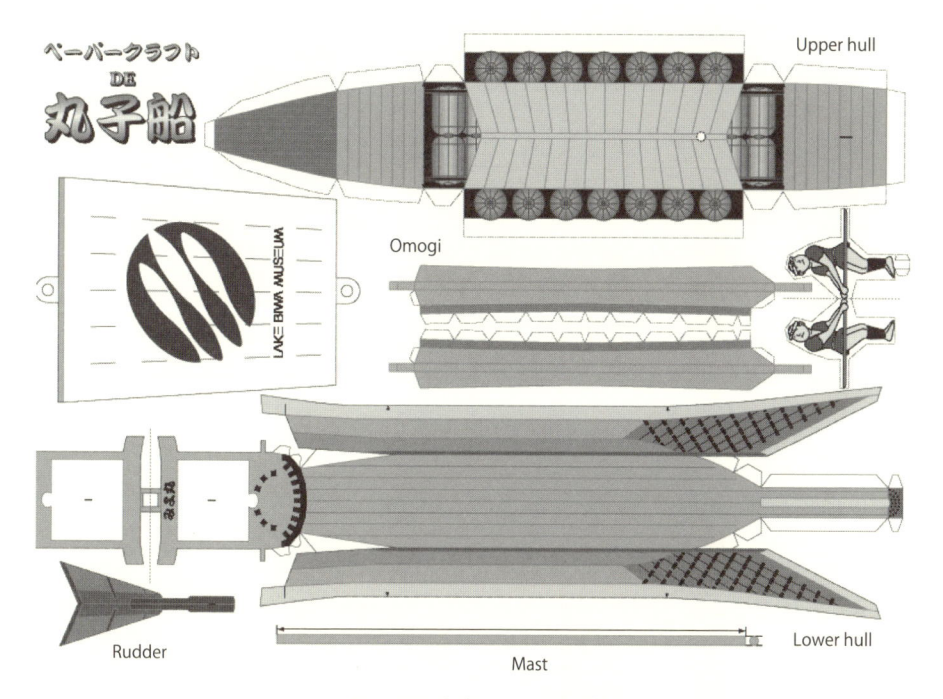

Fig. 4 Marukobune paper craft.

Photo. 34 The museum activities with the paper craft boat kit.

Chapter II Building the Marukobune Replica and Related Research

Fig. 5 Data base of traditional wooden boats in the Lake Biwa region.

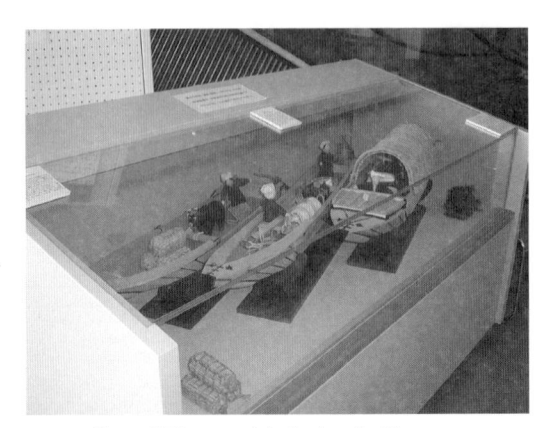

Photo. 35 Boat models displayed with cargo.

The third subject, the exploration of how traditional boats could be used in the future, was related to a plan discussed by the prefectural administration to revitalize lake transportation.[12] After the steady decline of lake transportation, Lake Biwa has been predominantly used for tourism. Revitalizing the lake as a transportation route was considered as part of a policy emphasizing the rising awareness of the human/spiritual aspects of the lake. Traditionally such values have been forgotten in light of modern technological progress.

In 1990 a plan to develop key ports for lake transportation was proposed based on the development projects of the region. The ports have terminals and services primarily for sightseeing ships, and terminals were constructed in Karasuma, Moriyama and Ayame from the south shore to the east shore, Adogawa in the west shore, and Takeshima. In 2002, another plan was proposed to assist an experimental lake taxi service in the northern Lake Biwa.[13]

Finally, an interesting idea for a modern use for marukobune was offered by a member of the Marukobune Tankentai. The proposal was to explore the use of marukobune in a natural disaster. Since Lake Biwa is a tectonic lake, there are many active fault lines in the surrounding region. In particular, the Hanaore fault, runs for 45 km from the north east part of Kyoto City to Imazu City in Shiga Prefecture, in a north north-easterly direction. This fault has drawn attention because the risk of seismic activity on the fault has become extremely high. The north side of this fault was hit by an earthquake in 1662 with a magnitude of 7.4. However, a study found that there have been only two seismic events on the south side of the fault, dating from 8000 to 7000 years ago and then again from 2500 to 1500 years ago. Thus, potential for an earthquake is considered high. Once an earthquake occurs, the current transportation system could be cut off, removing a vital lifeline to the region. If roads and rail lines are damaged, the only viable way to transport goods may be by water.

Notes

1. The project was inspected by the Marukobune Reconstruction Guiding Committee: Mr. Tetsuo Hashimoto, a folklorist of the region, Professor Emeritus Satoshi Matsuki of Kobe University of Mercantile Marine, Akiko Deguchi, Lecturer of Kansei Gakuin University, Mr. Yoshikazu Hasegawa of Shiga Prefecture Board of Education, Mr. Yoshiyuki Onuma of Shiga Prefecture Board of Education, and Mr. Shigeo Sugitate, a local researcher of the traditional boats of Lake Biwa. The record of the reconstruction was also compiled by A. Deguchi (Deguchi 1999).

2. Old marukobune built in 1952. This is the oldest existing marukobune, converted to a powerboat and used on the lake until recently. Since it was in a poor condition, it was restored in the fall of 2002. An ex-captain of a shipping company purchased it and asked Mr. Matsui for a major restoration to bring it back to life as a sightseeing boat. The lower part of the hull was rebuilt almost entirely, i.e. replacement of the lower side planking (furikake) and below, the lower half of the bow planking (heita), above the sheer strake (tana), and the internal part of the stem (shin). The remaining original parts were the side members (omogi), the upper part of the bow planking and the front surface of the stem.

3. About sail cloth, see also the report by S. Matsuki in Yoda & Makino (eds.) 1999.

4. These tools are kept in the Lake Biwa Museum.

5. Mr. Matsui, used kujirajaku, unlike most Japanese boatbuilders who use kanejaku (1sun is 3.3 cm on kanejaku, but 3.8 cm on kujirajaku). In general kanejaku was used to measure hard objects such as lumber by carpenters and construction workers, and the cloth measure was used when making clothes to provide room for fitting with a human body's soft curves. It is intriguing that cloth measure was used for marukobune considering its distinct round shape, even though the marukobune was constructed using hard materials.

6. The units relating to boat nails were ren, ami, and sunpo. Ren was used primarily in the Edo period, 1 ren was 400 momme (1,500 g), and the number of nails made from 1 ren is called ami, for example if 30 nails were made, the nail size was called 30 ami.

7. For the activities of Hashikake system, see The Lake Biwa Museum Annual Report Vol. 8, 2003, pp. 14-17.

8. The reproduction of historic scenes is being discussed also by the museum administration and private researchers. An example is in Furukawa, Onishi (ed.) 1992.

9. Miss. Miyo Nishiwaki of the Marukobune Tankentai contributed to the creation of the paper model boat, and another explorer, Mr. Mitsuo Osumi contributed entering data from the questionnaire into the database. These results are available on the Internet. http://www.lbm.go.jp/kumi/index2.html

10. The Marukobune Communication Desk was established as part of the marukobune

exhibition in the Lake Biwa Museum.　It was for collecting information from local people about traditional boats.　I owe much to museum staff, Tenji Koryuin, for interpreting this system to visitors.

11　Historic photographs valuable for understanding the history of Shiga Prefecture were taken by Mr. Takashi Maeno, mainly in the early Showa Period in various places in Shiga Prefecture.　He was born in 1916 in Akashi City, Hyogo Prefecture and moved to Otsu City, Shiga Prefecture in 1928.　His works include A Collection of Photographs by Takasuke Maeno 1993, Kaiseisha (『前野隆資写真集』,偕成社) and The Lake Biwa - Story of Water 1998, Heibonsha (『琵琶湖・水物語』、平凡社).　His works are also open to the public as "Pictorial Story, Now and the Past" in the Lake Biwa Museum web pages.

12　Planning Coordination Division, Planning Department, Shiga Prefecture 1990, 1994, 2002.

13　However, the proposal of "Reducing Unnecessary Automobiles by Revitalizing Lake Transportation" was considered unfeasible.　At the 2nd meeting of the committee for the improvement of the traffic congestion on the Otsu-Kusatsu route declared, "the feasibility is low because of the speed limitation of ships, and the service suspension in case of strong winds based on the social experiment of the lake transportation."　Meeting held on December 24th, 2003 at Piaza Omi hosted by Otsu Office of Public Works, Shiga Prefecture.

Chapter III
The Rise and Fall of Traditional Boats on Lake Biwa

(1) The Rise and Fall of the Traditional Boats as seen through the Life of a Shipwright

The Life of Mr. Sanshiro Matsui, the Last Marukobune Shipwright

As the last traditional shipwright of Lake Biwa, the life of Mr. Matsui reflects the decline of wooden boats in this region. Although the various types of wooden boats used on the lake disappeared at different rates, all types eventually succumbed to modernization and new technologies.

Mr. Matsui was born as the son of a stonemason in 1913. He was skillful as a child, and began his boatbuilding career as an apprentice when he was about ten years old. It was around the time when the traditional boats, particularly marukobune, were beginning to disappear (Fig. 1).

Mr. Matsui was not particularly keen on boats as a youth, and he did not intend to become a shipwright. Rather, his father wanted him to learn this trade and sent him to a boatyard as an apprentice. Matsui was one of six apprentices at the yard.

Life at the boatyard was not easy. Workers had only two days off a month, and worked 12 hours a day, from six o'clock in the morning. One day off was spent just washing dirty clothes. As an apprentice, Matsui was assigned only minor tasks, such as repairing nails or softening oakum, and he was not given regular woodworking tools until he turned sixteen. However, he learned by watching others, and steadily accumulated boatbuilding skills. Learning skills by watching others is the traditional way of training in Japanese crafts. He became a more than competent shipwright by the time he turned twenty, and he was well taken into his master's confidence. Interestingly, he was curious about other handicrafts, such as flower arranging and knitting, and during his apprenticeship he managed to teach himself these crafts in his spare time.

Marukobune were built until around the 1930s. Shipwrights worked

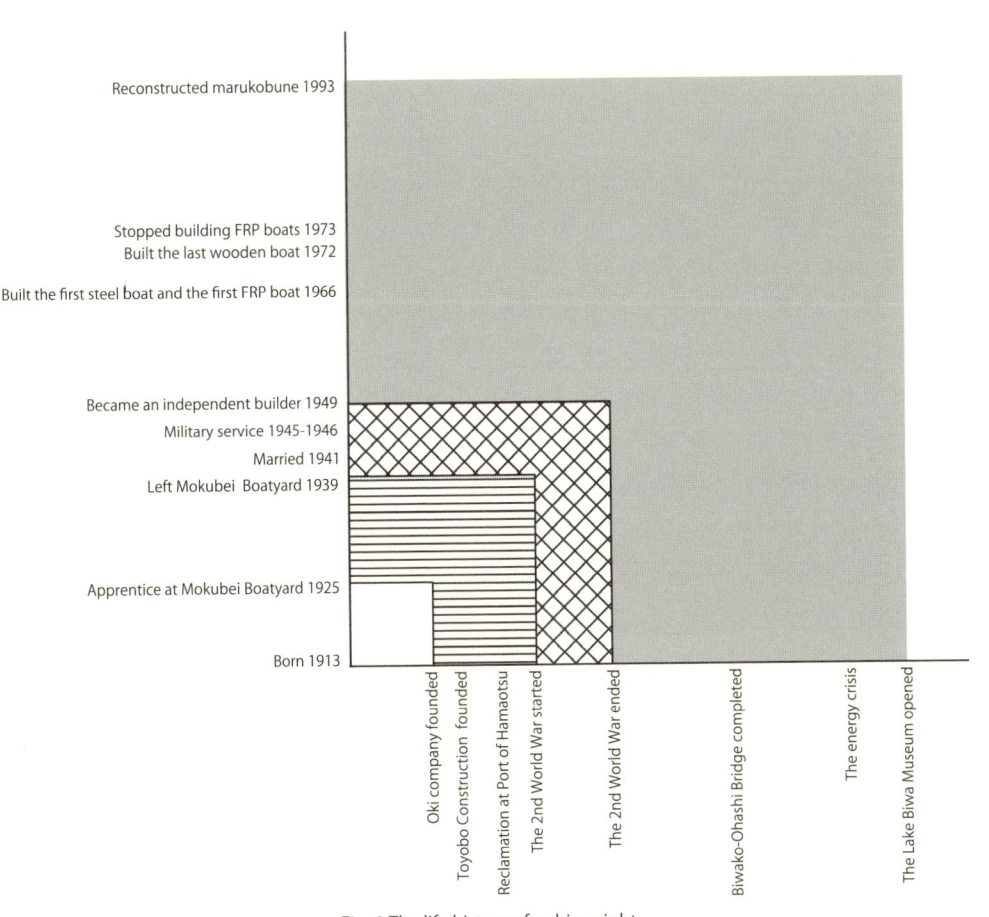

Fig. 1 The life history of a shipwright.

without any drawings; instead they relied on memorized dimensions and formulas. The reason for the lack of documentation was the secrecy endemic to the craft.

Most marukobune had a cargo capacity of 100 koku (15 t, 27 m^3) or 80 koku (12 t, 22 m^3), as these sizes conveniently passed through narrow canals and the swing bridges of the waterways feeding into the lake. In most cases, a marukobune was built by three men: two shipwrights and a

Chapter III The Rise and Fall of Traditional Boats on Lake Biwa

master shipwright. The latter was responsible for the overall design of the vessel. Matsui built four or five marukobune as an assistant to senior apprentices by the 1930s. From that point on, he worked as a master builder.

For omogi (see Chapter. II-(1)) and other building processes which required additional labor, other boatbuilders in the region would temporarily join in work together. There were 40 to 50 shipwrights in the region and they formed a consortium of boatbuilders.

In addition to new boat construction, repair work on marukobune was a frequent source of work. Minor damage was repaired by a vessel's captain, the owner, but major work, such as replacing bow planking and bottom planking, was 70 to 80 man-days work. In a typical three-man shop, major repairs such as this took about a month. During this period the captain stayed at the boatyard, and helped the shipwrights during the work day doing such things as cleaning the yard. Mr. Matsui related that, in the days before mass media, having a captain present in the yard provided an important opportunity to learn news from other regions of the lake.

(Numbers indicate months from January to December.)

Fig. 2 The process of making lumber materials for boats.

Changes in the Specialization of Workers

Traditionally timbers were supplied by a network of workers with specific skills and its process was dependent on the seasonal conditions (Fig. 2). These workers included: tombi (lumber surveyors), kobiki (loggers), yamashi, and dashi-no-oyakata all of whom were involved in getting timbers from the mountain forests to the lake. The tombi chose the timbers boatbuilders needed. The kobiki cut them down. The yamashi slid cut timbers down snow-covered mountain slopes to rivers, and the dashi-no-oyakata gathered the logs and eventually distributed them.

Tombi knew where to find particular species of trees. Tombi means 'black kite bird', so named for the layers of black mantles they wore over their kimonos when they went surveying in the mountains. There were several groups of tombi in Katata and other places around Lake Biwa such as Ogoto, Otsu and Hikone, as well as in other parts of Japan, and they exchanged information while tending to their clients' needs.

Yamashi coordinated the removal of logs from the mountains, and depended on the spring thaw to raise river levels and allow timbers to be transported. One of these river systems was the Ado River in Takashima County, where the mountains produced quality timbers. A spring log run from this region could provide a year's supply of timber for the boatbuilding in Otsu.

Dashi-no-oyakata were in charge of collecting the timber. Seven or eight dashi-no-oyakata waited near the mouth of the Ado River in Funaki. Each timber bore the seal of its owner, and timbers were assembled into rafts 2 jo (approximately 6 m) long for each owner. These rafts were towed with a long rope to the Otsu region.

During the initial phase of Mr. Matsui's career in the 1930s, the traditional social relationships between these types of workers had begun to change (Fig. 3). Boatmen and the association of boat carpenters still existed, but timber distributors and tombi had disappeared. As trucks began to transport logs,

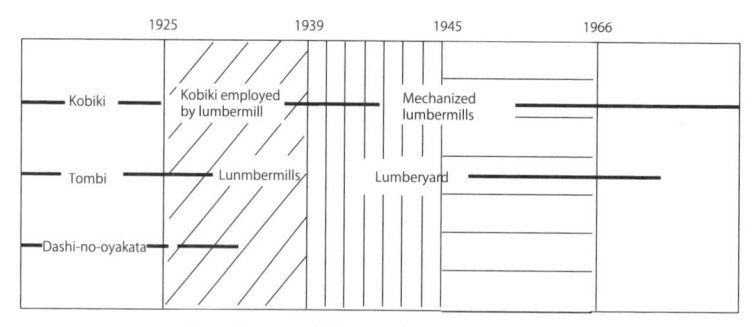

Fig. 3 Changes of the boat lumber professionals.

the timber distributors, and their expertise floating logs downriver, became obsolete. The tombi suffered as timber dealers began to look for suitable trees themselves in order to remain competitive.

By the 1950s, this market was taken over by lumberyards. The first lumberyard was founded in Katata as early as 1925. Loggers had worked independently in the early years, but they transitioned into lumber mills, and became sawmill workers. Mechanization of these mills after the 1930s would further limit this type of work. At the same time the entire region was rapidly changing, with new, large-scale construction and development projects, such as the establishment of the Toyobo factory in 1926 and the reclamation of the Hama-Otsu lakeshore in 1935.

Among these many changes, the disappearance of tombi had the most drastic effect on boatbuilding. Lumberyards primarily catered to the needs of the home building market, which required standardized materials. Boatbuilders typically needed bigger logs and special timbers. They also used different measurement standards than house carpenters. Without experts who could choose suitable timbers, it was left for the boatbuilders themselves to go into the woods and select trees. Mr. Matsui recalled having to laboriously search for trees in the mountains by bicycle or on foot. He remembered this as a particularly arduous task.

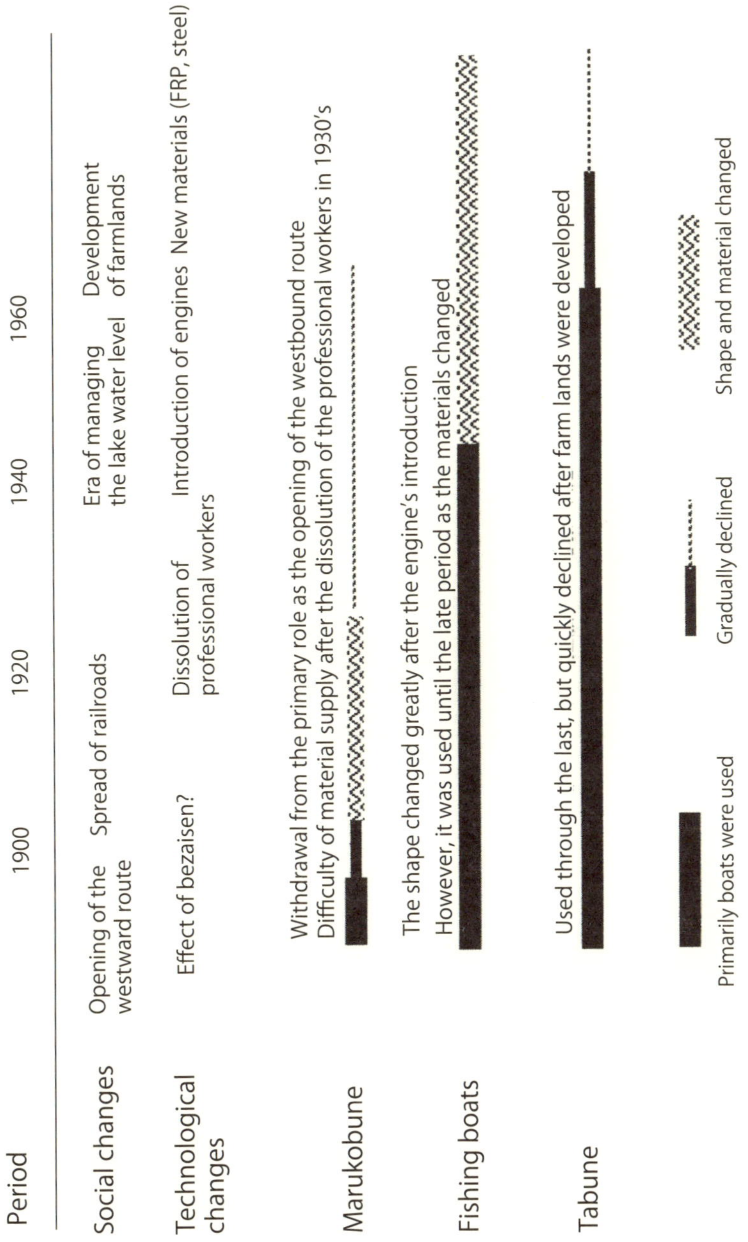

(1) The Rise and Fall of the Traditional Boat as seen through the Life of a Shipwright

Period	1900	1920	1940	1960
Social changes	Opening of the westward route	Spread of railroads	Era of managing the lake water level	Development of farmlands
Technological changes	Effect of bezaisen?	Dissolution of professional workers	Introduction of engines	New materials (FRP, steel)
Marukobune		Withdrawal from the primary role as the opening of the westbound route		
		Difficulty of material supply after the dissolution of the professional workers in 1930's		
Fishing boats		The shape changed greatly after the engine's introduction		
		However, it was used until the late period as the materials changed		
Tabune	Primarily boats were used	Used through the last, but quickly declined after farm lands were developed		
		Gradually declined	Shape and material changed	

Fig. 4 Rise and fall of the traditional boats on the Lake Biwa region.

The Disappearance of Wooden Boats

Marukobune and wooden fishing boats were popular through the 1920s (Fig. 4). However, in the 1930s new types of cargo boats began to be built, designed to carry specific materials. Marukobune, as a general-purpose sailing cargo vessel, became obsolete. Fishing boats continued to be built of wood, but the shape of wooden boats on the lake changed from the round, maruko-type construction to a simpler, flat-bottomed type known locally as hirata. Sailing vessels of all types also disappeared with the availability of marine engines.

Mr. Matsui built the last marukobune on Lake Biwa in 1933. He remembered that hundreds of marukobune were in use at least until that time. After the war, boat production shifted to sightseeing boats, pleasure boats and sailboats, which formed almost the entire boat production after the 1950s. The last marukobune were still in use after the war, and there were often calls to repair them, even after the 1950s. The last wooden boat Matsui built was in 1966: a cargo boat for carrying earth for a construction project. Matsui's story is common; another shipwright remembers that he rented his last wooden boat for the construction of the Biwako Bridge, which was built in 1964.

(2) Number and Usage of Marukobune

The Numbers of Marukobune in the Late 19th to Early 20th Century.

A common belief has been that marukobune largely disappeared at the end of the 19th century. The use of marukobune from the 1880s onward can be traced in the Shiga Prefecture Statistical Reports that have been issued annually since 1882, except for a lapse during World War II (Table. 1). [1]

The statistical reports, unfortunately, do not have a clear category defined as "marukobune" in their surveys. However, marukobune must be among the boats listed as transporting cargo and passengers. The categories of boats in the reports changed from time to time, with the introduction of such categories as Western-style, Japanese-style, small boat, sightseeing boat, and so forth. Fishing boats are not included in the list, as they are categorized separately in the fishing section of the reports. Steamboats were included in a separate category after 1899. Boats used for agriculture were included as small cargo boats beginning in 1902.

Notations of boat size in these reports provide invaluable information when trying to decide how marukobune were classified at any given time, and the classification of marukobune by size in the 17th century (Fig. 5) also helps. In the cargo boat category, Japanese-style boats with a cargo capacity exceeding 500 koku (in 1883) are large-size marukobune. Those boats less than 500 koku capacity (in 1883) and small cargo boats with a length of 10 ken (18 m) (1890-1894) are middle-size marukobune. Those with a length of 6 ken (10.8 m) (1895-1899) and 5 ken (9 m) (1889-1899) can be considered small-size marukobune, as there were no other Japanese-style boats of those sizes in the region. Small cargo boats with a length of 4 ken (7.2 m) and 3 ken (5.4 m) (1889-1899) could be very small marukobune, but this is not certain, as boats of this size were included among the ryosen in the 17th century (see above). Perhaps they were for transporting fish or fertilizer. The western-

113

Chapter III The Rise and Fall of Traditional Boats on Lake Biwa

Table. 1 Types and number of boats from 1904 through 1941.
M: Meiji period, T: Taisho period, S: Showa period

Year \ Type	Western style Sail	Western style Steam	Japanese style 500koku and over	Japanese style Under 500koku	Japanese style Utility/fishing/cargo boat	Tax exempt
1883(M16)	31	–	–	–	9,241	5,261

	Steam	Japanese style Utility/fishing/cargo boat	Tax exempt
1884(M17)	31	11,215	3,524
1885(M18)	Western style(steam) 30	13,472	10,219

	Western style Sail	Western style Steam		
1886(M19)	30	–	13,970	11,737
1887(M20)	27	–	14,229	946
1888(M21)	29	4	14,383	641

	Sail	Steam	Ko-kaisen (short-haul cargo boat) 3ken	4ken	5ken	Yusen (pleasure boat)	Tax exempt
1889(M22)	28	10	14,217	217	1	13	1,215

	Sail	Steam	Ko-kaisen (short-haul cargo boat) 3ken	4ken	5ken	10ken	Yusen (pleasure boat)	Tax exempt
1890(M23)	43	17	14,118	235	7	2	15	1,196
1891(M24)	24	4	14,060	230	7	2	36	577
1892(M25)	24	34	13,296	213	7	2	38	424
1893(M26)	24	37	13,848	211	7	2	66	425
1894(M27)				N/A				

	Sail	Steam	Ko-kaisen 3ken and under	4ken	5ken	6ken and over	Yusen (pleasure boat) (Under 3ken)
1895(M28)	24	48	13,664	199	4	1	82
1896(M29)	22	46	13,124	184	4	1	80
1897(M30)	24	48	12,536	193	6	1	81
1898(M31)	24	47	12,061	191	5	2	84

	Sail boat	Fugyosen, ko-kaisen, yusen, et al. (Utility/fishing/cargo/pleasure boat et al.)
1899(M32)	6	11,779 204 4 2 85
1900(M33)	60	13,465
1901(M34)	61	13,030
1902(M35)	35	12,975
1903(M36)	34	13,092

114

(2) Number and Usage of Marukobune

	Sail boat	Small boat		
	Western style	Fugyosen and ko-kaisen (Utility/fishing/cargo boat)	Yusen (Pleasure boat)	Rowing boat
1904(M37)	1	12,975		43
1905(M38)	1	12,681	72	40
1906(M39)	1	12,504	72	40
1907(M40)	−	12,321	68	38
1908(M41)	−	12,963	68	39
1909(M42)	−	12,963	67	36
1910(M43)	−	12,963	67	38
1911(M44)		12,775	67	37
1912(T1)		12,831	66	39
1913(T2)		12,719	70	39
1914(T3)		13,053	71	37
1915(T4)		12,924	31	39
1916(T5)		12,839	32	39
1917(T6)		12,667	32	20
1918(T7)		12,476	26	26
1919(T8)		12,366	24	22
1920(T9)		12,120	31	10
1921(T10)		12,223	32	15
1922(T11)		11,887	35	15
1923(T12)		11,357	42	24
1924(T13)		10,659	52	62
1925(T14)		10,947	52	62
1926(S1)		11,011	55	105

	Small boat					
	Fugyosen and ko-kaisen (Utility/fishing/cargo boat)		Yusen (Pleasure boat)		Rowing boat	
	w/o enigine	with engine	w/o enigine	with engine	w/o enigine	with engine
1927(S2)	10,344	73	56	1	140	17
1928(S3)	10,200	86	54	1	124	17
1929(S4)	10,239	142	54	2	141	19

	w/o engine	with engine
1930(S5)	10,018	181
1931(S6)	10,032	185
1932(S7)	9,784	182
1933(S8)	9,307	234
1934(S9)	9,674	263
1935(S10)	10,217	299
1936(S11)	10,401	337
1937(S12)	10,400	407
1938(S13)	10,380	386
1939(S14)	10,333	384
1940(S15)	10,348	306
1941(S16)	10,067	281

Marukobune

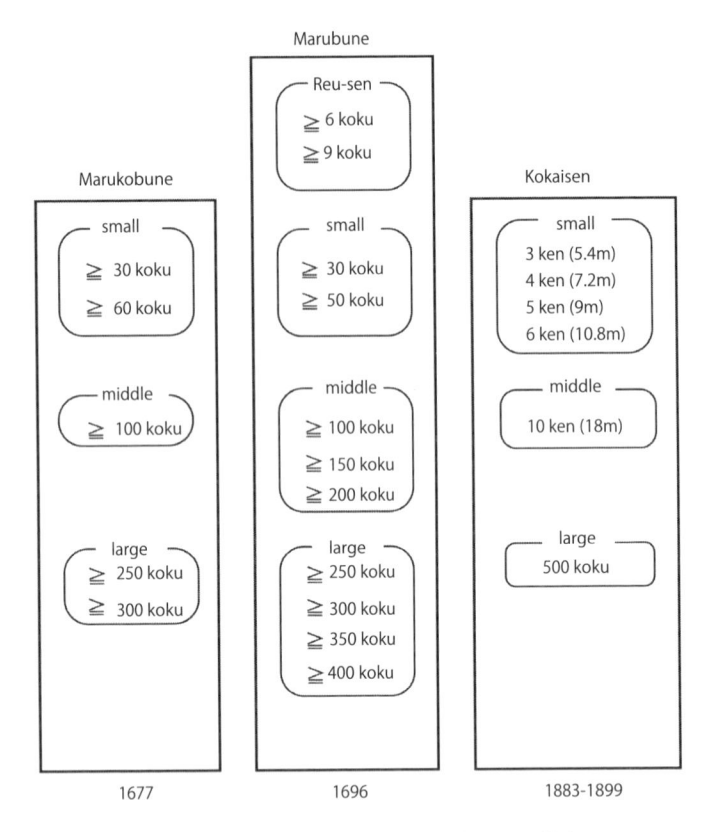

small
≧ 30 koku
≧ 60 koku

middle
≧ 100 koku

large
≧ 250 koku
≧ 300 koku

1677

Marubune

Reu-sen
≧ 6 koku
≧ 9 koku

small
≧ 30 koku
≧ 50 koku

middle
≧ 100 koku
≧ 150 koku
≧ 200 koku

large
≧ 250 koku
≧ 300 koku
≧ 350 koku
≧ 400 koku

1696

Kokaisen

small
3 ken (5.4m)
4 ken (7.2m)
5 ken (9m)
6 ken (10.8m)

middle
10 ken (18m)

large
500 koku

1883-1899

Fig. 5 Variation of sizes of marukobune, marubune, and kokaisen.

style boats and steamboats were introduced later, so they were definitely not marukobune. Given the definitions of boat sizes in the reports it seems certain that marukobune were used until at least 1899.

It is difficult to identify the category under which marukobune were included after 1900, because the statistics no longer provided a breakdown by size. However, presumably marukobune were always included in the small cargo category as mentioned above. Between 1930 and 1941, boats were classified only as with or without an engine and the "without engine" category should include marukobune, but there is no supporting information for this

(2) Number and Usage of Marukobune

Table. 2 Types and number of wrecked boats from 1904 through 1939.

	Steam boat		Japanese style sail boat			Small boat		
	Sank	Damaged	Sank	Capsized	Damaged	Sank	Capsized	Damaged
1904(M37)		2						
1905(M38)		1						
1906(M39)			1					
1907(M40)						1		
1908(M41)						1	1	
1909(M42)				1	1	1	3	
1910(M43)			1	1	1	4	2	1
1911(M44)						1	5	2
1912(T1)							22	6
1913(T2)					1		1	
1914(T3)				1			5	
1915(T4)						1	1	
1916(T5)						1	1	
1917(T6)						1		1
1918(T7)								2
1919(T8)				2	1		1	1
1920(T9)							1	1
1921(T10)				2		2	1	1
1922(T11)						1	2	1
1923(T12)						1	1	1
1924(T13)						1	1	
1925(T14)						1	3	4
1926(S1)						2	6	2
1927(S2)							2	
1928(S3)								
1929(S4)			1					
1930(S5)						1	3	
1931(S6)						2		
1932(S7)								
1933(S8)								
1934(S9)		2				6		200
1935(S10)								
1936(S11)								
1937(S12)								
1938(S13)								
1939(S14)								

M: Meiji Period, T: Taisho Period, S: Showa Period

supposition.

Statistics of wrecked boats were also included in the reports from 1904 to 1938, and they corroborate the conclusion that marukobune existed well into the 20th century (Table. 2). The wrecks are divided into three categories: steamboat, Japanese sailing boat, and small boat. Of these, Japanese sailing boat perhaps refers to marukobune boats, as it was the only sailing craft among the Japanese-style boats (again, fishing boats with a sail were listed separately, in the fishery statistics). If this interpretation is correct, these statistics confirm the existence of marukobune until the end of 1938. This

117

interpretation is supported by oral testimony that at least several hundred marukobune were active until the 1930s.

Based on the totals from categories that probably include marukobune boats, they were still in use as late as 1938. However, a drastic change was seen when publication resumed in 1949, after several years of interruption during and following World War II. In 1949, the list shows only the total number of sailing boats, without any detailed breakdown. Also, no boat numbers were published at all for the years 1951 and later. Thus, there is no precise information on the number of marukobune in use after 1950. We do know that the only remaining marukobune boat, with an engine rather than a sail, was retired in the late 1990s.

Contrary to common knowledge, the above information, based on official statistics, shows that marukobune remained in use well after 1889, when the railroads and modern modes of transport were introduced.

The Use of Marukobune in the Middle of 20th Century - Based on Oral Information

One quarter of boat-related information collected from local residents by the Lake Biwa Museum (Marukobune Communication Desk (see Chapter. II-note 10) described marukobune. The information revealed that marukobune were not just specific cargo boats, but also used for daily transportation as late as the 1960s. They were found throughout Lake Biwa and the surrounding waterways. The following are a selection of quotes gathered by museum researchers from visitors.

"From the Taisho period through the early Showa period there were many roof tile merchants along the Hachimanbori in Omihachiman City, and marukobune were used for transportation of roof tiles from there. We played by jumping onto the boats moored at the riverside. We knew them intimately." (Omihachiman City)

"Once I spotted a marukobune carrying firewood from Shiozu. Firewood was used as fuel for Hachiman roof tiles. And mud for tiles came from the rice field in Minamitsuda. It seemed a little bit larger than a 100 koku boat. It was sailed by two men. It was moving forward in the canal by pole. The canal became filled with mud and was dredged, and the mud was thrown onto the rice fields where the surface had been lowered from digging mud for tiles. As years passed, the mud hardened, and it became clayey. This was tile mud." (Omihachiman City)

"There used to be many marukobune, but they declined to ten boats or so around 1937. Hot-bulb engines were used then, and the boats left for various harbors with "pong, pong" sound from early in the morning. The boat on which I often rode was a little smaller than 100 koku, and it provided a kind of scheduled service to Nagahama. It left with firewood and brushwood, and returned with groceries, such as salt, soy sauce, and dry foods. The cargo was loaded the day before, and the boat departed the next morning after checking the weather. It brought mud for roof tiles from Hachiman, (the mud was) baked to tiles in Shiozu, and it brought finished tiles back to Hachiman. Sometimes it brought the mud directly to other ports. Before the War (World War II), there were a lot of ryokans (Japanese style hotels) and wholesale stores in Shiozu, and it was very busy. Peddlers' traffic was particularly high and, for example, blacksmiths visited from Kuwana after harvesting rice." (Shiozuhama, Nishiazai Town, Ika County)

"There was no land transportation yet, and people visited Nagahama and other places by boat. Boats from Oura sailed to Otsu loaded with brushwood and firewood." (Nishiazai Town, Ika County)

"When I was a child, I often saw marukobune with a cargo capacity of a little less than 100 koku. They transported brushwood, firewood and roof tiles on board from Shiozu (Osaki) to Hachimanbori. There were firewood and charcoal merchants and roof tile stores in a row along Hachimanbori, and probably they purchased the cargoes." (Omihachiman City)

"My brother living in Azuchi Town was actually building marukobune. I used to sail marukobune, and I transported stones for stone walls as well as straw rice bags from the Oki Island to Hachiman." (Omihachiman)

"I cut mud for roof tiles into cubes (Each weighed about 15 kg, and one side was similar to the length of a plow) at a rice field, loaded them on a small boat, brought through canals to marukobune on Lake Biwa, and loaded them on board. The mud was carried by hand, then by trolley, then marukobune, then a horse wagon, and an ox wagon. Brushwood and firewood were brought back, and Hachiman tiles were made by baking, fuelled with brushwood and firewood. (Omihachiman City)

"In Omihachiman I often saw them digging the soil (black and fertile) in a brick shape with a plow. The field was fertilized by algae from the Lake Biwa. Then, the mud was brought to the roof tile makers in Otsu on board marukobune. The soil in Omihachiman was best for making roof tiles." (Omihachiman)

"My family business had business with the roof tile merchants in Omihachiman and Shimosakamoto, the firewood and charcoal stores in Yamada region, and the bathhouses in Otsu. Now I can recall it was a really good business, but then came the automobile, and (marukobune) disappeared by the time I returned after the war." (Omihachiman)

"There was a captain in the same village, and he was a farmer and traded cattle on the side. Usually he made the Hachiman run by boat. He made a bid for brushwood from Mt. Isaki in Omihachiman and traded it. At that time a lot of brushwood was needed because people cooked plenty of food at their house when a wedding ceremony or a funeral was held. That's the reason why he was in that business." (Inae Town, Hikone City)

A few accounts of carrying gravel came from the Echigawa region and the Kusatsu shores. Transporting by boat was efficient, and was apparently common. Many of these descriptions suggest that people of the period were well aware of the weather conditions of the lake and knew how to handle boats safely.

"Wooden marukobune were used as gravel barges from Echigawa to the Port of Otsu. The length was similar (to the 100 koku marukobune exhibited at the Lake Biwa Museum), but it was slightly wider, I think. It wasn't equipped with an engine, and was operated by three men. There were engine-powered marukobune even before the war, but after the war it seemed the majority became engine-powered. The roof was fitted with wooden plates, but not straw mats." (Echigawa, Aisho Town, Echi County)

"I transported river gravel from Echigawa to Otsu. I actually sailed on board marukobune. Four men were on board and two each fore and aft. When we arrived in Otsu, it was unloaded by the four men. These marukobune carried only river gravel cargo, and I worked there for a long time." (Echigawa, Aisho Town, Echi County)

"I helped loading gravel on board marukobune. The gravel was washed and polished naturally and was all of a size. Not sure what they were used for, but they were for constructions if my memory is correct. And, when the tracks of Tokaido Line were laid, marukobune played a major role of transporting quite a bit of gravel to the Port of Nagahama." (Hikone)

"During my childhood, three marukobune used to arrive early in the morning at around five o'clock at the beach between Oyabu Town and Yasaka Town in Hikone. The gravel and rocks on the beach were loaded on the boat, and it sailed through the swinging bridge at Lake Matsubara (formerly the port of Matsubara) to the former landing place of the Biwako Steam Ships, and unloaded the cargo there. The reason why the gravel-carrying marukobune started work early in the morning was that the winds and waves on Lake Biwa were calm through the morning. It was important to load the cargo while the lake was calm and to return before noon at the latest. That's what my dad told me again and again." (Hikone)

"It was a 100 koku marukobune, and it was driven by a hot-bulb engine. It carried sands and gravel. An empty boat was sailed from the harbor of Oroshimo to around the current Maiami Beach, and it brought high quality gravel and sand from the Yasu River to Sugie Barasu (company name, meaning Sugie Ballast) and Yamazaki Jari (company name, meaning Yamazaki Gravel) in Hamaotsu. From winter through March, the seasonal winds were strong and I encountered danger many times while sailing. The north wind became stronger particularly from around the current Lake Biwa Bridge, and the waves became higher. There were choppy seas. Small boats were tossed and they occasionally capsized. Since marukobune were big, they didn't capsize. They carried heavy gravel, so the deck came down very close to the water's surface. The gravel was covered with boat planks - like a warship - to prevent water coming in. In those days, transporting by boat was efficient, and they could carry the cargo equivalent to 4 or 5 t trucks. The longer the bow, the more stable the boat was." (Oroshimo Town, Kusatsu City)

In the east shore region of the southern part of the Lake, such as Otsu, Kusatsu and Moriyama, boats were heavily used for transporting compost. The boats also transported aquatic grasses from Lake Biwa for the rice fields. Also, large quantities of night soil were brought from Otsu, and vegetables and other goods were brought back. This illustrates the importance in the past of organic matter, materials we now consider useless. Today we spend significant amounts of money to dispose of material that our forefathers used to fertilize their fields.

In some of the following descriptions, speakers refer to "boats with a capacity of over 100 koku.". This demonstrates that a large quantity of compost was traded, considering 100 koku corresponds to 250 straw rice bags.
"Water grasses of Lake Biwa were transported to fields for compost for green onions." (Shimogasa Town, Kusatsu City)

"Night soil in six barrels or so was brought from the Otsu area using a large marukobune with more than 100 koku cargo capacity. We sailed to Otsu with empty cargo or vegetables, and so on. The inside of the boat was so spacious that living there seemed possible, and kids were placed in the bow section." (Akanoi Town, Moriyama City)

"I sailed to Otsu from Moriyama to buy night soil, and went to Saigoshu to sell rice and buy firewood." (Moriyama City)

"I transported compost by marukobune. I loaded it on board by hand with two men. A power boat towed two or three boats linked. The sail was not used." (Konohama Town, Moriyama City)

"I used engine-powered marukobune traveling to Otsu to bring back night soil. And when I was in the elementary school, I used marukobune to go to school." (Otsu City)

"It was around 1948. I owned a marukobune as a member of the owner's group and sailed to Otsu City (Shimanoseki) or Kyoto City to get night soil, and brought it back on board marukobune. And, we transported more than 100 straw bags of rice on board to the rice storehouse near the current head office of the Shiga Bank, and transported river sand to hydroponic farms in Karasaki. I have a wonderful memory of the sound of a hot-bulb engine running smoothly, and sailing around Lake Biwa." (Otsu City)

"Once I had a ride on marukobune (larger than 100 koku cargo capacity) carrying night soils. It sailed to Otsu. They were transported by truck sometimes, but the boat was cheaper." (Otsu City)

Various necessities of life were transported to diverse places.

"(I transported) rice from Kusatsu to Otsu, and soy sauce and sake on the return." (Yamada Town, Kusatsu City)

"Rice and firewood produced in Shiga Town were brought to the Port of Hamaotsu, and chips of wood from logging to the east." (Wani, Otsu City)

"From Takashima, Oura and so on in the north shore, commodities like firewood, brushwood and rice were transported to Otsu along with stones from the Oki Island, and night soil from Otsu to Moriyama in Akanoi Bay."

"Brushwood and firewood from the Port of Oura to the Otsu region were transported." (Nishiazai Town, Ika County)

"Firewood and brushwood on the way, and foods, such as salt, soy sauce and dried fishes, were on the return." (Shiozuhama, Nishiazai Town, Ika County)

"When I was sailing marukobune with my father around 1937, it was a sailboat with a small foresail. We brought cattle to the Port of Shiozu for sale in Fukui." (Wani, Otsu City)

"I saw marukobune with large bags of cocoons on board which was moored in the canal of Hikone Castle. In those days, big houses in Hikone often had a cocoon storehouse." (Hikone City)

Cattle were used for cultivating the fields. And, silk yarn was one of the traditional products typical in Omi. It was used not just for fabric, but also for such things as the strings of a koto (Japanese harp).

"Once I was invited to get on board marukobune. It was moored at Nagahama, and I was treated with tea in the cabin. The cabin space was about the size of two tatami mats, and there were a small cupboard and a stove." (Nagahama City)

"In those times marukobune were carrying straw bags of rice and charcoal brought from the upper stream of the Ado River, I guess. (The owner of marukobune) lived on board with his family, and a baby was crawling on the deck. There were a couple of traditional Japanese restaurants in the harbour, and they were crowded with people. In the town a river was flowing down the middle of the road. People washed clothes there, and fished for small fish like minnows." (Omizo, Takashima City)

"My family business has been fishing since the Edo period. I started sailing marukobune with my father and brother since I was a little kid. Three crews were on board, and one of them was at the helm and handled the sail. During the flood in 1954 we sailed marukobune over the flooded land. We carried firewood, herring (for fertilizer), salted mackerel, and rice. We left the port at two o'clock in the morning. If the wind permitted, we arrived at Otsu in one day. It took two or three days occasionally. We put a straw mat over our heads, and warmed ourselves at the charcoal stove." (Shiozuhama, Nishiazai Town, Ika County)

"It took about three days to reach Otsu from Kaizu. We always worked as a group of two or three people. We transported charcoal, firewood, rice and so on. The shipping charge was about five thousand yen, and it may correspond to around five hundred thousand yen now." (Kaizu, Makino Town, Takashima City)

"Sailing marukobune was difficult, and there were occasions when a skipper fell in the water trying to row so vigorously." (Inae Town, Hikone City)

"I started sailing marukobune with my father. It was in its peak during the Meiji period (1868-1912). I inherited the business from my father." (Kaizu, Makino Town, Takashima City)

"During the peaceful period before the war, marukobune were briefly configured as sightseeing boats. We sailed to visit Chomeiji Temple with people, and every year we went on a sightseeing lake cruise during the summer vacation with our neighbours. The sailors (my grandfather and father) were excellent in forecasting weather. They watched the clouds in the morning and evening, forecast rain or wind, and they were very accurate. When they went sailing ignoring the forecast, often they encountered danger, so it seemed." (Omihachiman)

"We were running the transportation business with marukobune since my great-grandfather's generation. We transported rice to the Tokugawa lord at times. The previous generation and the generation before brought rice, salt, charcoal, herring (for fertilizer), and other goods to Hamaotsu, sold them there, and did extensive business. When marukobune appeared from the fog when I was sailing tabune on Lake Biwa, I was always amazed by its large size. The marukobune in Takashima were far larger than 100 koku." (Harie, Shinasahi Town, Takashima City)

"My father was a captain and sailed marukobune. His boat changed to a hot-bulb engine when I was in the lower grades of elementary school. I miss the name "Fukueimaru" drawn on its stern. There were four or five boats in the Port of Kitahira. Usually they could be sailed by a father and a son or two brothers, but my father was sailing alone because I was little. My father transported mainly firewood and brushwood from the west shore where mountains are close to the lake, to the east shore where the mountains are far away. I guess the boats were dedicated either for transporting firewood and charcoal, or for stones... I had a sleepover with my father on the boat during a summer break in my elementary school days. I recall when I woke up, we were heading back. Only when the boat was in a safe condition, did my father let me take the helm. Since I was scared of traveling far from the shore as a child, I steered unconsciously toward the shore, and my father had to correct me many times." (Otsu City)

"Marukobune was temporarily arranged as a sightseeing boat, and we sailed to visit Chomeiji Temple." (Omihachiman)

"It was during the festival at the Shirahige Shrine in the west shore. Small marukobune, a little smaller than 100 koku capacity, arrived calmly from somewhere. People on board prepared meals over a burner, and seemed to live on the boat. Besides, I heard when very wealthy people died, they were carried by marukobune to the mountain area in Adogawa called the Western Paradise and buried there. Not all the wealthy people, but only important people, like the head of a family, were treated this way, and the rest of the family members were buried in the local land." (Ukawa, Takashima City)

"It was similar to marukobune, and it was equipped with a so-called hot-bulb engine. I have a happy memory of sailing to nearby Chikubu Island by this boat." (Nishiazai Town, Ika County)

"Being a marukobune sailor was a sought after occupation for its high pay, and five or six of my classmates became sailors. There were lanterns in Shinden, but they were moved to the Lake Biwa Bridge. In Shinden, sand on the beach around Yoshikawa was brought by a small boat to a marukobune waiting offshore, transferred, and five or six of the boats were towed together by a hot-bulb engine boat to Hamaotsu. (Konohama Town, Moriyama City)

"Children went to elementary school by marukobune." (Otsu City)

"During my elementary school days, I used to play on a moored marukobune. We stepped through the side deck, swam and dived under marukobune in summer, and we were scolded for it. Some kids got a ride on a returning marukobune, jumped into the water about 500 m from shore, then swam back to shore. But these kids were older." (Inae Town, Hikone City)

"In my childhood, we peeled off the copper plate mounted on a marukobune while its captain was away from the boat, sold it to a scrap metal broker, bought candies, and boasted to each other. The copper was called "aka/datekasugai" (see Chapter. II-(1), "Caulking") and we used to say "let's go get aka." (Otsu City)

"When I was a kid, I sailed out on Lake Biwa in a small boat with my friends, but drifted near Otsu during a typhoon. We wondered what to do and just cried in loud voices. Then a big boat, looked like a marukobune, came in sight and it towed us back to Yamada." (Yamada Town, Kusatsu City)

"During the summer vacation our neighbours gathered and enjoyed sightseeing sailing on the lake."

(3) Number and Use of the Farming Boat, or Tabune

Tabune, a Boat Used for Farming

Tabune is a small boat used for farming (see figures in this section). The catchment area of Lake Biwa is known as a rice-growing center. Comparisons show this region to be characterized by a high rice field ratio, a high part-time farmer ratio, and smaller cultivated land area per household compared to national data (Table. 3)[2]. Tabune were an important form of transportation for traveling through the water channels in the rice fields, as well as the handiest way to move among fields and transport materials and farm products.

According to research by the Lake Biwa Museum,[3] 67% of the traditional Japanese boats locally were tabune in 1993 (Table. 4), and more than half of them were in well-maintained condition. This indicates they were used until

Table. 3 Characteristics of agriculture in Shiga Prefecture.

	Shiga Prefecture	National average	National ranking
Total number of farm households	46,970	64,421	31
Number of commercial farm household	36,600	47847	31
Full-time commercial farmers ratio(%)	5.4	20.6	45
Semi full-time commercial farmers	21.3	24.7	36
Part-time commercial farmers ratio(%)	73.4	54.8	3
Farm land area(ha)	55,300	101,319	30
Farm land area/household(ha)	1.18	1.57	21
Rice field ratio(%)	92	54.7	2

Table. 4 Variety of existing traditional boats.

Basic types	Number of boats	Condition			
		Good	Partially damaged	Greatly damaged	Unknown
1. Heitabune (Heita bow boat)	524	287	152	82	3
A. Marukobune	6	1	3	2	0
B. Mid-size heitabune	60	19	22	17	2
C. Small-size heitabune	445	259	123	62	1
D. Minamihamabune	13	8	4	1	0
2. Kensakibune (sharp bowed boat)	92	70	13	9	0
A. Large-size kensakibune	10	2	4	4	0
B. Mid-size kensakibune	78	65	9	4	0
C. Passenger kensaki boat	4	3	-	1	0
3. Others	51	39	7	3	2
A. Yakatabune (houseboat)	19	15	3	1	0
B. Amiuchibune (cast net fishing boat)	8	6	2	-	0
C. Punt	17	13	2	2	0
D. Ayukakebune (Ayu fishing boat)	4	3	-	-	1
E. Others	3	2	-	-	1
Total	667	396	172	94	5

relatively late. The distribution of these boats (Table. 5) was concentrated in the coastal region on the east side of the lake. They were also seen in the southern and western ends of the lake, but rarely in the north. Research showed that tabune were a convenient form of transportation for farmers, just like bicycles or cars today.

The era of modernization, led by the government, from the end of the

Table. 5 Distribution of tabune.

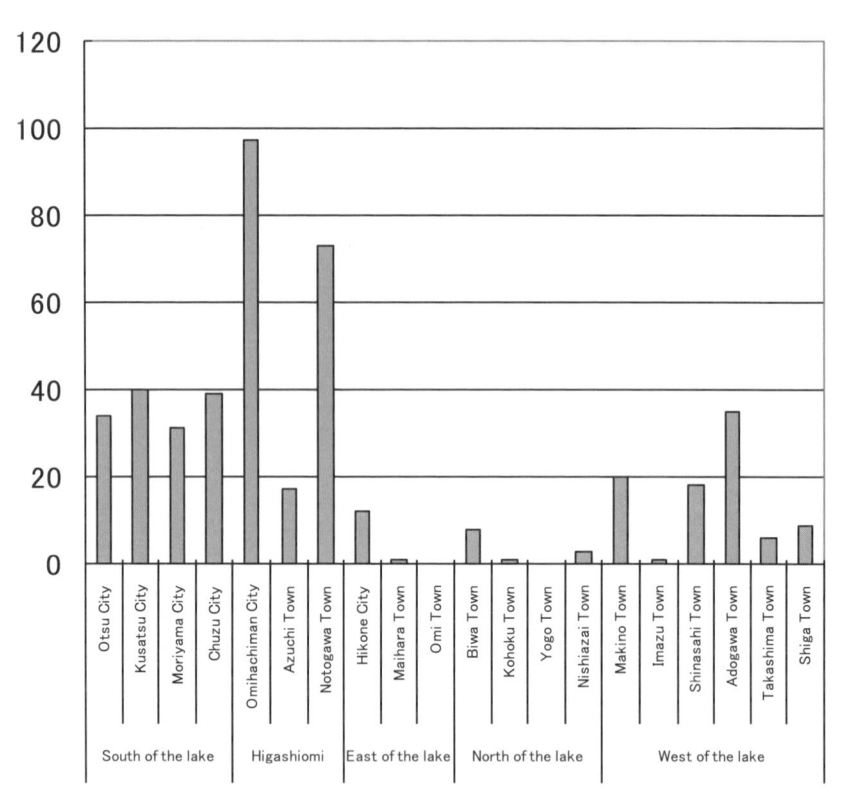

Region	Location	Count
South of the lake	Otsu City	~34
South of the lake	Kusatsu City	~40
South of the lake	Moriyama City	~32
South of the lake	Chuzu City	~39
Higashiomi	Omihachiman City	~97
Higashiomi	Azuchi Town	~17
Higashiomi	Notogawa Town	~73
East of the lake	Hikone City	~12
East of the lake	Maihara Town	~1
East of the lake	Omi Town	~8
North of the lake	Biwa Town	~1
North of the lake	Kohoku Town	~1
North of the lake	Yogo Town	~3
North of the lake	Nishiazai Town	~1
West of the lake	Makino Town	~20
West of the lake	Imazu Town	~1
West of the lake	Shinasahi Town	~18
West of the lake	Adogawa Town	~35
West of the lake	Takashima Town	~6
West of the lake	Shiga Town	~9

19th century through the present period, created significant changes in tabune use. Water level control of Lake Biwa, disaster prevention, and the modernization and the expansion of agricultural production, significantly changed the condition of the shoreline and the swamps that are the most important factors influencing the use of tabune.

The shoreline at the end of 19th century was much more complicated than at the end of 20th century. The total area of swampland is now smaller (Fig. 6). This change was caused by several administrative policies concerning land use. At the end of 19th century, Shiga Prefecture took over the water management of Lake Biwa, controlling the water level, and draining excess

(3) Number and Use of the Farming Boat, or Tabune

Table. 6 Events impacted the shoreline and the water level of the Lake Biwa.

Year	Events
1868(Meiji 1)	Otsu Prefecture was established. The water management of the Lake Biwa became under the control of the Prefecture.
1872(Meiji 5)	Major flooding in May. The Seta River was dredged.
1874(Meiji 7)	The Torii River water gauge was set up in the shore of the Lake Biwa near the Karahashi Bridge.
1890(Meiji 23)	The 1st Lake Biwa Canal was completed.
1905(Meiji 38)	The Nango overfall weir with a length of 180m was completed. The water level control was improved.
1944(Showa 19)	A decision was made to reclaim the swamps including Matsubara-naiko and Sonenuma.
1948(Showa 23)	Plans for Comprehensive Development of the Lake Biwa. Unprecedented flooding by the 13th typhoon of the year.
1954(Showa 29)	The master plan for river improvement was established. The Seta River was dredged.
1957(Showa 32)	The construction of the Amase Dam started. (-1964) Dredging of the Seta River began.(-1962)
1961(Showa 36)	Seta River overfall weir completed. Comprehensive Development Plan of the Lake Biwa was published.
1964(Showa 39)	The New Act on River was approved. The master plan of the water administration of the Lake Biwa was decided.
1966(Showa 41)	The reclamation of Dainakanoko was mostly completed.
1967(Showa 42)	Shiga Prefecture published "Master Plan of Comprehensive Development of the Lake Biwa".
1992(Heisei 4)	The Lake Biwa Development Project (by The Water Resources Development Public Corporation) was complete.

water (Table. 6). In the middle of 20th century "the Land Infrastructure Development Plan" began, resulting in the modernization of agriculture, and the implementation of disaster prevention projects. These measures greatly influenced the water level and the shoreline (Table. 7 left). A total of 1,618.17 ha of land were developed, and 170 ha of swamps in the inland water

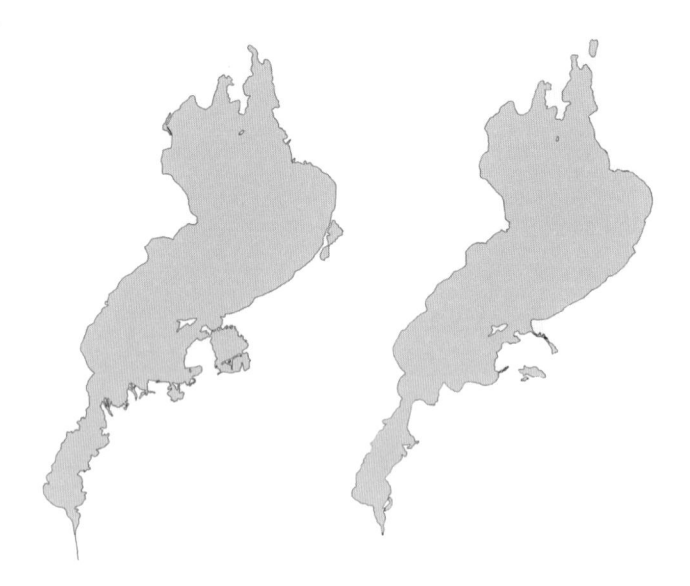

Fig. 6 The shoreline in 1869 (left) and the current shoreline (right).

region of Lake Biwa were reclaimed in the early 1970s. Another project, to foster highly productive agriculture through the development of the land infrastructure and the modernization of agriculture, began in early 1960s. In this effort, small rice fields were consolidated and readjusted to be more manageable. The road system was developed so that modern agricultural machines could be introduced. As a result, the total cultivated area shrunk about three quarters by 2002 compared to 1960. The ratio of improved farm fields showed an increase (Table. 7, right).[4]

Development projects intended to maintain stable water levels on Lake Biwa began in the early 1970s, and continued for 25 years.[5] These projects built riverbanks, roads for lake management, and water drainage facilities along the lakeshore. Development also took place on rivers that flowed into the lake, including the overfall weir of the Seta River, and the dredging of the Seta River.

As the result, half of the south basin had disappeared by 1983, and the total area of the lake, compared to 1908, had shrunk from 686.3 m^2 to 672.8

(3) Number and Use of the Farming Boat, or Tabune

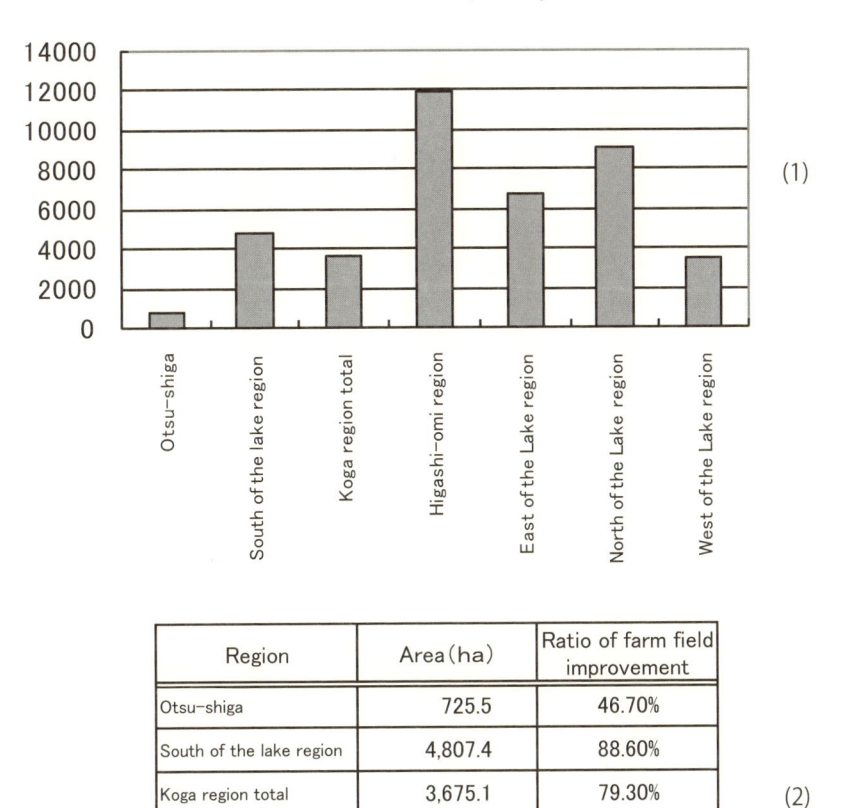

Table. 7 The area(1) and the ratio(2) of the farm field improvement in FY 2002.

(1)

[Bar chart showing values for: Otsu-shiga, South of the lake region, Koga region total, Higashi-omi region, East of the Lake region, North of the Lake region, West of the Lake region]

Region	Area (ha)	Ratio of farm field improvement
Otsu-shiga	725.5	46.70%
South of the lake region	4,807.4	88.60%
Koga region total	3,675.1	79.30%
Higashi-omi region	11,889.3	89.00%
East of the Lake region	6,686.8	92.90%
North of the Lake region	9,069.3	92.60%
West of the Lake region	3,477.5	86.10%

(2)

m^2. The length of the shoreline decreased from 240.8 km to 188 km. The north-south length of the lake was 63.49 km in 1997, which was nearly identical to the length (63.3 km) in 1908. The shortest east-west width in 1997 was 1.35 km and it was 300 m shorter than 1.62 km in 1925.[6] Such changes to the swamps and the reduction of shoreline would have considerably impacted the number of boats.

The Use of Tabune in the Middle of the 20th Century - Based on Oral Information

Oral information sources from local people regarding tabune provided information mostly on the region from the south of the lake to the north of the lake which overlapped the distribution of rice fields, and they were particularly concentrated in the Omihachiman area. The period of the information was mostly from the early Showa period (late 1920s) through the mid 1950s, but newer information from 1970s and 1980s was also collected, and it coincided with the period preceding the farm field improvement.

"Every household had such a boat (tabune) and it was essential." (Before the Second World War, Zeze, Otsu City)

"In those days we used to move around the rice fields in the Noda area by a boat, and it was an important tool. Women mastered steering the boats with long poles. Boats were busily sailing with anything on board, such as products from the rice field and even cattle." (Early Showa period, Noda, Yasu City)

"Once Suikei Town was a 280 ha swamp, and the land reclamation started from around 1947. Before the land reclamation, the roads were just wide enough for a person to walk, so rice was carried by tabune, which had a length of about 10 m. They were rowed by oar, but engines were installed around 1953. Since traveling to Chomeiji by oar was a little hard, we paid a visit by an engine-powered boat." (Around 1960, Omihachiman)

"I had experience onboard tabune. It was transporting rice crops. It was also used for fishing on the lake, such as casting nets and sade (dip net). I guess it was rowed or poled depending on the situation." (Through around middle of 1950s, Konohama Town, Moriyama City)

In addition to farm products like rice and vegetables, tabune were used for transporting night soil and compost, both important products in farming regions.

"I sailed a 7 to 8 m tabune usually with an oar, and with a bamboo pole in the shallows. I transported harvested rice and compost. At the beginning I struggled rowing as the oar came off. In those days there were lots of water channels." (Early Showa period, Imazu Town, Takashima City)

"I sailed to Otsu or Kyoto with farm products like Japanese radish to sell, and came back with about six barrels of night soil carried on board." (Zeze, Otsu City, Before the World War)

"Tabune were used for sailing to Zeze from the Moriyama area to obtain night soil, and they went to particular houses at the same time and day of every month to exchange it for cash or vegetables." (Before the war through after the war, Zeze, Otsu City)

"I often sailed to Otsu by tabune to purchase night soil. I carried 20 to 30 barrels each time, and visited there more than once a month." (Till around 1959, Yamada Town, Kusatsu City)

"The tabune I used was almost identical to the fishing boat in Katata in terms of shape and size. I transported harvested rice and straw for roofing, sailed to Zeze to sell rice and vegetables, and used the money to buy night soil. I used it for cutting algae as well." (Between around 1950 and 1955, Niihama Town, Kusatsu City)

One reason why these boats were so convenient closely relates to the fact that water channels connected houses and the work fields.

"I went to the rice fields by tabune every day. During the rice planting season, I transported seedlings by boat. And, in the harvest season I went to the rice fields carrying the threshing machine, and returned with finished un-hulled rice on board. Boats were used to go to the rice fields in both Chuzu

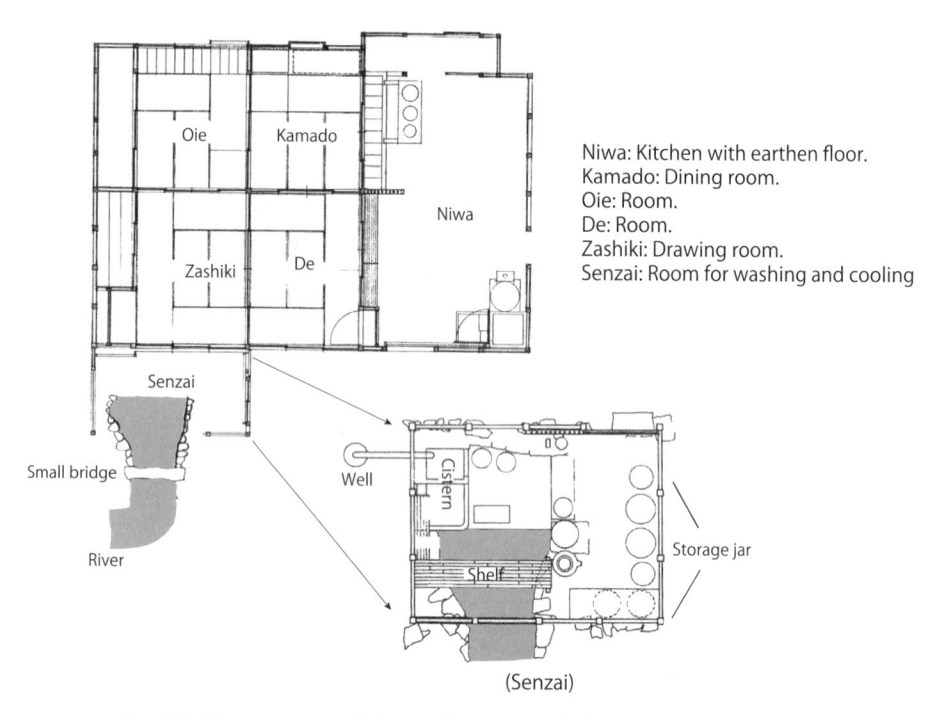

Chapter III The Rise and Fall of Traditional Boats on Lake Biwa

Niwa: Kitchen with earthen floor.
Kamado: Dining room.
Oie: Room.
De: Room.
Zashiki: Drawing room.
Senzai: Room for washing and cooling

Fig. 7 Washing space example(Kawaya) in Tomie family dwelling in Honjo Ward, Hikone.

Town and Omihachiman. Water channels (canals) were built around the rice fields. A pole was used in the shallows to push boats, and oars were used where the pole didn't reach the bottom. A dock was located near houses, and a boat was always moored there. People living in a house not adjacent to a water channel were inconvenienced. They had to carry threshing machines or other stuff by two-wheeled cart to the water channel, and had to load them on a boat. It was hard work." (From 1945 through around 1965. An outboard engine was used in around 1965, Yasu City, Omihachiman City)

"A river was running behind my house, and it connected to rice fields via water channels. Kawado[7] (the similar type "kawaya", see Fig. 7) was like a primary entrance of the house, and stuff like threshing machines were carried from there to the rice field. When loading a machine or something on board, a plank was laid on the boat. Lifting the machine from the boat to the rice field was difficult and it was the kids' job to suppress the boat's rolling by holding a bamboo pole against the bottom." (1957, Kusatsu City)

"When visiting a farmhouse to sell compost or buy rice, there were only roads in the area wide enough for one man to walk or bicycle, therefore goods like compost were transported by tabune. Now, the road ("the Lakeside Road") has been developed, and farmers are pleased with the convenience." (From 1980 through around 1985, Maki Town, Omihachiman)

"I went to the rice fields with cattle, a farm tractor or some stuff on board, and helped working in the rice fields. In those days each household had a boat. When loading a farm tractor on board or unloading it from the boat, sometimes it got stuck in the river." (1963, Kusatsu City)

In the past, cattle were an essential work force for farmers.

"I carried cattle on board tabune. Cattle often fell off the boat on the way, and I remember I saw a cow swimming." (Omihachiman)
"The shape of the boat looked exactly the same as tabune, but it was bigger, and it crossed the river with cattle on board for farm work." (Through around 1955, Furutaka Town, Moriyama City)

Tabune appeared to be used occasionally in conjunction with farm tools as well.

"When I was a boy, in order to fill water in the rice fields from May through mid August, tabune with water wheels on board were placed at the inlet of a rice field. A man rotated the wheel by stepping on it, and water filled the rice field. The length of the tabune was about 4.5 m." (1940-1950, Sugoshi Town, Hikone City)

Tabune seemed to be more than a tool for daily life, but an object that people shared intimate memories of, especially when remembering using the boats outside of work.

"I was not living near the lake shore, but we used it for doing funayuki (touring by boat) once a year during my elementary school years. Funayuki was pleasure boating on Lake Biwa. We borrowed a tabune from our friend, and enjoyed a sukiyaki party. I really looked forward to it as a child, and it's a good memory." (About 50 years ago, Omihachiman)

"I was living in Kawaguchi Town of Hamaotsu, and came to Akanoi using the Taiko Steamships, and often enjoyed fishing dabugai (a kind of clam) and minnows from tabune. On my way home from school, I caught lots of shijimi clams in a bucket along the Obana River." (1930s, Akanoi Town, Moriyama City)

"When I visited my old home, the festival of Hyozutaisha Shrine was held, and my relative brought me on a short cruise down the river. I looked at the reeds and water grasses and it was lovely." (1961, Noda, Yasu City)

"When I was 15 or 16 years old, I played at rowing tabune on a farm pond. That tabune was for feeding carp. The farm pond was used as a reservoir for the rice fields. It was too much just for a reservoir and was used for raising carp. In fall the pond was drained, and all villagers went there to catch fat carp. There are carp in the pond still, but sewage flows in it making the water polluted, and not many people eat them since they smell. Tabune was able to carry two or three people." (From 1930s till before the War, Oshinohara, Yasu City)

"We visited Chomeiji by tabune on August 1st every year. We had a meal on the boat." (Around 1940s, Shimotoyoura, Azuchi Town, Gamo County)

The museum's oral history sources were particularly concentrated in the Omihachiman region. Most respondents' memories are from the early Showa period to the mid Showa 30s (1926-1960), but some stories were from the

(3) Number and Use of the Farming Boat, or Tabune

1960s and 1970s, past the era of large-scale fishing.

"Since my father engaged in farming, he owned two boats, a tabune and an engine powered wooden boat. He transported rice by tabune. He used the wooden boat mainly when he went to buy night soil. He sailed between Kusatsu and Otsu. He had kept the boats until around the farm field consolidation 25 years ago." (Around 1960, Kusatsu City)

"Until the farm field improvement was complete, each farm household had tabune. Everything was transported through the water channels. There was a harbour in the village, we carried stuff there by pulling a two-wheeled cart, and went to the rice field by boat." (Around 1955, Fukudo Town, Higashiomi)

"Now the farm field improvement is done, and farm products can be easily transported by truck. However, in around 1960s no road was there, and we transported anything for farming (rice and wheat farming) by tabune." (Around 1960s, Fukudo Town, Higashiomi)

(4) Statistical Data of Traditional Boat Use in Each County in the Early 20th Century

The "Shiga Prefecture Statistical Report" and the "Shiga Prefecture Product Report"[8] provide various statistical data on the Lake Biwa region from the Meiji period to the Taisho period (from the end of the 19th century to the early 20th century). The latter in 1880 includes population, number of households, and occupation data on towns and villages in Shiga. In this report 226 villages out of 1,399 villages in 13 counties are noted to have boats, and their types and numbers are recorded (Fig. 8). They are classified based on their use for fishing, transportation, and farming. Though not all villages present the boat types by use, the existence and types in these villages can be judged based on their general description and the list of products.

Summarizing the above-mentioned data, the total number of boats in Omi as a whole was 11,100, and the boat types and the distribution are summarized in Fig. 9. It shows boats for transportation at about 40%, and boats for farming and fishing at 20% to 30%. The types of boats in villages where the number of boats is not known exactly appeared to be mostly for transportation or farming, according to the description in the record. Because of this, the ratio of fishing boats to the whole is estimated to be less than the above percentages.

Examining the data, one can see significant differences in the use of boats in coastal versus inland regions. During this period nearly 90% of all boats were in coastal regions, and a little over 10% were in inland regions. In the coastal region, 40% were for transportation and about 30% or less were for fishing and farming. By contrast, in the inland region nearly 50% of the boats were for transportation, about 40% were for farming, and about 10% were for fishing. In the inland region the highest number of boats was in villages at the junctions of major roads.

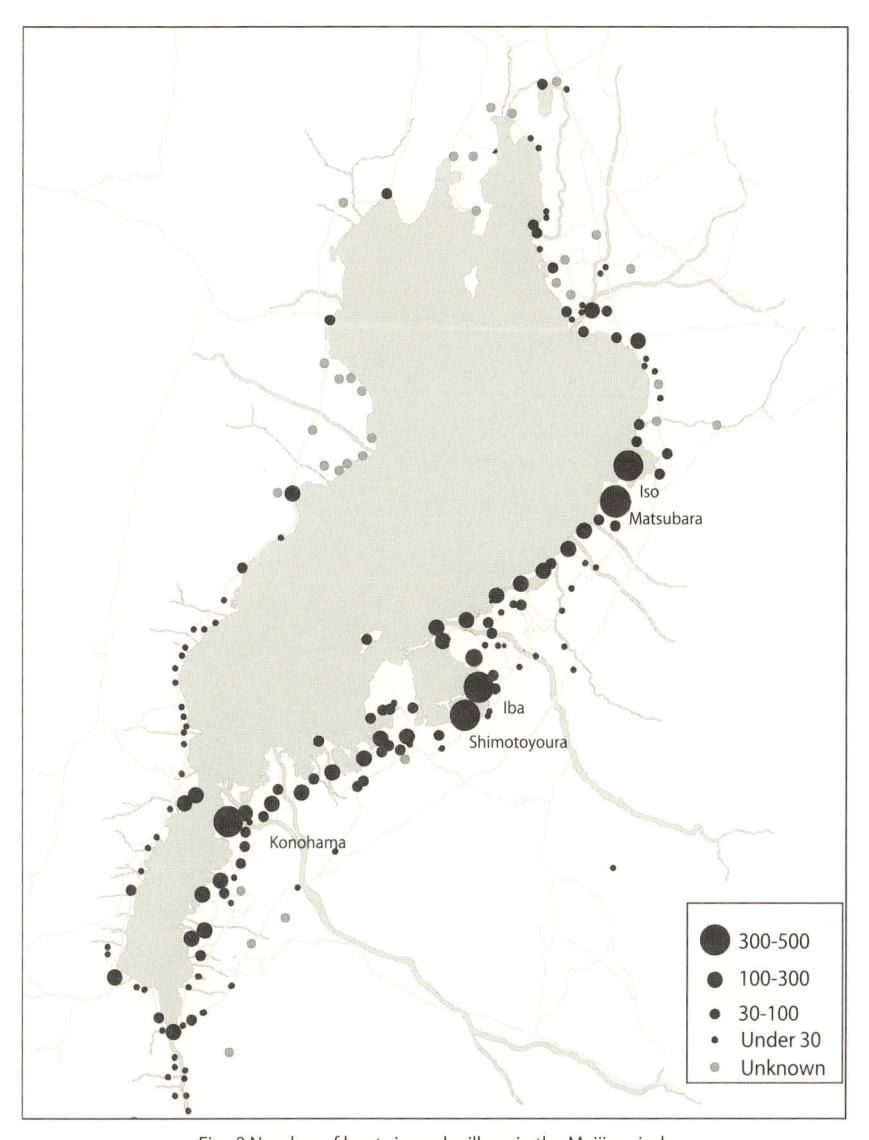

(4) Statistical Data of Traditional Boat Use in Each County in the Early 20th Century

Fig. 8 Number of boats in each village in the Meiji period.

Chapter III The Rise and Fall of Traditional Boats on Lake Biwa

Distribution of coastal and inland region.
- Coastal region 88%
- Inland region 12%

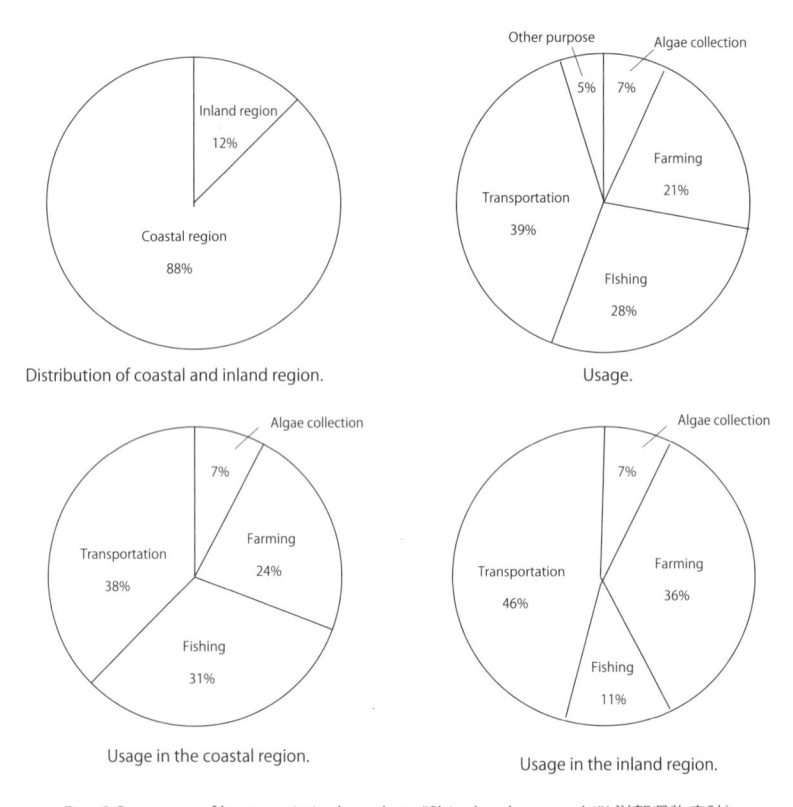

Usage.
- Transportation 39%
- Fishing 28%
- Farming 21%
- Algae collection 7%
- Other purpose 5%

Usage in the coastal region.
- Transportation 38%
- Fishing 31%
- Farming 24%
- Algae collection 7%

Usage in the inland region.
- Transportation 46%
- Farming 36%
- Fishing 11%
- Algae collection 7%

Fig. 9 Summary of boat statistics based on "Shigaken bussan-shi"(滋賀県物産誌).

Records for two counties - Nishiazai and Takashima - unfortunately do not appear in the Shiga Prefectural Statistical and Product Reports. However, other documents mention boats in these counties, but without any detail or numbers. While Mr. Matsui was unable to provide statistical information, he did provide information on the types of boats once used in these and the other counties in the Lake Biwa region. Matsui could recall sizes, designs, construction details, and patterns of use for the region's watercraft.

A detailed examination of the boat types in each county reveals that they can be classified into two types: one for a specific use, and the other for multiple uses according to the season and the location. A typical example

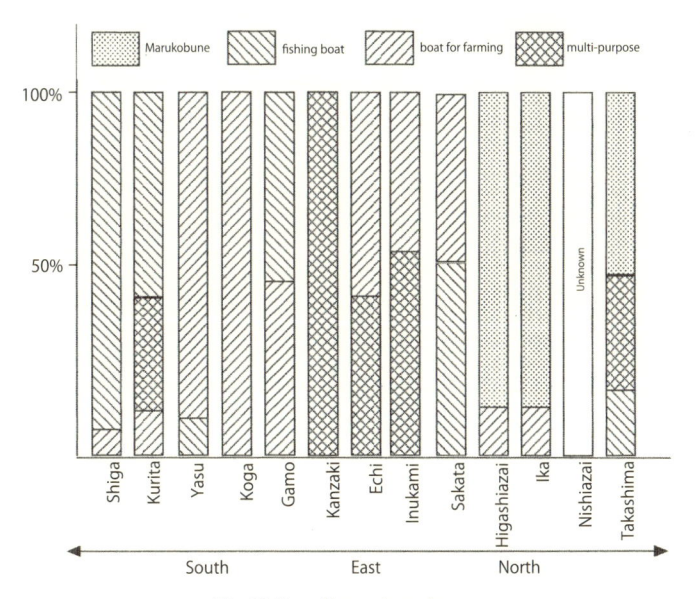

(4) Statistical Data of Traditional Boat Use in Each County in the Early 20th Century

Fig. 10 Use of boats in each county.

of a specific-use boat is the fishing boat of Oki Island (Okishima), which was used for various kinds of fishing throughout the year, but not used as tabune for farming. Whereas, an example of a multiple-use boat is the tabune of Yamada, which was used both for fishing and farming.

The counties can be divided into two groups based on how boats were used. The counties that had multi-use boats include Kurita, Yasu, Echi, Inukami and Takashima. The counties that did not have multi-use boats include Ika, Higashiazai, Sakata, Gamo, Koga, Yasu, and Shiga (Fig. 10). The regions with multi-use boats are in the lake's ecotone, regions characterized by a transition between wet and dry areas.

The advent of powered small boats created a convergence in boat design. A standard hull design developed so that by the 1960s the regional diversity in fishing boats had all but disappeared.

The following is a description of the boats in each county.[9]

Shiga County (Fig. 11)

The east side of the county borders Lake Biwa and the south side is bordered by the Seta River and Kurita County. Its shape is long north-to-south and narrow east-to-west. In the west are the Hiei and Nagara Mountains. There are a few rivers between the mountains that flow into Lake Biwa. The region is not well irrigated and farmers use springs. The coastal area has good water access for transportation, and roads run north and south, and to Kyoto. The major occupation in the coastal villages was fishing. Villages with fishing boats and cargo boats, and villages with only cargo boats, spread along nearly the entire coast. In particular, Otsu, Honkatata and Imakatata had over 200 boats, respectively. Katata's fishing grounds were near Oki Island (Okishima). Katata's fishermen used a small fishing boat, called ankobune (Fig. 12). These boats were narrow and deep but could sail quickly. They were not stable and it seems that sometimes fishermen brought three or four children on board for stability. In Bamba, Bessho, Nishikori, Hieitsuji, Enoki, Minamifunaki, and Minamihira there were around ten boats for collecting algae, and there were eleven ferryboats in Terabe and one in Senmachi. Tabune were used to go to the rice fields in the south from Karasaki along the Lake Biwa shore, as well as to sail on the lake, hence they were heavily built and relatively large. Their hulls were deep but they did not have topside planks,[10] the bottom was fairly flat longitudinally. They were stable and easy to sail. Their cargo capacity was comparatively large, supposedly capable of loading the rice from a 1 tan (around 1,000 m^2) rice field.

Dambebune of Sakamoto were designed specifically for carrying lumber from the Hiei Mountains. Lumber was shipped across the lake to villages such as Kurita, Yasu, Akanoi, and Omagari, as these villages did not have a local source for quality lumber. Timber was carried by ox wagons to Sakamoto, and shipped to the other side by dambebune. These were long and fairly large boats, capable of carrying logs of over seven meters in length.

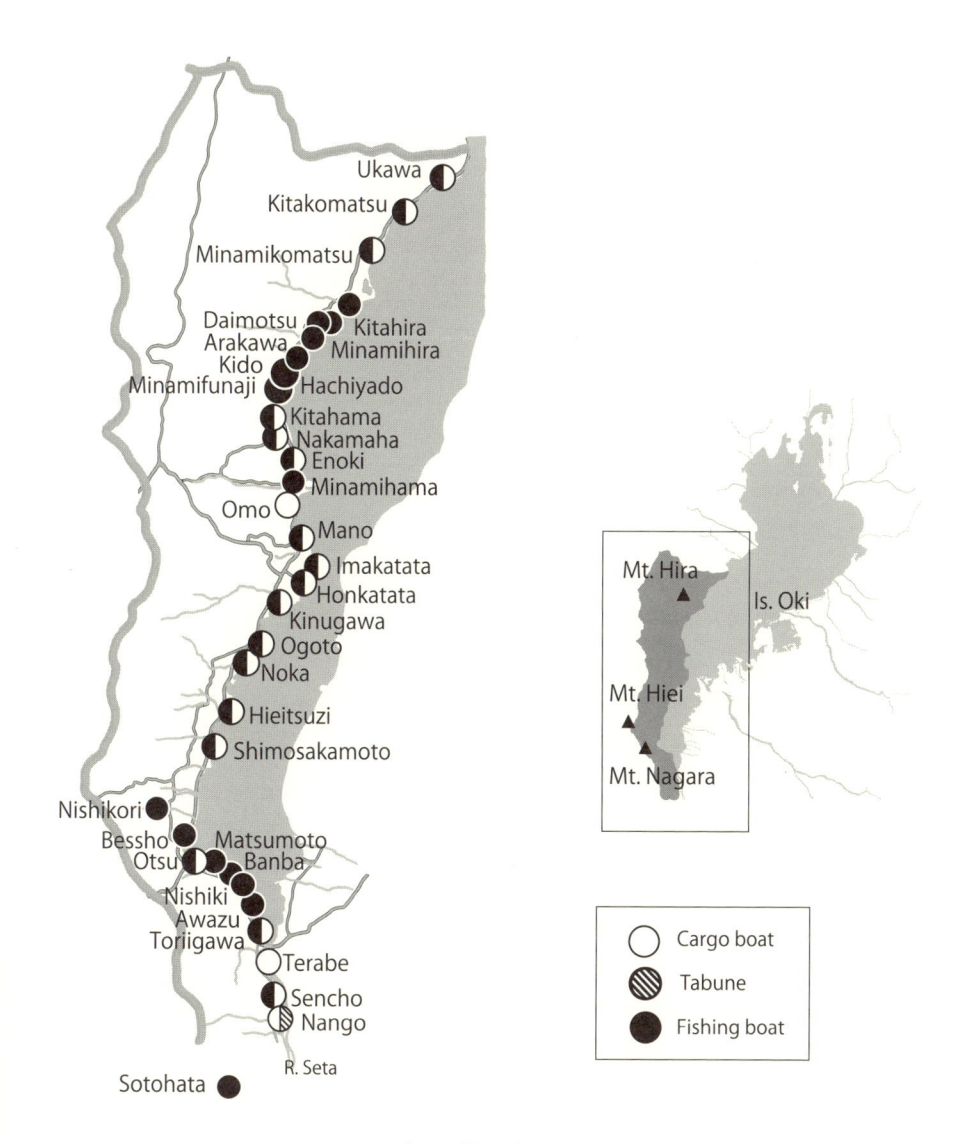

(4) Statistical Data of Traditional Boat Use in Each County in the Early 20th Century

Fig. 11 Shiga County.

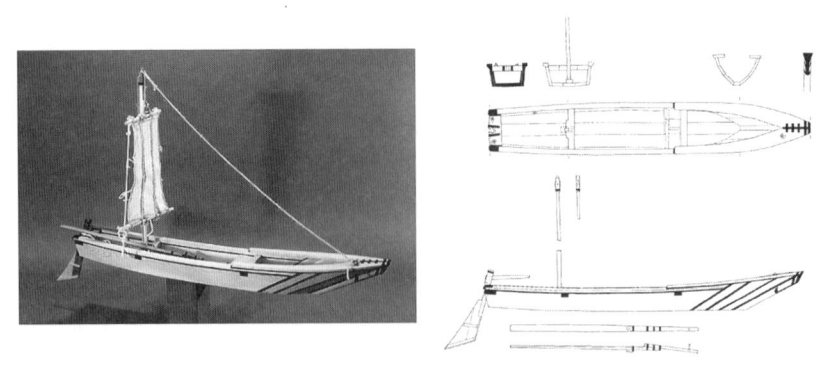

Chapter III The Rise and Fall of Traditional Boats on Lake Biwa

Fig. 12 Fishing boat in Katata region.

Sosuibune (Fig. 13) were canal boats. In the Lake Biwa region the first canal was dug in 1890, and it was 11 km long. The canal was built to supply Kyoto with water, and also to provide transportation and irrigation. A second canal was opened in 1912 between Otsu and the Kamo River in Kyoto, and also used for power generation. Sosuibune was used to transport firewood along these canals. These boats could carry 30 koku (75 straw bundles), and they made round trips between Shiga and Kyoto in one day. They also transported rice and firewood from Shiga to Kyoto, returning with kimono fabrics, salt and sugar from Kyoto. The dimensions of the boats were determined according to the depth and width of the canals, and it appears that the canal boats' midship beam was 6 shaku (1.8 m), depth was 2 shaku (0.6 m), and the length of the cargo space was 9 shaku (2.7 m). The majority of the canals were inside tunnels, and therefore the boats did not have a roof to protect from rain. The pole's tip was a little sharper than those commonly used because the canals had concrete beds. The pole was held under the arm when pushing against the bed.

The total number of cargo boats passing through the canals was 7,127 in 1893, 14,647 in 1902, and the total number of passenger boats was 12,540 and 21,025, respectively.[11] After World War II roads were constructed and automobile transportation spread in the region, and the canals were used

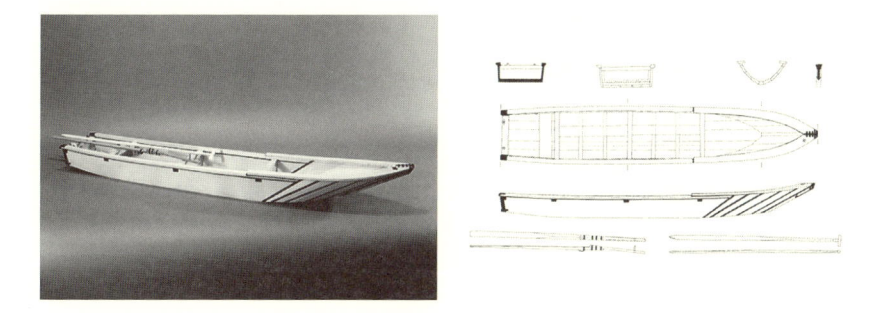

(4) Statistical Data of Traditional Boat Use in Each County in the Early 20th Century

Fig. 13 Sosuibune.

less for cargo transportation and boat traffic steadily declined. The number of passengers was 111,514 in 1906, but it dramatically declined to 25,610 in 1914. Finally, transportation via the canals ceased on November 16, 1948.

Kurita County (Fig. 14)

In the south eastern part of Kurita County are the Shigaraki Mountains, the Konze Mountains and the Tanakami Mountains. To the west of these regions there is the Seta hill country followed by alluvial plains running to Lake Biwa. The Hayama, Kusatsu, and the Okami Rivers, among others, flow through these regions. Many reservoirs are scattered to the south of the Kusatsu River.

A total of over 250 fishing and cargo boats existed in Hashimoto near the mouth of the Seta River. Several types of fishing boats are known to have been used in the Seta River. These include shijimikakibune (Fig. 15) for shijimi clam fishing, amiuchibune (Fig. 16) for cast net fishing (relatively large fish), and tsuribune (Fig. 17) for small fish like minnows. The latter were also used for transporting fish to yakatabune. The amiuchibune and tsuribune were small and agile boats well adapted for the flowing waters of the Seta River. The yakatabune (Fig. 18) can still be found today in the Seta as sightseeing boats.

The villages of Minamiyamada, Shimodera and Oroshimo had 53, 30 and

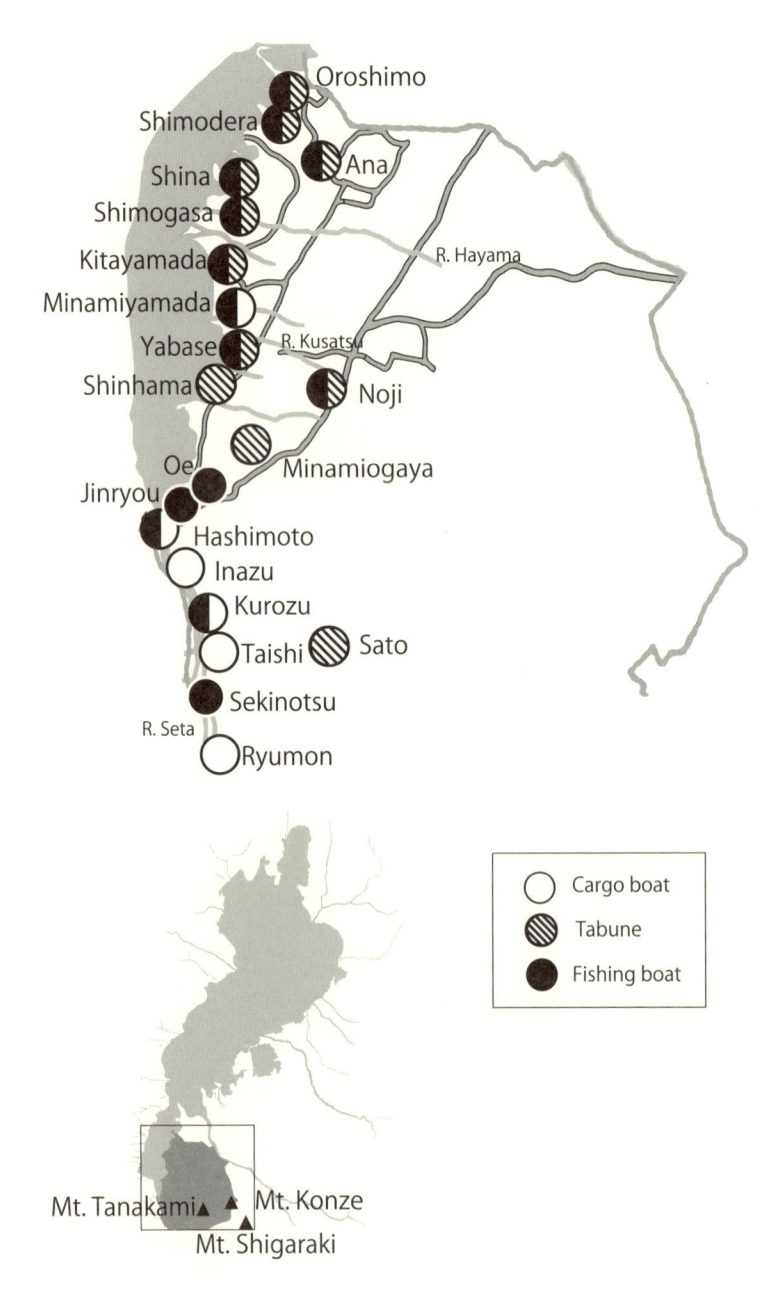

Chapter III The Rise and Fall of Traditional Boats on Lake Biwa

Fig.14 Kurita County.

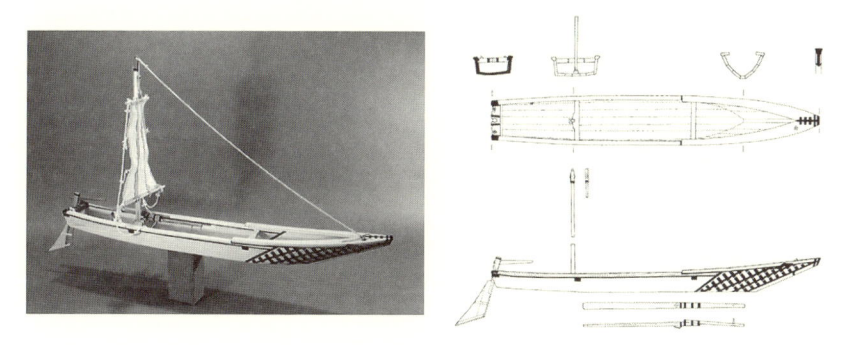

(4) Statistical Data of Traditional Boat Use in Each County in the Early 20th Century

Fig. 15 Shijimikakibune.

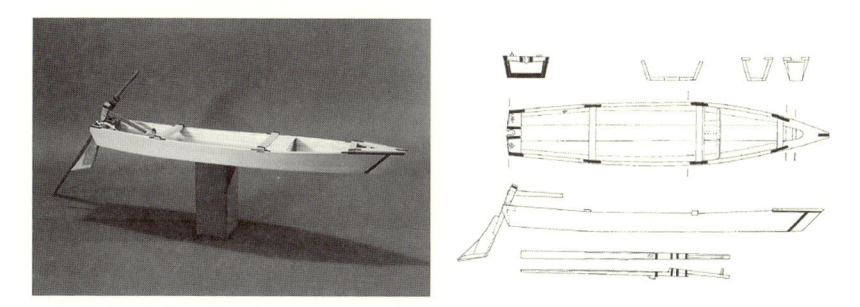

Fig. 16 Amiuchibune.

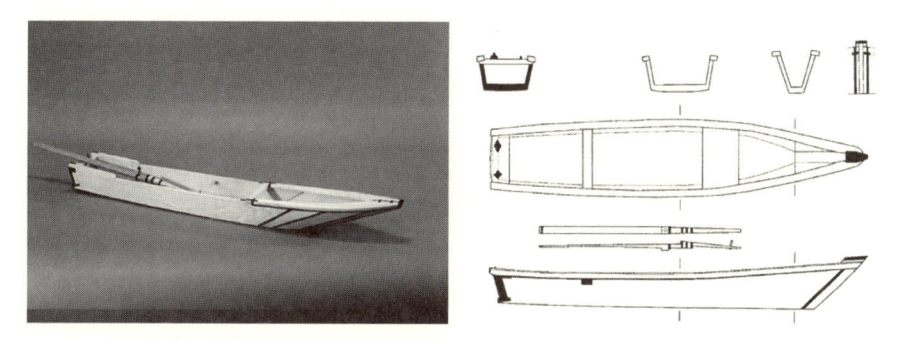

Fig. 17 Tsuribune.

149

Chapter III The Rise and Fall of Traditional Boats on Lake Biwa

Fig. 18 Yakatabune.

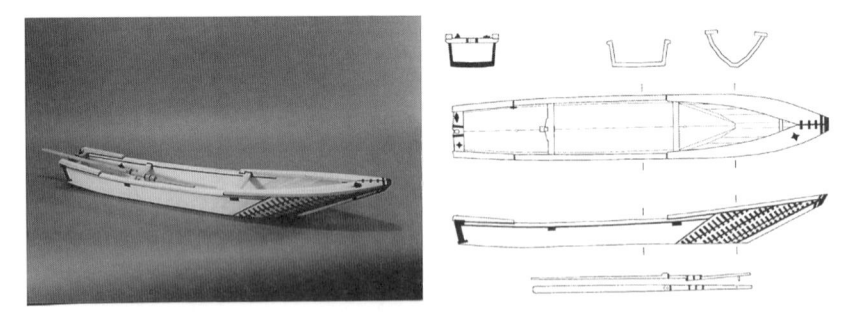

Fig. 19 Boat in Yamada region.

91 boats respectively used for fishing, as well as collecting algae. Since these boats were used for both purposes, they needed to be able to sail in swamps; therefore they were shallower and narrower than typical fishing boats. The boats reflected several distinct features. The boats in Yamada (Fig. 19) did not have pole rests (saozashi); and boats in the Akanoi and Oroshimo region (Fig. 20) had a lowered transom (fubuki). Both boats were used for transporting vegetables to Otsu where their owners exchanged for bundles of

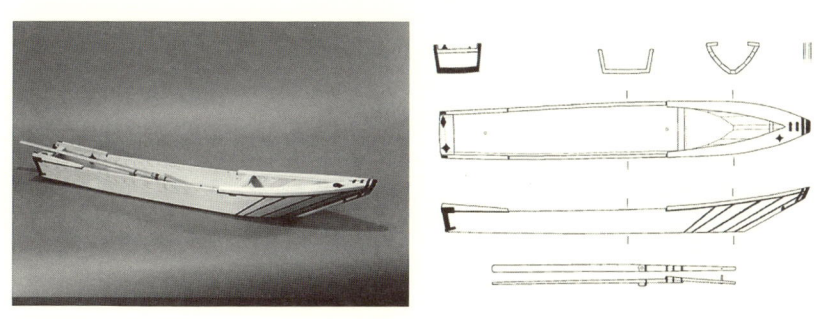

(4) Statistical Data of Traditional Boat Use in Each County in the Early 20th Century

Fig. 20 Boat in Akanoi and Oroshimo region.

straw or compost.

In Shinhama and Minamiogaya only tabune were used. Yabase was located at the gateway to Otsu and it had 4 large boats. Shimogasa was slightly inland and it had over 250 tabune and 4 large cargo boats. These tabune were exclusively for farming. The boats in Yamaga

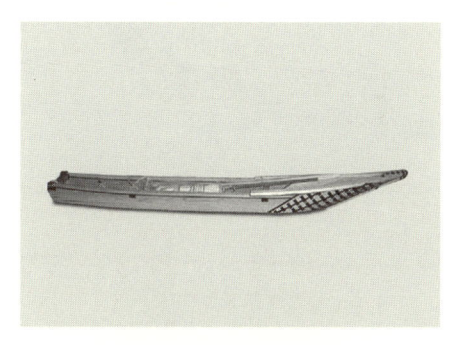

Fig. 21 Boat in Yamaga region.

(Fig. 21) and Shimogasa were sailed between these villages and Otsu to transport vegetables, returning with night soil from Otsu. Occasionally, vegetables were exchanged for glutinous rice. The boats in this region that sailed on Lake Biwa, instead of shallow swamps, were slightly larger and deeper than the typical tabune, and their bows were higher and their hulls had higher freeboard. They were equipped with sails as well.

Yasu County (Fig. 22)

In the southeast region of Yasu County there are the Yasu and Hino Rivers, which flow to the northwest. Between the two rivers is a fan shaped alluvial plain with rice paddy fields. In its north, the old Nakasendo highway runs

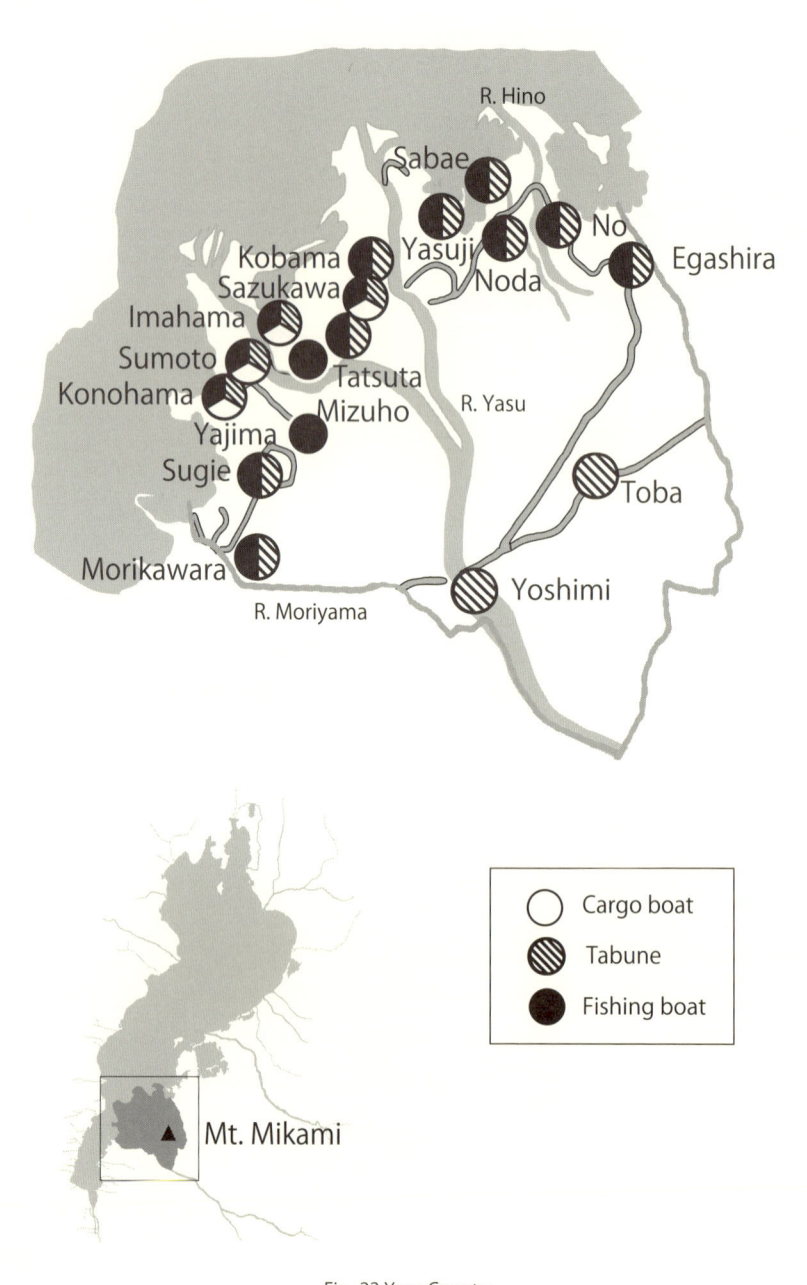

Chapter III The Rise and Fall of Traditional Boats on Lake Biwa

Fig. 22 Yasu County.

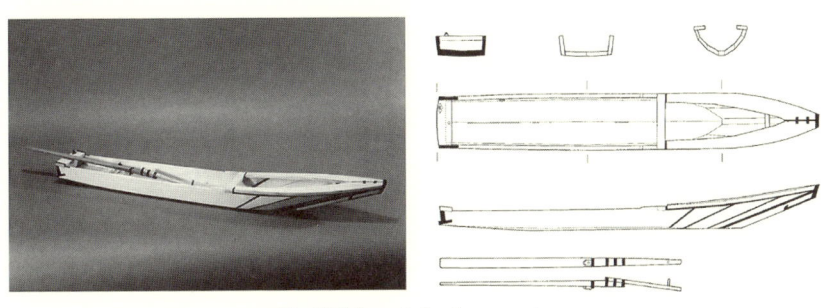

(4) Statistical Data of Traditional Boat Use in Each County in the Early 20th Century

Fig. 23 Tabune in Imahama region.

Fig. 24 Ushibune.

through the mountains. There is also the Moriyama River, and all three major rivers provided good water transportation, and the majority of the area except around Mt. Mikami was suitable for farming.

The villages with tabune spread along the main road and inland. Yoshimi had ten boats and Tonami had seven. Boats were heavily used because the shorelines of the period were complicated, with a couple of big rivers flowing through the county to the lake. Some of the villages along the shore had over 200 boats. Konohama had 350 boats, for example. They were used primarily for transportation and farming.

In Imahama, the relatively shallow tabune were used only in swamps and canals but not on Lake Biwa itself (Fig. 23). Ushibune (cattle boats) were used to carry cattle for rice farming, and used during the rice planting periods

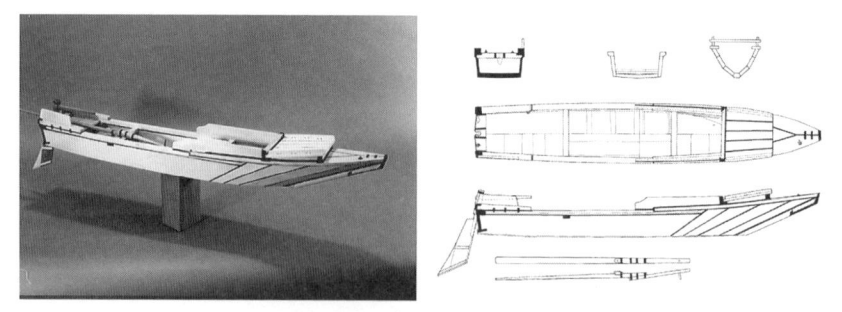

Fig. 25 Fishing boat in Ayame region.

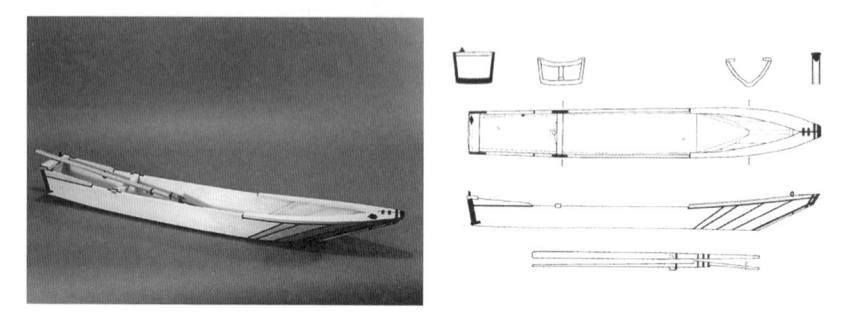

Fig. 26 Tabune in Konohama region.

in spring and fall (Fig. 24). The swamp region from Yasu along the Noto River had many rice fields not accessible by land, and these paddies were scattered like islands in the swamps. Therefore, every farmer had to own at least one ushibune.

Fishing boats in Ayame (Fig. 25) were exclusively for cast net fishing. Nets were thrown by a fisherman standing in the boat, so there were boards added between the midship and the bow to prevent the fisherman from falling overboard. The net was pulled onto kakiita, a plank mounted on the bow.

The boats of Konohama (Fig. 26) were used for farming and building eri, a fish trap fixed to the lake bottom. (see Chapter. I-Fig. 16) Eri fishing involved sailing to shallows carrying cut bamboo (su). Once at the fishing grounds, the fisherman built eri by driving the bamboo into the bottom of the lake while working from the bow of the boat. In these boats, the ikura, the quarter beam,

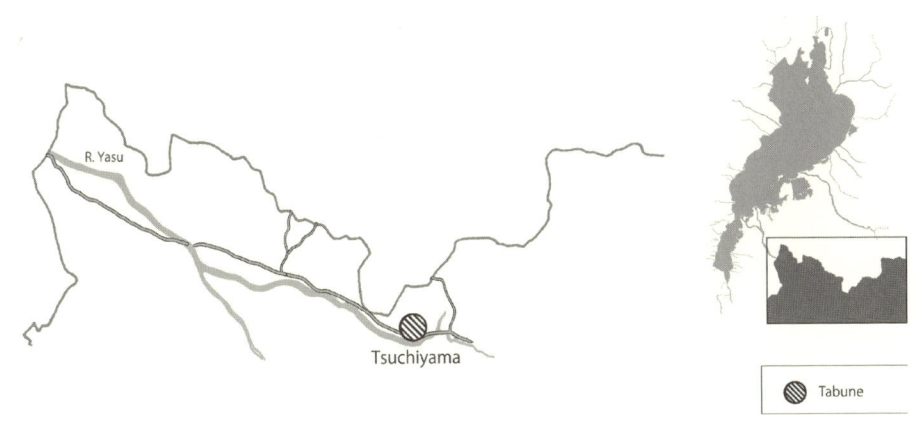

(4) Statistical Data of Traditional Boat Use in Each County in the Early 20th Century

Fig. 27 Koga County.

was placed further aft than usual to facilitate this work. The middle of the ikura was lowered to hold the bamboo, and the bow was slightly higher than usual.

Koga County (Fig. 27)

In Koga County's eastern region are the Koga Mountains. South are the Shigaraki Mountains, and in the north the Minakuchi Hills spread where the Yasu River flows westward and an alluvial plain was formed along the river valley. It was an important location historically connecting Omi to Iga and to Ise. It also had a strong connection to Yamashiro and Yamato. The old Tokaido road ran east and west along the Yasu River. Tsuchiyama was the only village owning boats, where there were 3 boats, presumably for farming. Information about the type of these boats is unknown.

Gamo County (Fig. 28)

The Hino River flows roughly in the middle of Gamo and its source is in the Suzuka Mountains in the east of the county. To the west were swamps of various sizes. Chosenjinkaido, Nakasendo, Godaisankaido, Happukaido,

155

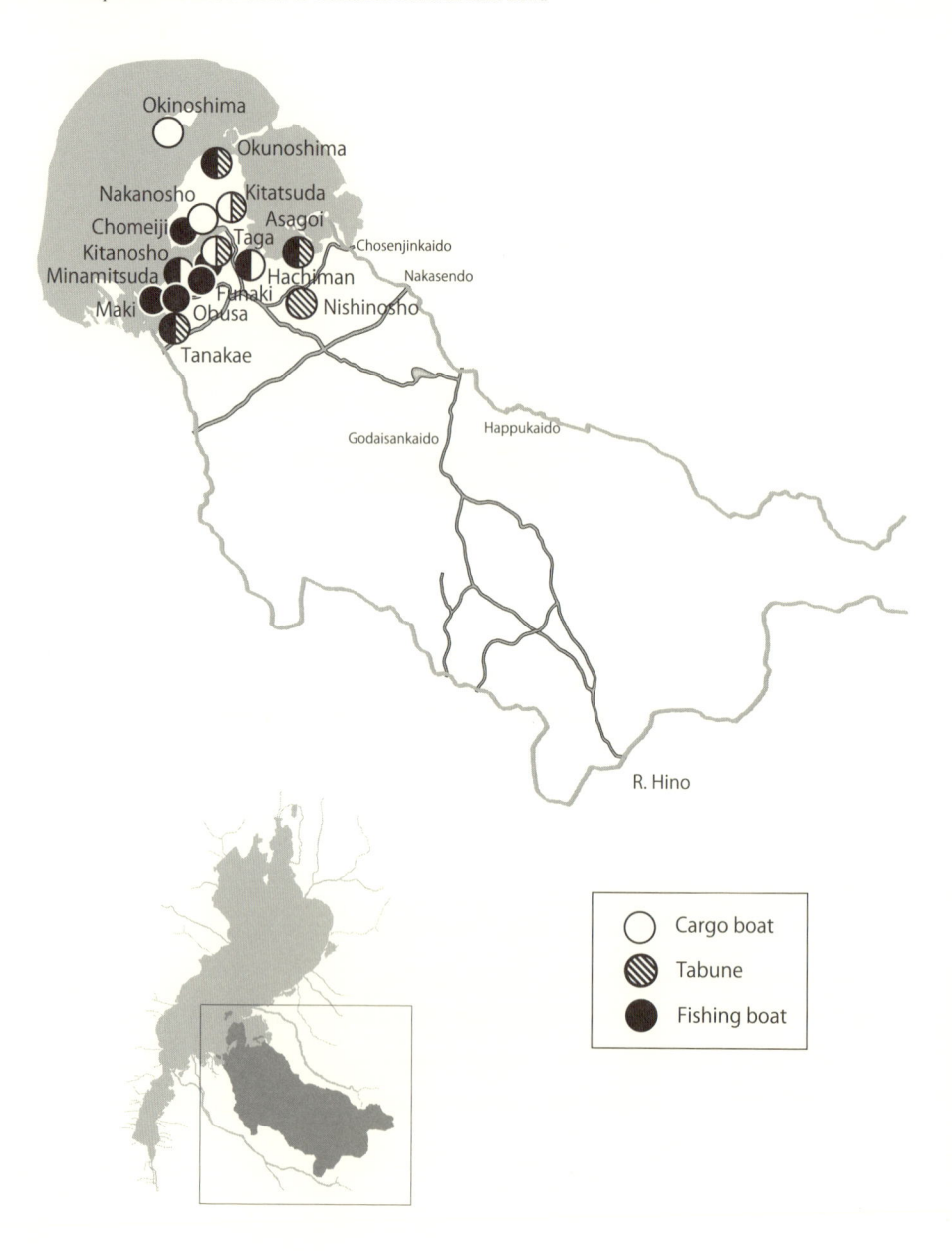

Fig. 28 Gamo County.

and some other routes ran through the county. Hino, Yokaichi, Gokasho were important villages for the Omi merchants. Oki Island (Okinoshima) is located off the north coast.

Villages owning boats were concentrated in the shoreline region. Many villages had specific types of boats. Maki, Obusa, Funaki, Chomeiji, and Taga had only cargo boats. Oki Island had fishing and farming boats, while Nakanosho had only fishing boats. Nishinosho had only tabune. The majority of these boats were small with a length of less than 3 ken (5.4 m). Shimotoyoura had a large number of boats, 366 boats for cargo and farming. Maruyama and Asagoi had around 100 boats used for algae collection and farming.

The region from Omagari to Hachimanbori was not engaged in fishing, and the boats were dedicated to farming (Fig. 29). The dimension of their boats was 0.3 m in depth and 0.9 to 0.93 m beam, slightly shallower and narrower than usual. The boats in the region were built with a lower bow in order to navigate under the bridges in Hachimanbori. The boats apparently left with bundles of straw and returned loaded with vegetables.

Oki Island (Okinoshima) boats were dedicated to fishing (Fig. 30). People on Oki Island were engaged in various kinds of fishing throughout the year, such as koitoami (gill net) fishing and shijimi (clam) fishing. Thus, they had fishing boats built for each purpose. The waves can be high in the waters surrounding the island, particularly on the west side. Therefore, the fishing boats were deep and wide for stability with washboards mounted on both sides to raise their freeboard.

The Oki Island had boats dedicated to farming as well (Fig. 31). There were no rice fields on Oki Island, and Oki's farmers had to sail across the lake to Omihachiman. The waves are generally calm early in the morning when farmers left for the mainland, but the waves were high when they returned. Therefore, large and deep tabune similar to their fishing boats were used. Since the men dedicated themselves to fishing, tabune was mostly used

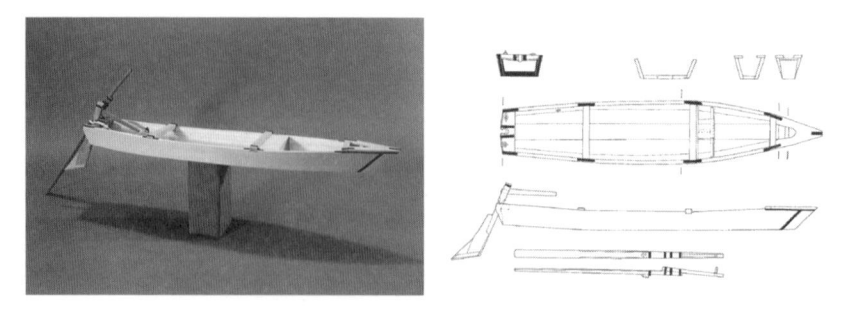

Fig. 29 Tabune in the region between Omagari and Hachimanbori.

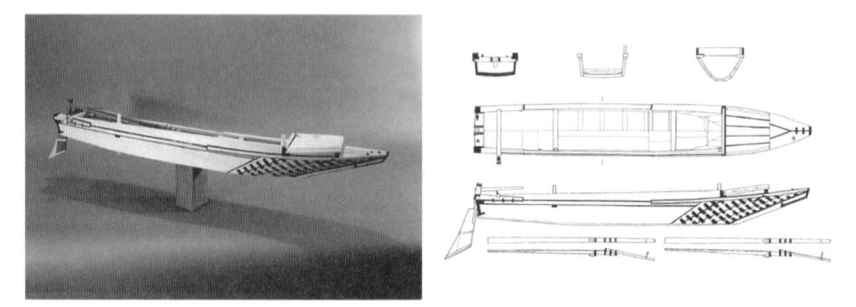

Fig. 30 Fishing boat in Okinoshima.

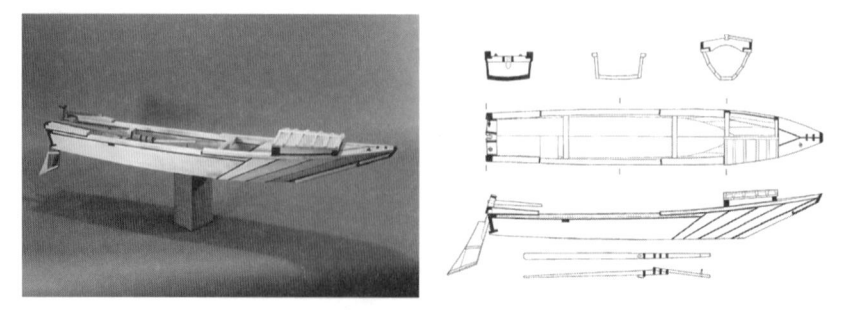

Fig. 31 Tabune in Okinoshima.

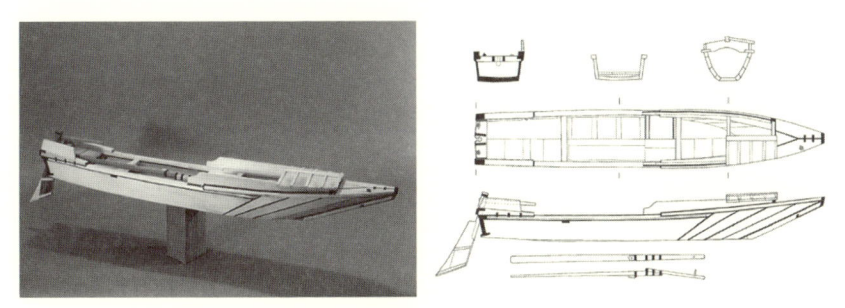

Fig. 32 Fishing boat in Chomeiji.

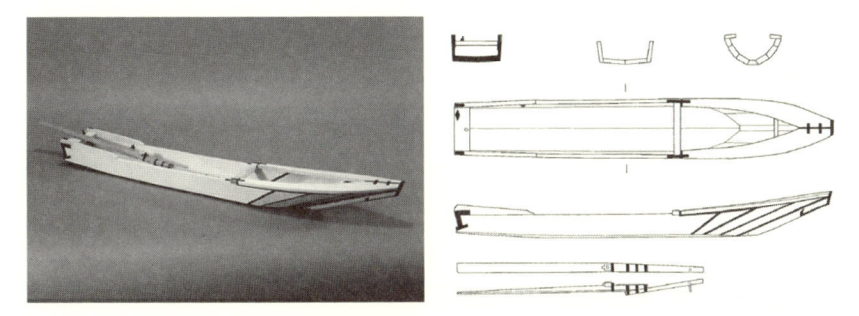

Fig. 33 Tabune in Notogawa region.

by women, who commuted daily to the mainland by boat (about 1 km) to work in their fields.

The fishing boats of Chomeiji were used exclusively for gill net fishing (Fig. 32). Some of the boats were large, but a slightly narrow and a light weight boat were preferred. Tabune were used exclusively for farming (Fig. 33), and they were slightly deep and equipped with saozashi (pole rest) as they sailed between the swamps and Lake Biwa.

Kanzaki County (Fig. 34)

The Echi River has its source in the Suzuka Mountains, and forms low marshes and swamps such as Dainakanoko and Syonakanoko. The villages near the shore are well watered as well as fertile. Boats were used

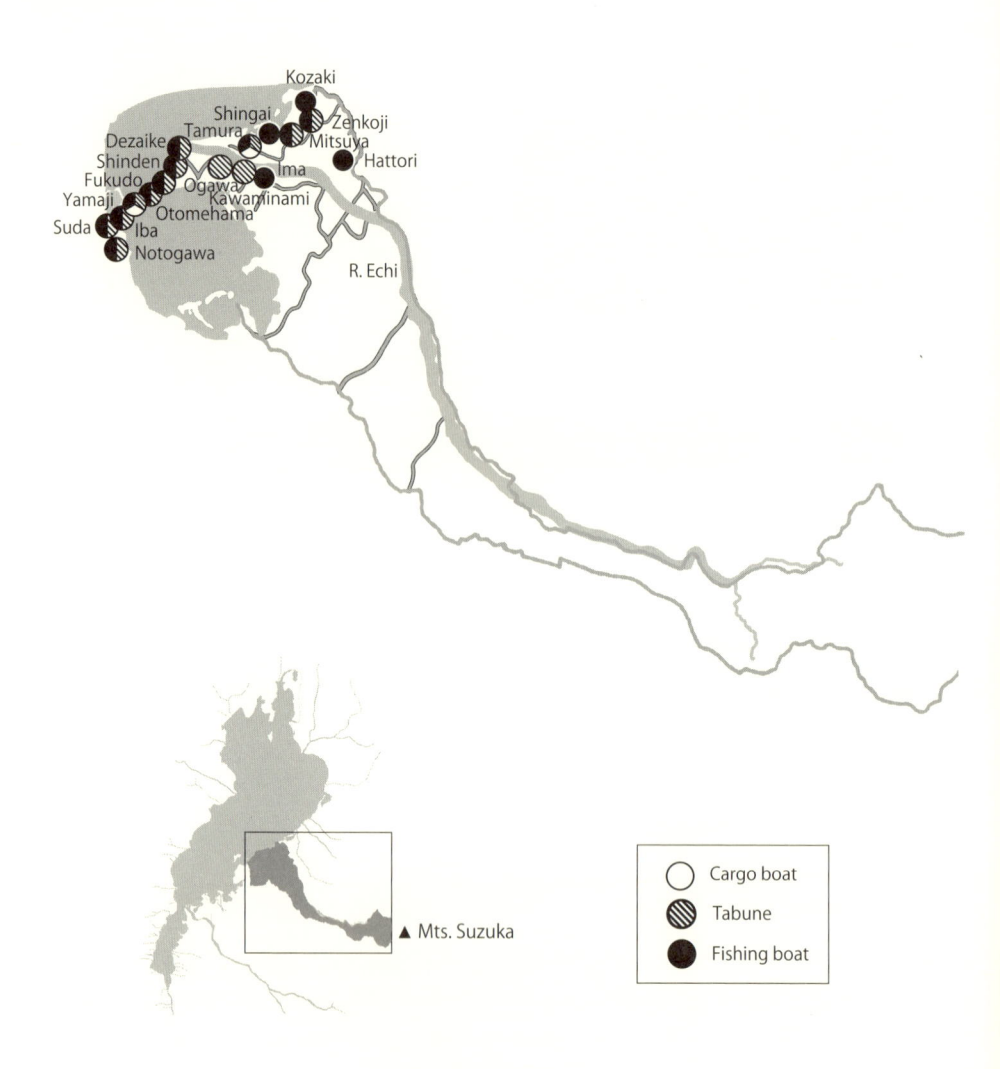

Fig. 34 Kanzaki County.

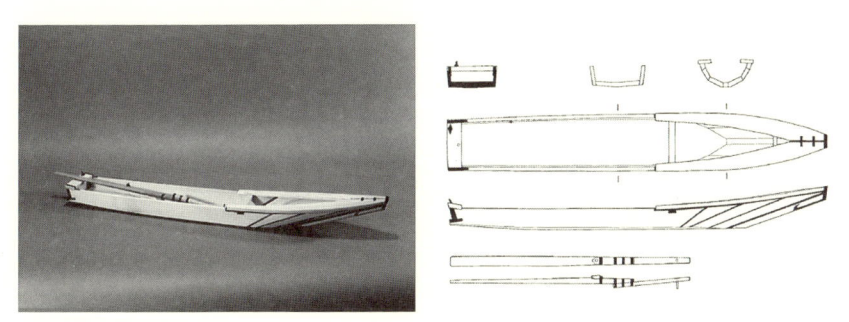

Fig. 35 Tabune in Notogawa region.

extensively for transportation and farming. Ushibune, or cattle boats, were used by farmers. In Notogawa Village tabune were essential for transporting compost and rice plants to and from the rice fields. The tabune of Notogawa (Fig. 35) had oibana (V-shaped foredeck) mounted on ikura (beams), and it did not have saozashi (pole rest). Iba village had the largest number of boats among the coastal villages of the Lake Biwa, nearly 500. Ima Village and Hattori Village had a ferryboat on the Echi River.

Echi County (Fig. 36)

Echi County spreads from the border of Mie Prefecture in the Suzuka Mountains to the shore of Lake Biwa. Ishidera and Satsuma on the lakeshore had more than 100 boats and they were used for fishing, transportation, and farming. Nishikawa Village is located slightly inland and had 32 small boats for both transportation and farming. The types of boats are unknown.

Inukami County (Fig. 37)

Inukami County is in the basin of the Inukami, the Seri and the Uso Rivers. The western part of the county is an alluvial plain, and many swamps were in the shore region including Irienaiko and Matsubaranaiko.

Water transportation was mostly dependent on rivers. Matsubara was the largest port, adjacent to Hikone, which was located along the main

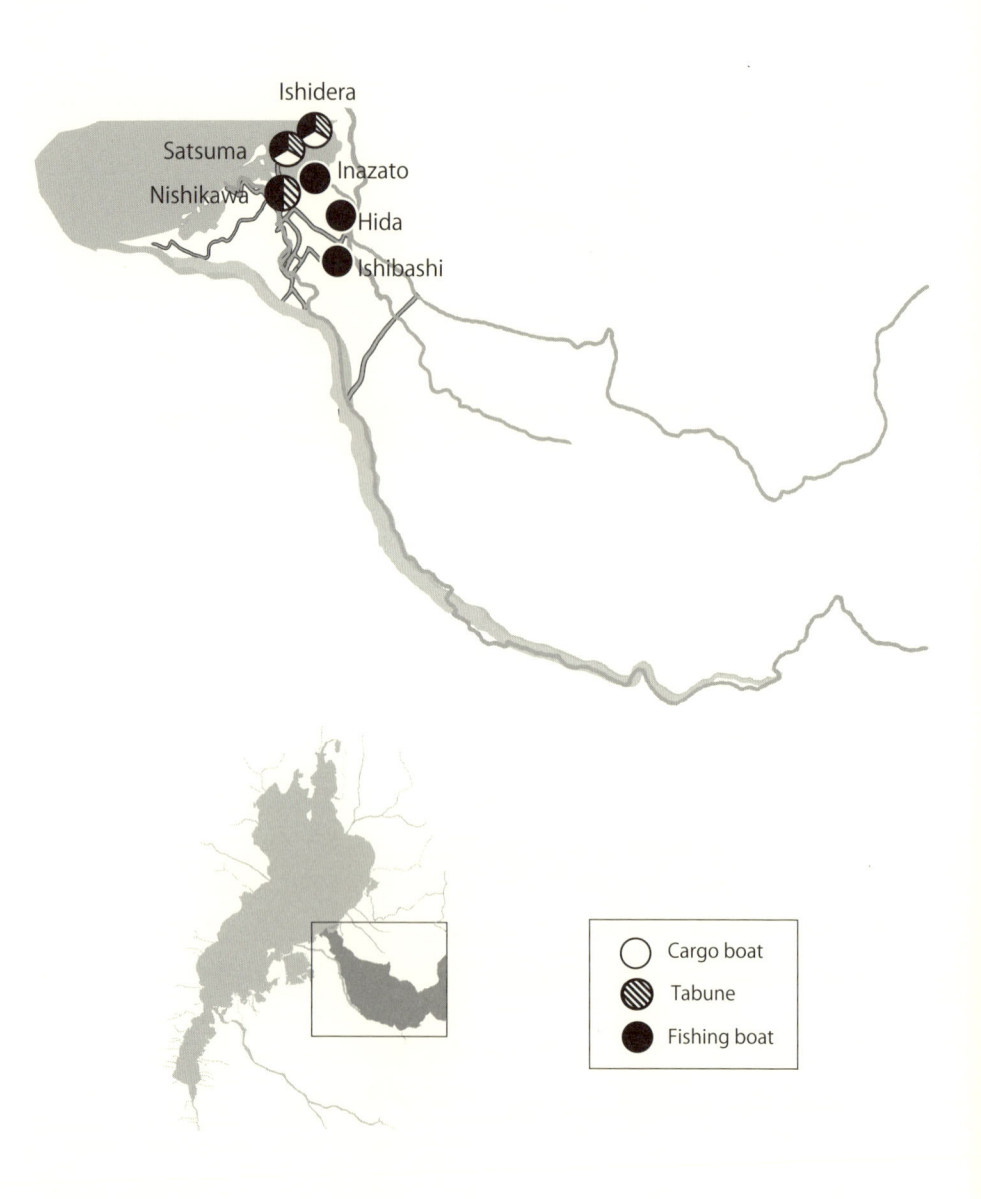

Chapter III The Rise and Fall of Traditional Boats on Lake Biwa

Fig. 36 Echi County.

162

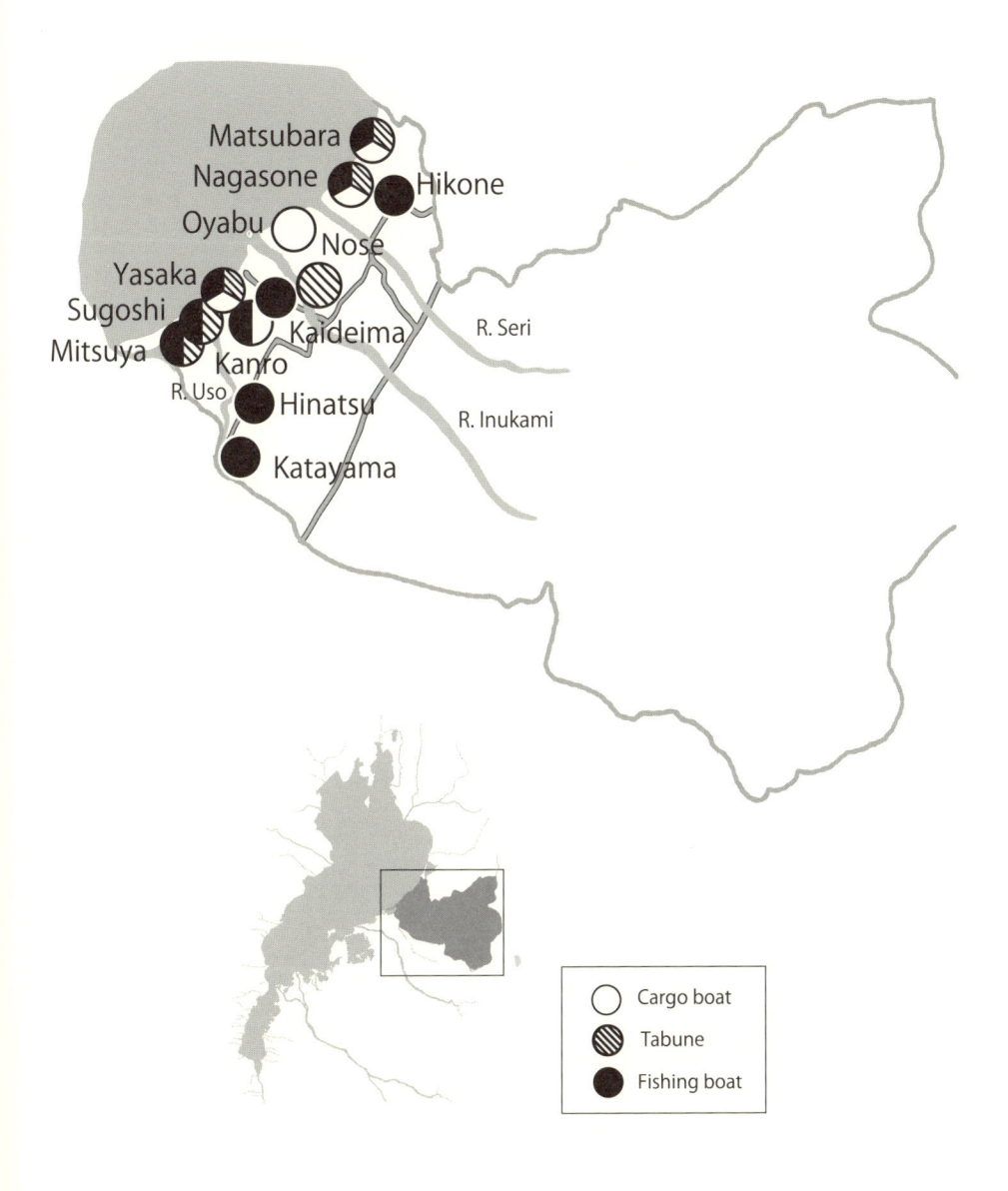

(4) Statistical Data of Traditional Boat Use in Each County in the Early 20th Century

Fig. 37 Inukami County.

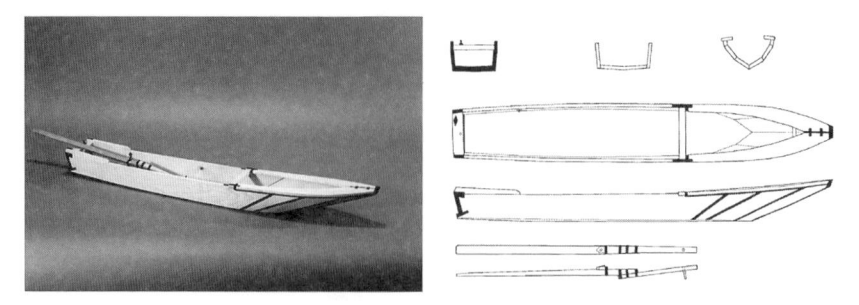

Fig. 38 Fishing boat in Mitsuya region.

transportation route, and it had 284 small boats for fishing and farming. 45 large boats were used for refugees during flooding and 38 marukobune were used for transportation. Hikone had boats for both transportation and algae collection. Among other villages Oyabu, Yasaka, and Mitsuya had over 100 boats. The boats of Oyabu and Yasaka were largely for fishing, and the boats of Mitsuya were mainly for both farming and transportation. The fishing boats of Mitsuya (Fig. 38) do not have a stem (shin), and this appears to be unique to southern Hikone. The tabune in this region and the kawabune (river boats) of Anegawa had the same type of bow construction.

Sakata County (Fig. 39)

Mt. Ibuki is in the northeast of the county. Mt. Ryozen in the southeast and the low Yokoyama Mountains occupy the central region. The Ane River flows along the northern border, and the Amano River flows through the south. The west side faces Lake Biwa.

Sakata has many rivers and the major roads, such as Hokkokukaido and Nakasendo, ran through the county and connected north, south, east and west. Water transportation was well developed. The largest port town was Nagahama, and it had 15 large cargo boats, 3 steamboats and 131 small tabune. In terms of number of boats owned, Iso Village had the most: over 300 fishing boats. Umegahara Village had 88 algae-collecting boats.

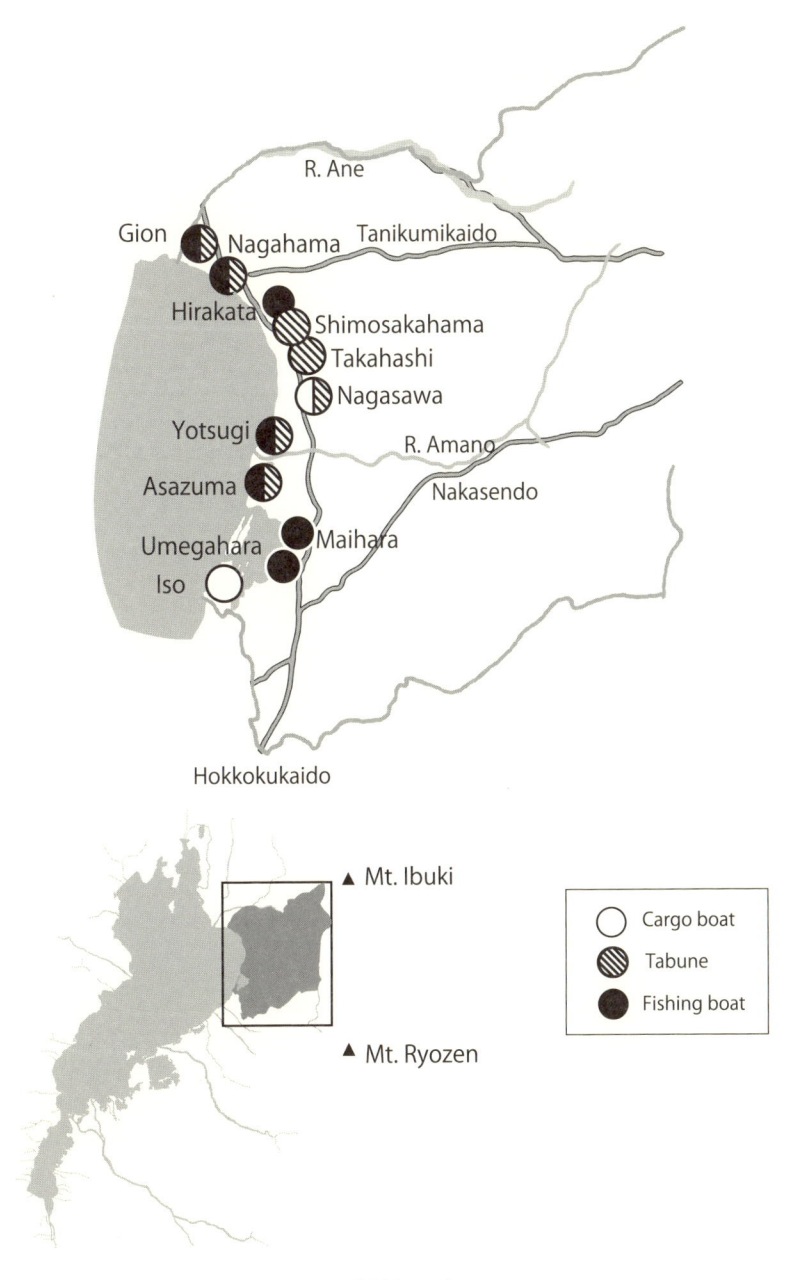

(4) Statistical Data of Traditional Boat Use in Each County in the Early 20th Century

Fig. 39 Sakata County.

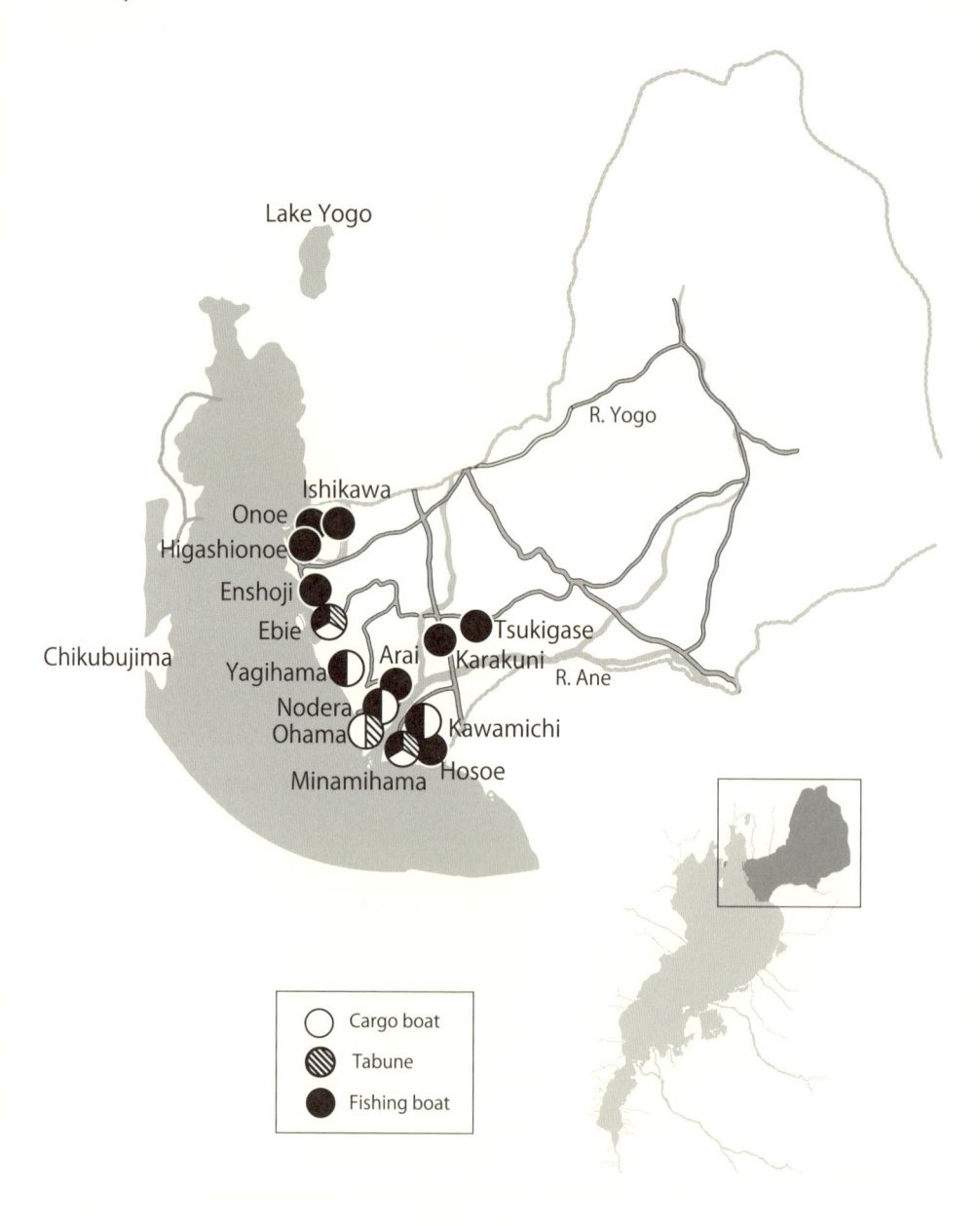

Chapter III The Rise and Fall of Traditional Boats on Lake Biwa

Fig. 40 Higashiazai County.

Higashiazai County (Fig. 40)

The east part of this county is mountainous and the west is flatland. Its west side faces Lake Biwa. Chikubu Island (Chikubujima) is part of the county. The major rivers in Higashiazai are the Ane, Takatoki, and Yogo.

The eastern region is fairly mountainous and no village owned a boat according to historic records. The villages in the south along the Ane River, such as Kawamichi, Minamihama, Ohama, Nodera, and Arai, owned primarily cargo boats and fishing boats. Among these villages, Kawamichi Village had 155 boats. Upstream villages in the inland regions, including Tsukigase and Karakuni, had 4 and 5 cargo boats respectively. In the north Onoe, Higashionoe, and Ishikawa had total of more than 100 cargo boats. The exact types of boats are unknown.

Ika County (Fig. 41)

The region from the north to the central part of Ika County is mountainous and stretches to the Yokoyamadake Mountains. The rivers include the Takatoki River, the Yogo River, and the Oura River flow from there to the flatlands in the south. The major roads in the county were Hokurikudo along the Yogo River and Hokkokuwakiokan along the Takatoki River.

There was plenty of farmland in the region, and a few villages owned tabune and cargo boats. Kawanami Village had the largest number of boats: a total of 70 cargo boats and small sized tabune called habune. Shimoyogo Village in the north had 21 habune. Boats in the south were used for transportation of lumber and other goods. Katayama Village had 15 cargo boats and Yamanashi Village had 14 cargo boats. Iura Village on the lake's shoreline had 8 small cargo boats, as well as marukobune and steamboats. The cargo boats were occasionally used for fishing.

Nishiazai County (Fig. 42)

The south side of this county faces Lake Biwa, and the Hibakari Mountains

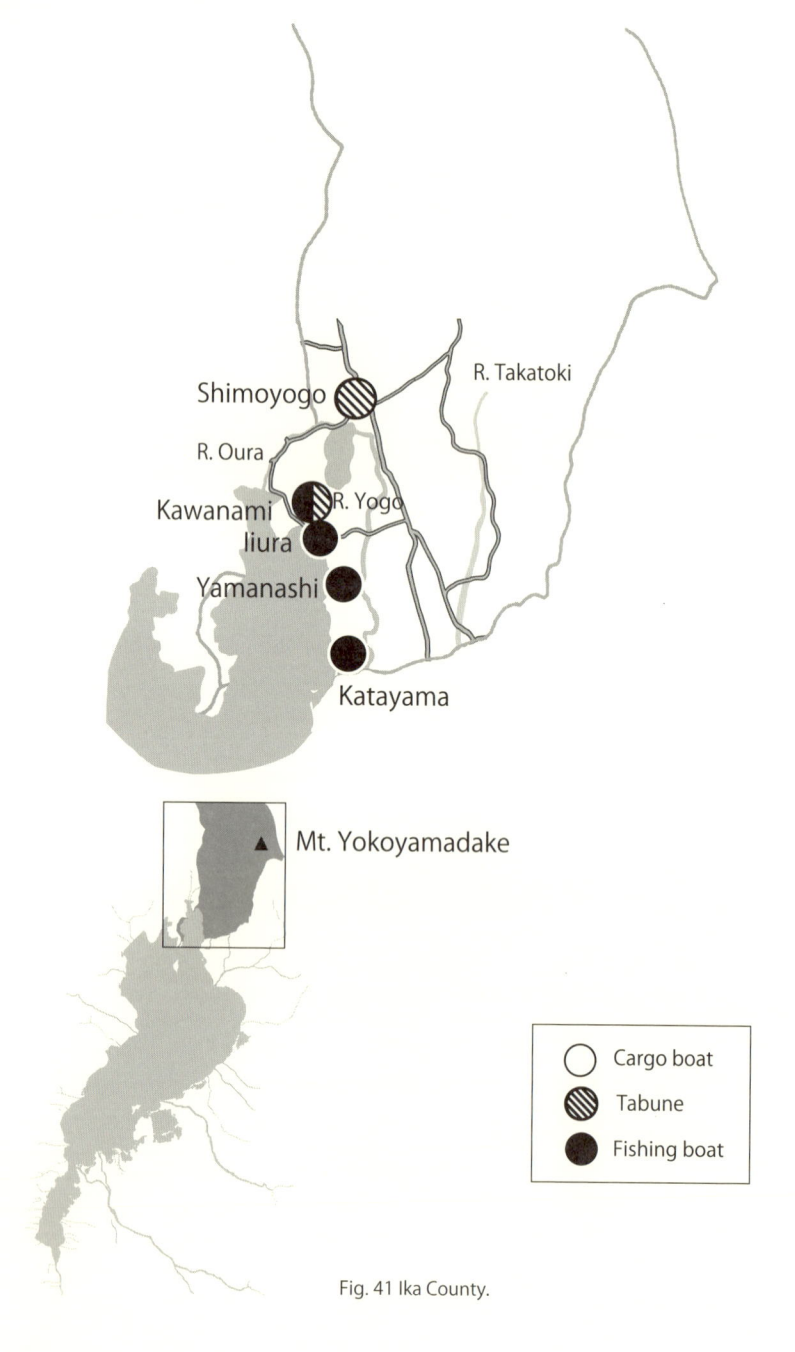

Chapter III The Rise and Fall of Traditional Boats on Lake Biwa

Fig. 41 Ika County.

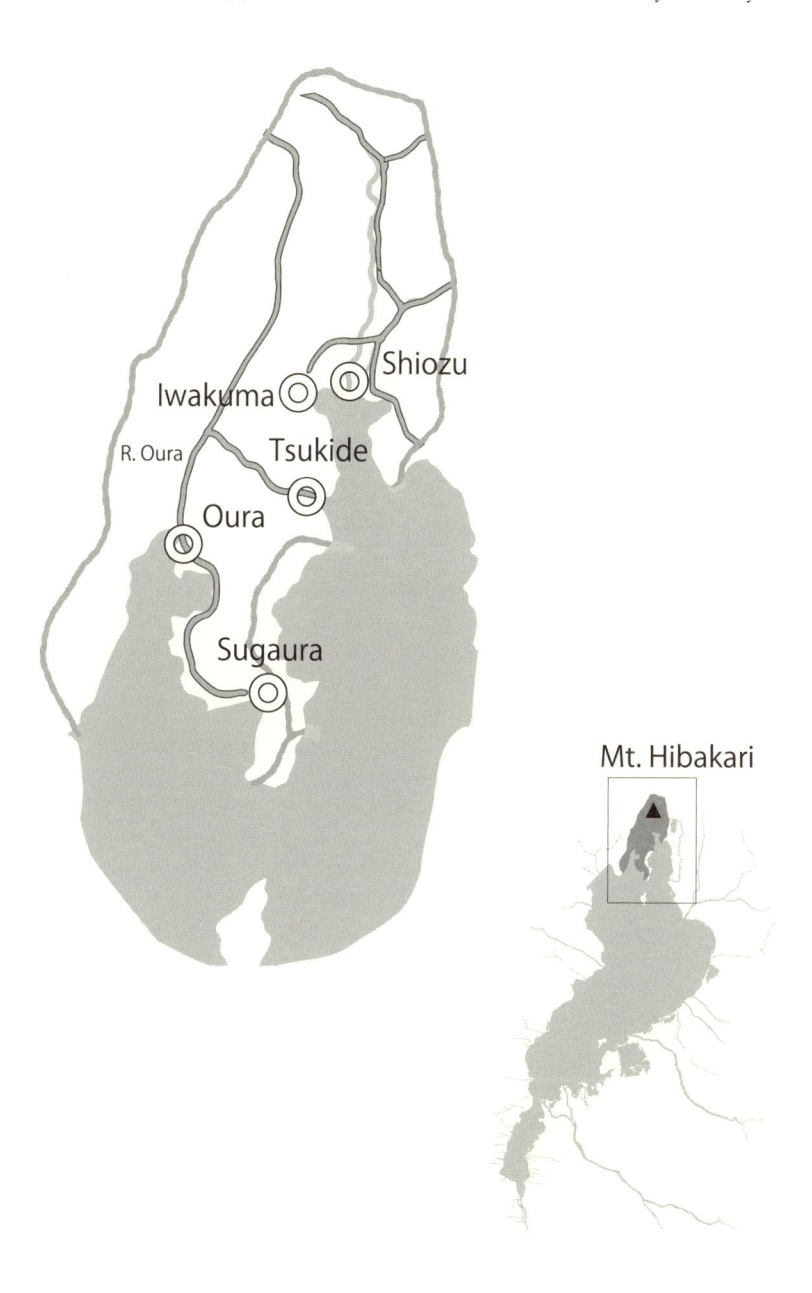

(4) Statistical Data of Traditional Boat Use in Each County in the Early 20th Century

Fig. 42 Nishiazai County.

extend from north-to-south in the middle. The major roads are the route to the north along the Oura River connecting Shichirihangoe (road) and Shiozukaido running from Shiozu to Tsuruga. Shiozu, Oura and Sugaura were major ports, and they prospered from lake transportation and fishing.

The traffic at the ports along the shore was busy for transportation. In particular Shiozu was the gateway between Otsu and Tsuruga, and steamboats ran to Shiozu. Shiozu, Iwakuma, Yamada, Sugaura, and Oura supposedly had many boats, though the actual numbers are not written in the "Shiga Prefecture Statistical Report" or the "Shiga Prefecture Product Report" without any reason. Shiozu and Iwakuma obviously had fishing boats, and the primary purposes of the boats in other villages were transportation and farming. The county records show 231 boats. The villages along the shore, such as Sugaura, Oura and Shiozu, should have owned around 100 boats. The types of these boats are unknown.

Takashima County (Fig. 43)

The east side of Takashima County faces Lake Biwa. The Nosaka Mountains and the Hira Mountains spread to the shore, and the county lacks flatland. The Chinai River in the north, the Ishida River, the Ado River and the Kamo River flow in parallel, and rice fields and farmlands spread around the rivers. Since ancient times, the shortest route between Kyoto and Hokkoku ran through the mountains in Kutsukidani along the Ado River. The road starting from Imazu and running west was called Kurihangoe, and it was a major route connecting Wakasaobama to lake transportation on Lake Biwa. In addition, Shichirihanngoe, starting from Kaizu to north, was an important route connecting Echizentsuruga and Lake Biwa. Lumber transportation (Soma) in the Ado River and the Ishida River prospered here from historic times.

The traffic of steamboats and sailing ships at the ports along the major roads was heavy. Katsunotsu had 145 boats and it was the largest number in the

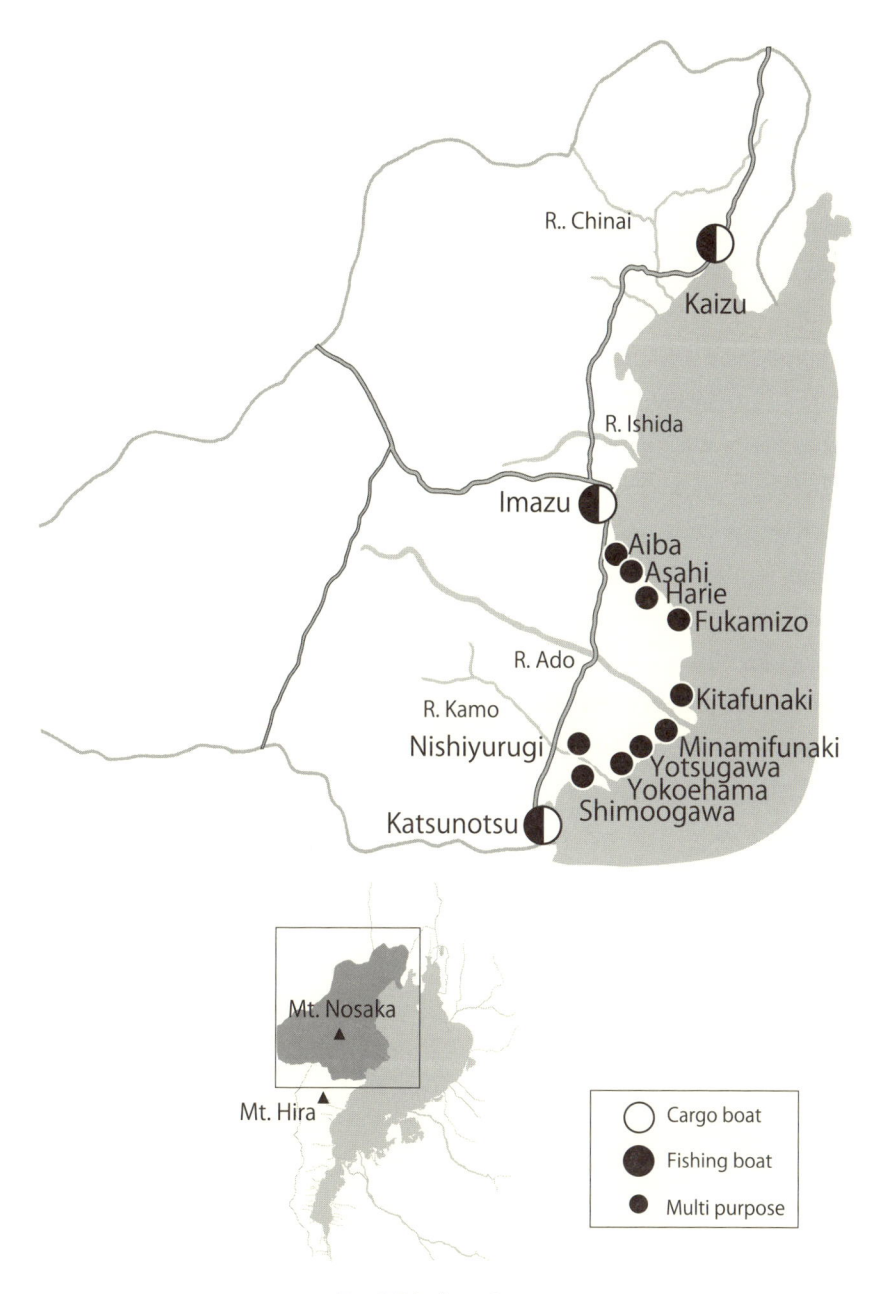

(4) Statistical Data of Traditional Boat Use in Each County in the Early 20th Century

Fig. 43 Takashima County.

county. 86 boats in Imazu and 35 boats in Kaizu were used for fishing and transportation.

In other small villages along the shore, such as Harie, Fukamizo, Kitafunaki, Minamifunaki, Yotsugawa, Yokoehama, and Shimoogawa, multipurpose boats for transportation, farming, and fishing were used. The boats of Nishiyurugi, located inland along a major road, were used for both farming and transportation. No specific numbers of these boats were recorded, but a total of 1, 869 boats existed in 1883 across the county.

The land was fertile in the region and a large number of villages were engaged in farming. Commuting to rice fields in Imazu required tabune, and tabune was used nearly throughout the year (Fig. 44). However, these boats were not used exclusively for farming. In the spring they were used for gill net fishing while farming was slow. The stern of these boats was low to facilitate pulling a net on board, and it had saozashi (pole rest).

Another village, Kitafunaki, was small and its lands were connected by paths. Therefore, tabune was not required for farming, and fishing boats were used only in spring for gill net fishing (Fig. 45). The fishing boat of Kitafunaki differed slightly from that of Imazu. It did not have saozashi (pole rest), and its hull was a bit deeper to cope with high waves.

In addition, there were boats for raft-assembly (Fig. 46) and boats for raft-towing (Fig. 47). These were required for log transportation. Kasturagawa and Kutsuki are two villages in the mountains in proximity to the upper reaches of the Ado River, an area that produced high quality timber. The annual harvest was thrown into the river during the spring thaw (see Fig. 2), and seven or eight workers called oyakata collected them at Minamifunaki downstream. Logs bore a seal of their owners and the logs were assembled into rafts with a length of 2 jo (approximately 6 m). The rafts were towed with a long rope to the Otsu area. The distance was 16 km by land but it was slightly shorter (12 km) via the lake. Men on shore pulled the raft by hand with ropes, while a boat simultaneously towed. During a storm the

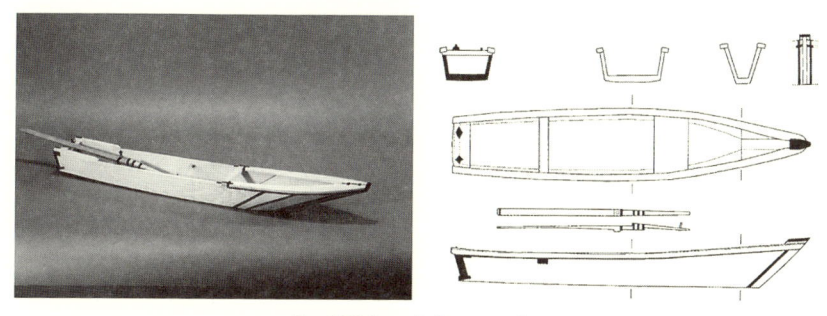

(4) Statistical Data of Traditional Boat Use in Each County in the Early 20th Century

Fig. 44 Tabune in Imazu region.

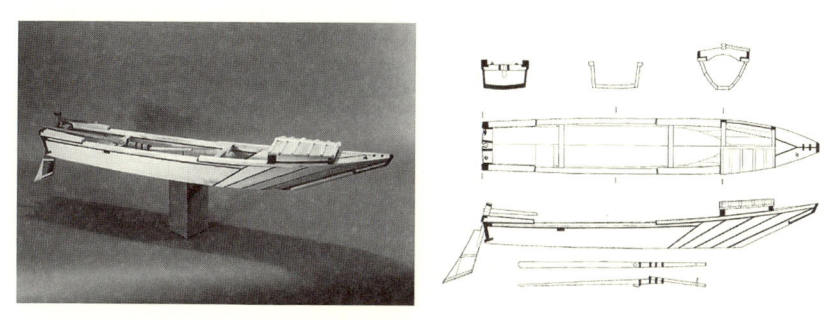

Fig. 45 Fishing boat in Kitafunaki.

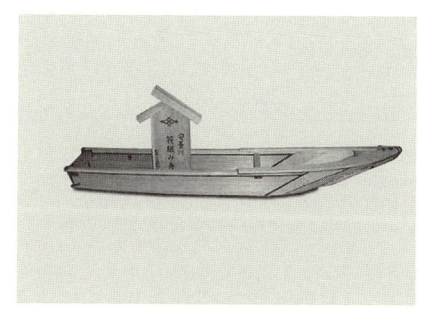

Fig. 46 Ikadakumibune
(raft assembly boat).

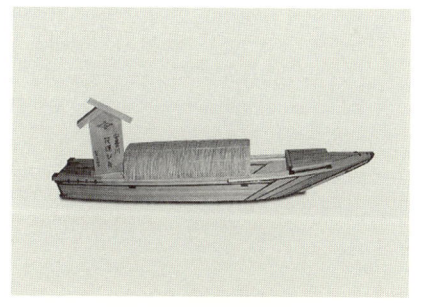

Fig. 47 Ikadahakobibune
(raft towing boat).

men waited in the boat for better conditions. The boat was capable of accommodating seven or eight men. It took normally three days to bring the log rafts from Funaki to Otsu; however, it took up to seven days depending on the weather.

Notes
1. Shiga Prefecture, General Affairs Section (ed.), 1882-.
2. Shiga Prefecture, Agricultural Administration Division (ed.), 2003, p. 24.
3. Naisuimen Gyoro Kenkyukai (ed.) 1999, pp. 1-74.
4. ibid., p. 32.
5. The fundamental principle was to preserve the rich natural environment of Lake Biwa and to restore the water quality. In order to utilize the resources effectively, comprehensive measures for the preservation, development and management of Lake Biwa and its surrounding region are promoted.
6. Ebise 2000, p. 2.
7. It is also called as "kawato", "kabata", "kawaya" and so forth depending on the location. It means steps down a river, a river itself, or a pond to hold spring water. Before the World War II it was not only used as a harbor, but it was also used as a water place for drawing drinking water and domestic water. After around the middle of 1970's, the rivers were modified and became narrow for an easier access by automobiles, hence kawado disappeared. However, there still exist kawado in use for daily life around the Lake Biwa region. (see the detail example of "kawaya" in the house of Tomie family in Hikone city in Kada & Furukawa 2000)
8. Shiga Prefecture (ed.) 1962. It consists of a preamble and 17 volumes in 36 books. Among these, 33 books through Volume 13 are compiled in Shiga Prefenture (ed.) 1967.
9. Boat models were prepared by Mr. Sanshiro Matsui and are kept in the Lake Biwa Museum.
10. Mr. Sanshiro Matsui, a shipwright, called such structures without tana, hirata-bune.
11. Otsu city office (ed.) 1982.

Chapter IV
The Hull Structure and Evolution of Marukobune: A Hypothesis

(1) Shiki-Expanded Structure

The Origin and Comprehensive Evolution of Japanese Traditional Boats

The origin and the comprehensive evolution of traditional Japanese boats have been studied by several scholars (Fig. 1). S. Nishimura proposed an evolution of boats starting from a log, evolving into a raft by tying logs transversely to increase cargo capacity, followed by a dugout made by hollowing out a log (kuribune), a skin boat (kawabune), a sewn boat (hogosen) and a planked boat (kozosen).[1] N. Matsumoto assumed that the log, raft, and dugout coexisted,[2] and proposed that multiple logs tied together, and the catamaran with two dugouts tied together, are the predecessors of the outrigger.[3] This evolution is a transverse expansion in cross section. By contrast, vertical expansion is found in semi-planked boats, with additional side planks added to raise the upper edges of a dugout. Longitudinal expansion is the enlargement of a dugout with planks added fore and aft. Furthermore, T. Miyamoto emphasized the important role of the raft: it contributed to the emergence of the planked boat.[4] In addition, T. Ishizuka, K. Ishii, and K. Sakurada studied the evolution from dugout to planked boat, and examined two scenarios. One is tanaitazukuri (plank construction), which consists of side planks called tanaita added above a plank keel. The other is omogizukuri (omogi construction) where omogi sawn from a log are placed on both sides of a plank keel and topside planking is attached above.[5]

Later on, A. Deguchi summarized the entire evolution process in a graphic diagram (Fig. 2), where various types of wasen (traditional Japanese wooden boats) are classified two-dimensionally according to their evolutionary phase.[6] The X-axis is transverse (bottom plank) expansion, and the Y-axis is vertical (side plank) expansion. In this diagram, the single piece log kuribune (Fig. 2-O) evolved vertically (Y-axis: side plank extension) into a semi-planked

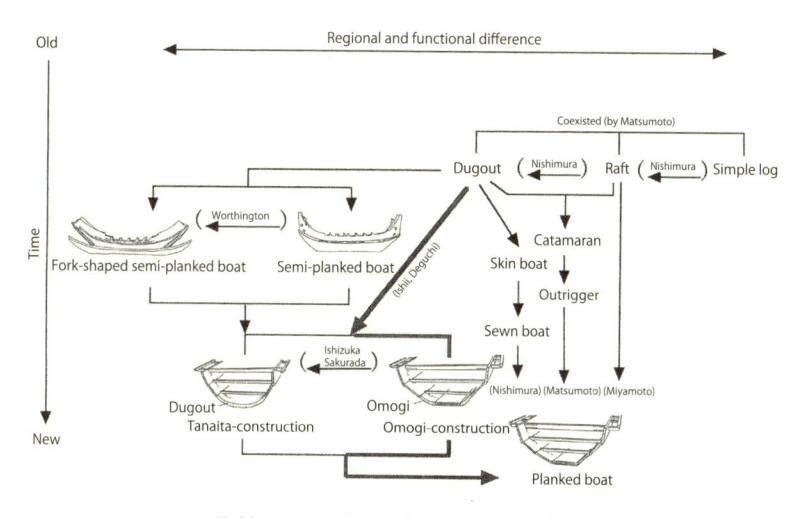

(1) Shiki-Expanded Structure

Fig. 1 Evolution phases of boat.
(Bold arrow: marukobune's evolution formerly assumed.)

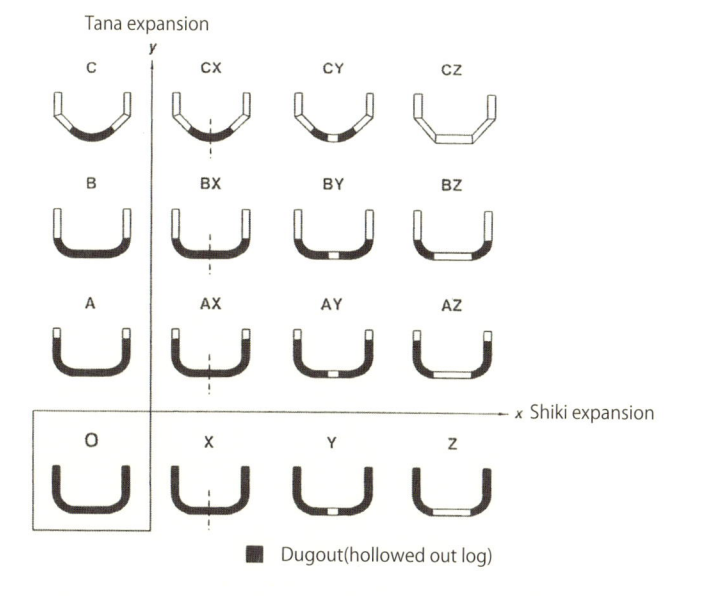

Fig. 2 Classification of dugout's cross section according to the development of shiki and tana.

177

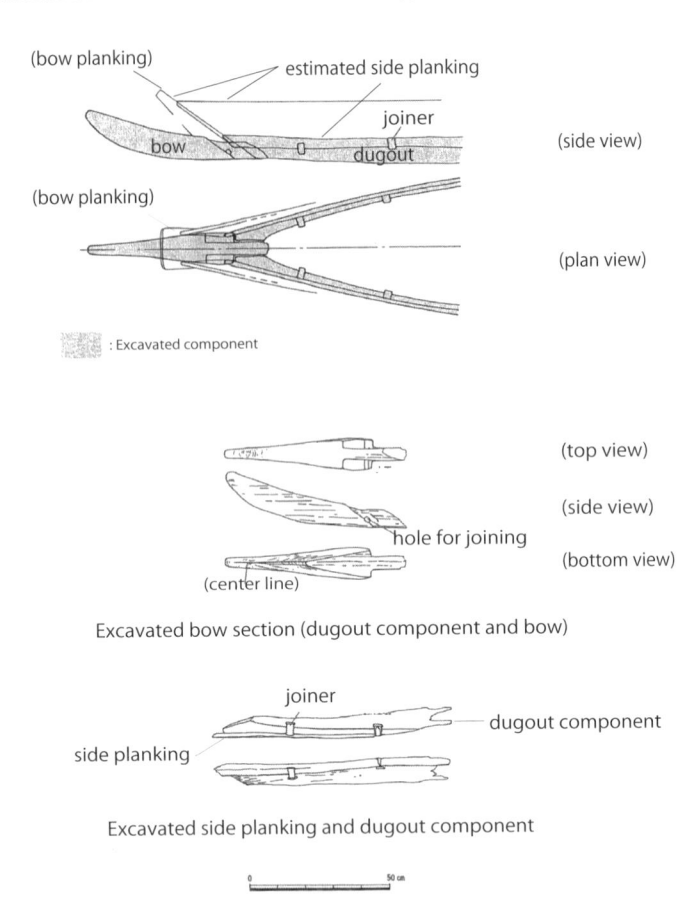

Chapter IV The Hull Structure and Evolution of Marukobune: A Hypothesis

Fig. 3 The restored shape of the semi-planked boat excavated from the Shimonaga site.

boat (Fig. 2-A, B, C) by adding planks upward to increase its capacity, and it evolved transversely (X-axis: bottom plank expansion) into a different type of semi-planked boat (Fig. 2-X, Y, Z) by adding bottom planks to expand its breadth. Meanwhile, it evolved both vertically and transversely into derivatives of a semi-planked boat by adding side and bottom planks, with hollowed log components remaining (Fig. 3-AX, BX, CX, AY, AZ, BY, CY, BZ). Finally, it evolved into a fully planked boat without the hollowed log components, by adding more side and bottom planks.

(1) Shiki-Expanded Structure

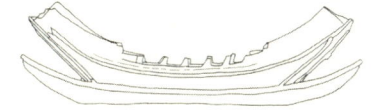

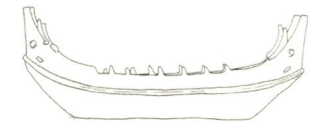

Fig. 4 Boat models of fork-shaped semi-planked boat (left) and semi-planked boat (right)

Archaeological evidence of semi-planked boats with vertical expansion exists from the Kofun period, and even from the Yayoi period, around 200 B.C. (Fig. 3). These boats are built on a dugout keel, with planks joined at the bow, stern and both sides to expand capacity, and their structures can be classified into two types. The first type has a tateita (bow plank), which stands at the middle of the keel and is separated from the bottom dugout forming a fork shape.[7] The second type has bow and transom planking attached at either end and does not form a fork (Fig. 4).

Regarding semi-planked boats with the fork-shaped bow, E. B. Worthington classified the various dugouts on Lake Victoria into six phases, including a simple dugout, a semi-planked boat consisting of a dugout and joined planks added above, and a semi-planked boat with a fork-shaped bow.[8] If one looks at the evolution of their shapes, it is evident that the dugout component comprising the bottom part gradually shrunk downwards. Thus, the semi-planked boat with a fork-shaped bow is considered the final phase in the disappearance of the dugout component, within the evolution of the tana-expansion of the dugout.

Boats classified as the shiki (bottom plank)-expanded semi-planked boats in other parts of Japan include eguribune (hollowed out boat) (Photo. 1) and dobune of Oga Peninsula, katabune of Hachirogata, kanaorekakko of Sanriku Town in Iwate Prefecture, maruta of Ofunato City, kawabune of Yamagata Prefecture and Niigata Prefecture, dobune of Toyama Prefecture, sasabune of the Jintsu River, marukibune and dobune of Ishikawa Prefecture, beka, marukibune and kochibune of Fukui Prefecture, tomobuto of western Wakasa

Chapter IV The Hull Structure and Evolution of Marukobune: A Hypothesis

Photo. 1 Eguri bune in Oga peninsula, Akita prefecture.

Photo. 2 Morotabune (right) in Miho shrine in Shimane Prefecture.

Bay, marukobune of the Tango Peninsula, as well as the tomodo, morotabune and soriko of Shimane Prefecture (Photo. 2). These are predominantly found in the regions along the coast of the Sea of Japan. Additionally, they are found in the inland regions (marutabune of Lake Suwa in Nagano Prefecture), the coast of the Pacific (marutabune of Lake Hamana and bocho of the Atsumi Peninsula), the Tokara Islands (marukibune), and the Korean Peninsula (kumei).[9]

A Sabani is a semi-planked sea boat that evolved from a dugout (Photo. 3). It is believed the sabani was developed at the end of 19th century in the

(1) Shiki-Expanded Structure

Photo. 3 Sabani in a private collection of Mr. Y. Arashiro in Ishigaki island in Okinawa Prefecture.

Itoman region of the main island of Okinawa. Traditionally, in this region dugouts were made of locally available trees, such as ryukyumatsu (a type of pine) and akagi (of the species Euphorbiaceae). However, because of a decrease in the number of large timbers, the Ryukyu Dynasty issued a ban on the building of the dugout ("yama-bugyosho-kibo-cho", 1737). This triggered the creation of the sabani, which is made of Japanese cedar from Kyushu with planks joined to a bottom dugout component. This is a perfect example of a vertical expansion of a dugout. Its cross section is V-shaped. This hull shape allowed the sabani to pierce waves smoothly and to make less leeway under sail.

Deguchi concluded that it was highly probable that the shiki-expanded semi-planked boat evolved as a result of technology exchanges between Japan and the Korean Peninsula and southern China, because in addition to the above-mentioned domestic distribution, they are also found in regions between the southern part of Tohoku and the Tokara Islands, to the south, as well as commonly found in neighboring parts of Asia including the Korean Peninsula, southwestern China, and Myanmar. Furthermore, the tana-expanded semi-planked boats are distributed throughout the regions ranging from the middle and lower reaches of the Amur River to Sakhalin, Hokkaido, the northern Tohoku region, and the islands of southern Japan. These regions are separated from where the shiki-expanded boats are distributed (Fig. 5, 6).[10] The method of expanding capacity by increasing the number of shiki planks might have originated in raft-building traditions, as they have a common technique. Unfortunately, any evidence of using rafts in ancient societies is difficult to find.

The vertical expansion is considered an influence of the ancient fork-shaped semi-planked boat (Fig. 7). The upper part of the topsides of a fork-shaped boat was excavated in the Lake Biwa region.[11] It was described: "Its whole surface is covered with adze scars. It is a sheet of straight-grained Japanese cedar. Its size is 20 cm in width and 1.5 cm in thickness, and 130 cm of its length is remaining. The front edge was cut straight at a 55 degrees angle and holes were bored at the upper edge. Rectangular holes are observed 22 cm apart at the lower edge where a string of bark passed through them."[12] Furthermore, a bow section with a length of 64.5 cm and a width of 10.5 cm, and two pieces of topside planking with a length of 93.5 cm and a thickness of 3 cm, and a length of 21.9 cm and a thickness of 3 cm were discovered at a site from the Kofun period.[13] Among the topside pieces the larger one has mortises through which strings of cherry bark with a width of 2.3 cm are wrapped two to three times to join it to the bottom part. Then, wedges were driven in the mortises to prevent the wrapped bark strips from loosening (Fig. 3, bottom). Tateita, the upper parts of the fork attached to the bow section, were also excavated.[14] Based on these findings it was determined that the semi-planked boat of the Lake Biwa region was constructed in order to add topsides and tateita to a dugout bottom. The topsides were joined to the sides of the dugout by bark string fastenings through bored holes, and both the tateita and the bow have mortises bored, where wooden plugs were driven to join them together.[15]

Is the Marukobune Shiki-Expanded or Tana-Expanded?

The shiki (bottom planking) is an important component for the boat's

(1) Shiki-Expanded Structure

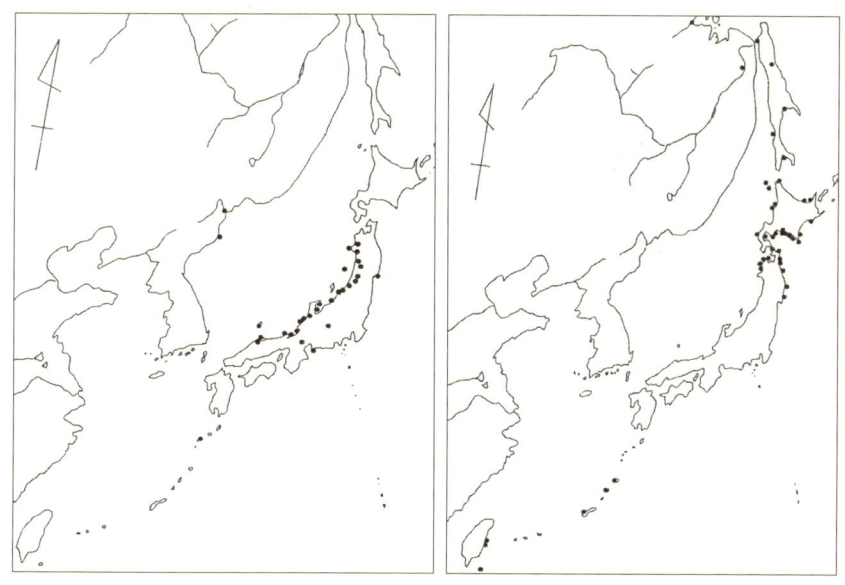

Fig. 5 Distribution of Shiki-expanded dugouts.　　Fig. 6 Distribution of Tana-expanded dugouts.

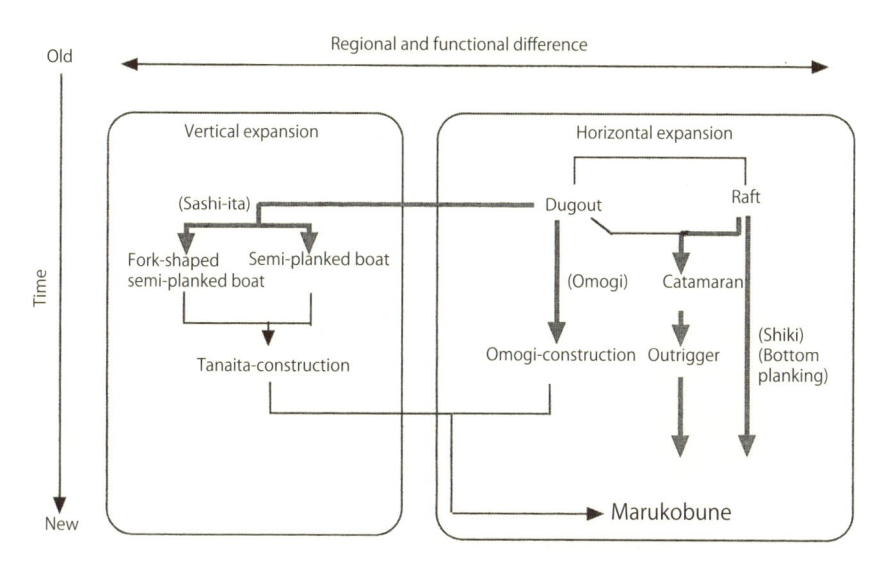

Fig. 7 Elements of Marukobune evolution.

(Bold arrows: Proposed in this study to indicate evolution elements of Marukobune.)

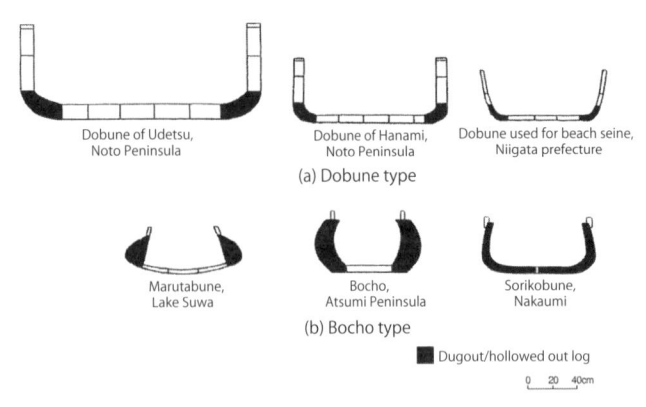

Chapter IV The Hull Structure and Evolution of Marukobune: A Hypothesis

Fig. 8 Dobune type vs. bocho type.

transverse expansion (see Preface-Fig. 1, 2). Examples of semi-planked boats with expanded bottom planks, classified as bocho-type boats (Fig. 8-b)[16] include maruta on Lake Suwa, bocho of the Atsumi Peninsula, sorikobune on Nakaumi Lake, and marutabune on Lake Hamana. However, all of these boats are smaller than the typical marukobune and their beams are roughly 1.5 m, and the number of bottom planks used is from one to three. In the case of the marutabune on Lake Suwa, "There were quite a few boats with shiki made of just two planks side by side. It became three-plank shiki then, and after World War II, because of the scarcity of wide timber materials, even four-plank shiki were built."[17] This reveals that the number of shiki planks increased because of the scarcity of planks of the required width, rather than an increase in beam. Similar trends are commonly seen in other bocho-type boats, and there were no other boats that increased the number of shiki planks in order to widen the beam except for the marukobune.

The hull dimensions of a marukobune with a capacity of 100 koku are: 17 m in overall length (19 m with the rudder lowered), 2.4 m beam, 1 m of draft, and a mast with a height of 12 m. In comparison, a 200 koku marukobune is 80 to 100 cm wider, 3 m longer and 15 cm deeper. Conversely, an 80 koku marukobune is 1.5 m shorter, 15 to 20 cm narrower, and 5 cm shallower (Fig.

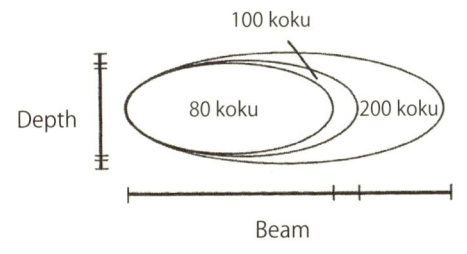

Fig. 9 Cross section comparison of marukobune with different cargo capacity.

9). These differences in the cross section indicate that the beam expansion is more significant than changes in draft. That is to say, the capacity is increased primarily through the expansion of the beam. This expansion rate of the beam is clearly higher than that of other shiki-expanded semi-planked boats in general, where the beam is 1.5 m and consists of one to three bottom planks. The technique of expanding the capacity by increasing the number of bottom planks might have originated in the raft tradition, as mentioned above. In the Lake Biwa region, raft-building traditions go back at least to the Nara period. This is because timbers used for building materials were transported to build the capital in Kyoto via the Lake Biwa water system. According to folklore records, rafts were also used in the Korean Peninsula and the regions surrounding Southern China (Fig. 10).

The vertical expansion of marukobune can be found in the furikake (lower side/bilge planking), omogi (side member), tana (top side planking) and sashiita (washboard). These components are built upward from the bottom planks in that order. Looking at cross sections of marukobune of different sizes, vertical expansion is not so obvious, compared to shiki expansion, as the capacity of a vessel is increased. However, when loaded with its maximum cargo, the hull sinks to the upper edge of the omogi, so sashiita are added amidships on both sides in order to prevent swamping (Preface-Fig. 1, 2). In the case of a marukobune with a cargo capacity of 100 koku, three sashiita made of podocarpus are mounted longitudinally on both sides. Each sashiita

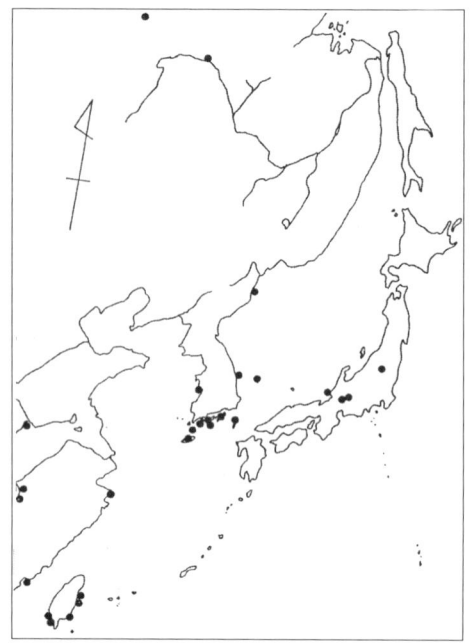

Fig. 10 Distribution of rafts.

is a 47 cm high rectangular plank, of which 1.5 cm is inserted into a groove, and the length is 193 cm. A manual of traditional Japanese boat building from the 18th century describes marukobune thus: "its hull is long, narrow and deep, and side planks are joined to the bottom plank forming a round form but it does not have tana".[18] This implies that there was no vertical expansion, although the addition of sashiita was itself a vertical - though temporary - expansion to some extent.

The cross sections of two marukobune of different sizes show the transverse expansion is more significant than the vertical expansion (see Fig. 1, arrow). This is because the number of bottom planks increased for more cargo capacity; therefore the marukobune is classified as a shiki-expanded semi-planked boat (or bocho-type). Thus, marukobune is, in essence, a horizontal expansion type of boat, with a limited degree of vertical expansion as well.

(2) Function of Omogi

Is the Omogi of the Marukobune Considered a Dugout Element or just a Plank?

The omogi is the key element that gives the round shape to the marukobune. The function of the omogi has been discussed by several scholars. Ishii considered omogi an alteration of a dugout component in the bottom, becoming a part of the tana (top side planking) through evolutionary phases; from semi-planked boat to planked boat (Fig. 11).[19] He emphasized the similarity between marukobune, and hokkokubune or hagasebune.[20] They are all cargo boats that played important roles in coastal transportation in the Sea of Japan during the first part of the Edo period. He also emphasized

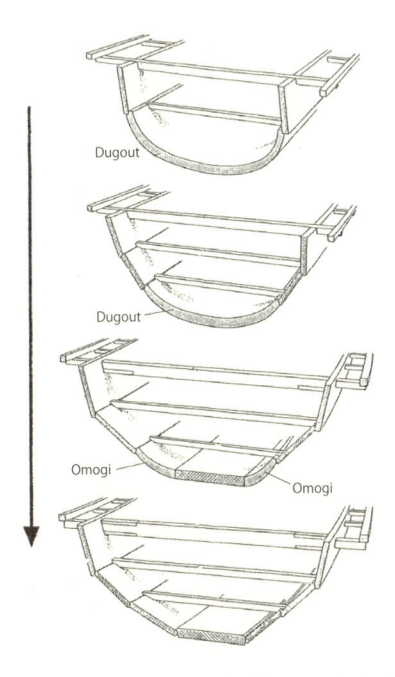

Fig. 11 Evolution from semi-planked boat to planked boat.

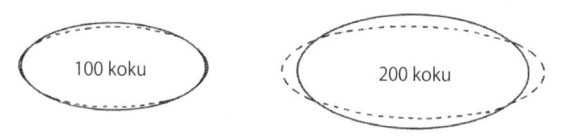

Chapter IV The Hull Structure and Evolution of Marukobune: A Hypothesis

Fig. 12 Cross section comparison of marukobune in different period.
Oval: Data from "Senpaku-shihousho"(from the last part of the Edo period to the beginning of the Meiji period.
Oval with dotted line: present.

marukobune's similarity with the dobune (Fig. 8-a), which still exists on the Sea of Japan coast. Omogi are also used in the construction of dobune. These boats had a pair of structural components called omoki in common, and apparently the omoki has a different role from the omogi of the marukobune as will be explained later. Other scholars viewed marukobune as a semi-planked boat because omogi were made of logs and in other contexts these are hollowed-out timbers.[21]

The cargo capacity of a boat can be enlarged by increasing its length, width, and/or draft. As mentioned above, the cargo capacity of marukobune was increased more by beam expansion than by draft expansion. The omogi determine the draft. As hull size grew, larger logs were required for the omogi. Tana planks and topside planking, were added as cargo capacity went up, but that did not increase the capacity of the hull itself. Perhaps, with time, it became more difficult to acquire the large timbers needed to make omogi for larger boats.

The dimensions kept by shipwright today show slight differences from the dimensions recorded in a document from the end of the 19th century (Fig. 12).[22] The beam and draft of a 100 koku marukobune of that period are 7.8 shaku (2.3 m) and 3.7 shaku (1.1 m), whereas a 200 koku boat has a beam of 9.7 shaku (2.9 m) and a draft of 4.7 shaku (1.4 m). That is a 60 cm increase in beam and a 30 cm increase in draft. This indicates that marukobune in the past were narrower and deeper than what present-day shipwrights understand. The cross section of the 19th century boat is more rounded

(2) Function of Omogi

as well. There is no evidence in the historic documents that the draft was increased by the addition of tana. Therefore, the draft might have been increased by the added height of the omogi, indicating a greater availability of larger Japanese cedar timbers in the past.

The position of hollowed-out log components is another question. All the semi-planked boats found in Japan have their hollowed-out components at the bilge between the bottom and the side planking, regardless of their hull expansions, whether tana (vertical) or shiki (transverse). The connecting component between a flat shiki (bottom planking), and the flat tana (side planking), creates a round bilge, and it is believed that a hollowed-out component was effective for preventing water leaks when used for joining planks. This construction technique is common to dobune-type boats, and their hollowed-out components are called omoki.

The bilge of marukobune, however, uses furikake (bilge or chine planking), and a hollowed-out component is not used there. Shiki and furikake meet at an angle to form a chine. This implies that marukobune's omogi should have had a role associated with its side position. It has been widely accepted that marukobune has a connection to the dobune type boats, but the above-mentioned structural difference suggests the connection is only limited to the name of its component: omogi versus omoki. The marukobune cannot be classified as a semi-planked boat if the definition is that a hollowed-out component is used as the bilge. Furthermore, the omogi of other semi-planked boats are actually hollowed-out logs. The marukobune uses a log ripped in half, but its interior surface is not hollowed out, but left flat. No other boat found thus far uses a log without hollowing it out. One noteworthy exception is the maruta, used as a fishing boat on Lake Suwa.[23] Maruta (Fig. 8-b, left) is essentially a hollowed out log, but its central section is left partially intact.

From the above discussion, the function of omogi can be understood as a side member. However, it was made of half-logs. The reason for this construction should be found elsewhere.

Is Marukobune a Combination of a Raft and Dugout?

Marukobune seems to be a combination of a raft and a dugout. Rafts and dugouts are found in various parts of the world, and in particular, rafts are seen in inland waters and relatively warm sea areas,[24] while dugouts are of a type of boat widely observed in wooded regions. It is worth noting that the size in diameter of locally available timbers influences the type of boats used. If large timbers are available and a dugout with enough cargo capacity can be built with them, dugouts are used. However, if such timbers are difficult to acquire, rafts assembled with small timbers are used. For example, not many dugouts existed in the northern part of the Korean Peninsula where large trees, such as kusunoki (camphor tree), do not grow. From Anap Pond in Gyeongju, shiki-expanded boats were excavated which are similar to rafts, with three logs, hollowed in the middle, and fastened side-by-side (Fig. 13).[25] Furthermore, nimble dugouts were used in relatively calm conditions, such as inland waters, for light loads, with a small number of crew, whereas dugout catamarans, raft-type boats, and dugouts with outriggers were used for heavy loads in rougher waters. There is historical evidence that social rank determined the type of boat used: the lower strata used dugouts, and the higher social classes used raft boats, bundled boats, or catamarans.[26]

The width of dugouts excavated in Shiga prefecture was compared with finds from other prefectures. The comparison revealed that dugouts from Shiga prefecture are slightly narrower than others (Fig. 14).[27] This indicates that the dugouts from Shiga prefecture might have been used for daily operation, but it would have been difficult to transport large amounts of cargo with them.

Some expatriates from mainland China came to the capital via Lake Biwa, and migrated to the surrounding regions during the Kofun period (Chapter. I-(2)). These people formed a stratified society and local lords strengthened their authority through land ownership. Their control of

(2) Function of Omogi

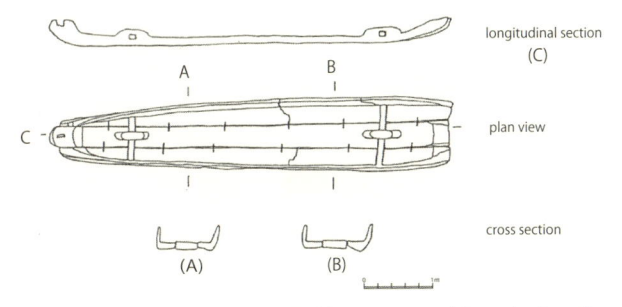

Fig. 13 The restored shape of the semi-planked boat excavated from the Anap Pond, south Korea.

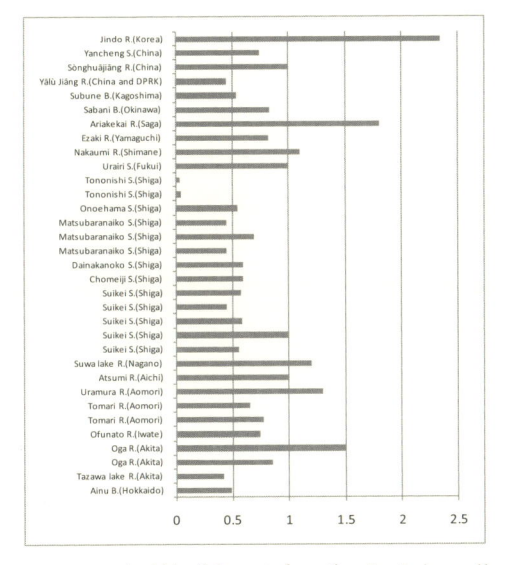

Fig. 14 The max preserved width of dugouts from the sites in Japan, Korea and China.

lake resources and the improvement of ports increased the amount of goods transported by boats. After the Yamato Imperial Court was established, and the transportation system of Lake Biwa came under court control, roads surrounding the lake were improved and tolls were imposed. The court had ties with the eastern provinces via the Lake Biwa region, so rice as tax, as well as large amounts of timbers and roofing tiles for building were transported to the capital via the lake.[28]

It is unclear whether dugouts were tied together to form catamarans for added cargo capacity, but there are several festivals in the Lake Biwa region, with origins in the Medieval period,[29] where two large traditional Japanese boats are tied together to carry a large mikoshi (portable shrine). Another interesting example of this practice is the tomobuto of the Tango region. Tomobuto is a bocho-type boat like the marukobune, and it was used as a catamaran in rough conditions.[30] Also, the ancient documents describe the aristocracy along the lower rivers of Lake Biwa using boats called nigawara, which means twin boats. These are classified as semi-planked boats consisting of a dugout and a kumibune, meaning connected boats, and are classified as catamarans.[31]

The surface area of Lake Biwa is 670 km^2, and its catchment area is 3,174 km^2, which is about five times as large as the lake. Furthermore, the shape of the lake, before the land reclamation in the modern period, indicates that the surface area historically was far larger than today (Chapter. III-Fig. 6). This probably indicates that historically boats had to navigate much more shallow waters. Consequently, marukobune and other boats had to evolve by widening their bottoms like rafts, while maintaining as much draft as possible for a semi-planked boat, in order to retain seaworthiness in occasionally choppy waters.

Comparing the current boats in the Lake Biwa region with those of other regions (Table. 1), the length-to-beam ratios of boats of the Lake Biwa region are under 5, and under 4.5 in other regions. Also, the boats in the Lake Biwa region are longer. The length to draft ratio is under 13 in both cases, but in the Lake Biwa region the ratios varied slightly depending on tonnage.

Compared with the current fishing boats used in the Lake Biwa region (Table. 2), the dimensions of models and actual fishing boats used primarily during the 1930's (Table. 3) had more slender shapes. The length-to-beam ratio of the current boats is under 5, whereas the ratio of past boats

(2) Function of Omogi

Table. 1 Round haul netters in other regions.

size (ton)	length/width	length/depth	width/depth
3	＜4.50	＜13.00	2.35≦ ＜3.60
4	＜4.50	＜13.00	2.35≦ ＜3.60
5	＜4.50	＜13.00	2.35≦ ＜3.60
6	＜4.50	＜13.00	2.35≦ ＜3.58
7	＜4.50	＜13.00	2.35≦ ＜3.56
10	＜4.50	＜13.00	2.35≦ ＜3.56
12	＜4.50	＜13.00	2.35≦ ＜3.53
15	＜4.50	＜13.00	2.25≦ ＜3.50
20	＜4.50	＜13.00	2.15≦ ＜3.50
30	＜4.50	＜12.00	2.15≦ ＜3.40
40	＜4.50	＜11.00	2.15≦ ＜3.30
50	＜4.50	＜11.00	2.15≦ ＜3.20
60	＜4.60	＜1110	2.10≦ ＜3.10
70	＜4.60	＜11.20	2.10≦ ＜2.90
80	＜4.60	＜11.30	2.10≦ ＜2.80
90	＜4.60	＜11.40	2.10≦ ＜2.70
100	＜4.60	＜11.50	2.10≦ ＜2.60

Table. 2 Size of modern fishing boats used on Lake Biwa region.

size (ton)	length/width	length/depth	width/depth
3	＜5.00	＜13.00	2.00≦ ＜3.20
4	＜5.00	＜12.88	2.00≦ ＜3.15
5	＜5.00	＜12.76	2.00≦ ＜3.10
6	＜5.00	＜12.63	2.00≦ ＜3.00
7	＜5.00	＜12.50	2.00≦ ＜3.00
8	＜5.00	＜12.33	2.00≦ ＜3.05
9	＜5.00	＜12.17	2.00≦ ＜3.03
10	＜5.00	＜12.00	2.00≦ ＜3.00
12	＜5.00	＜12.00	2.00≦ ＜2.95
15	＜5.00	＜12.00	2.00≦ ＜2.90
19	＜5.00	＜12.00	2.00≦ ＜2.81

Table.3 The size of the traditional wooden fishing boats on Lake Biwa.

No.	Length (cm)	Width (cm)	Depth (cm)	length/width	length/depth	width/depth
1	1,020	148	72	6.89	14.2	2.05
2	852	128	56	6.66	15.2	2.29
3	756	100	36	7.56	21	2.78
4	696	108	36	6.44	19.3	3
5	644	124	44	5.19	14.6	2.12
6	564	108	36	5.22	15.7	3
7	1,592	104	40	15.31	39.8	2.6
8	1,112	152	80	7.32	13.9	1.9
9	1,060	180	80	5.89	13.25	2.25
10	1,210	190	120(90)	6.37	13.4	2.11
11	1,080	220	110	4.91	9.8	2
12	870	130	60	6.69	14.5	2.17
13	1,210	140	120(90)	8.64	13.4	1.55
14	1,230	140	120(90)	8.79	13.7	1.55
15	860	140	60	6.14	14.3	2.33
16	750	140	50	5.36	15	2.8
17	1,080	160	70	6.75	15.4	2.28
18	690	140	70	4.93	9.8	2

(No. 9 to 18 are mesured from replica models.)

is mostly 5 and over.[32] It is assumed that the introduction of motors led to the enlargement of the beam. Moreover, the length-to-draft ratio of current fishing boats is under 13, while the same ratio in historic boats is over 13, except for only two cases, so earlier boats are more slender in this respect as well. Regarding the beam-to-draft ratio, historic and current fishing boats are nearly identical, and the ratio is 2.0 or more, but under 3.0. Thus the introduction of new technology caused boats to become wider relative to their length, but did not alter their draft.

(3) Transition of Marukobune's Role Reflected in its Bow Shape

Evolution of Marukobune's Bow Shape

The shipwrights who built marukobune refer to the bow section as the boat's face, and call the shin (stem) the nose, the tips of the tsuna-kukuri (rope bitt, an athwartships beam that pierces the bow, supports the bow planking, and serves as a bitt.) the ears, and the patterns drawn on the upper part of heita (bow planking) in black ink, the eyes (Preface-Fig. 2). They also call the forward surface of the stem, the tsura, which means face in Japanese. All of the marukobune we are aware of today have the distinct stem as seen in Fig. 15-a. However, marukobune drawn in old paintings do not necessarily have a stem (Fig. 15-b). Marukobune with bow sections built with vertical planks (tateita) joined around the centerline without a stem (shin) are shown in old paintings and drawings. They are portrayed this way in several documents and drawings from the 16th to the early 19th century.[33]

One reason why stems are missing from early drawings has been explained as simply an omission of detail by early artists. However, in one 18th century folding screen,[34] boats with and without shin are pictured, and both types are called marukobune. In other documents from the same period,[35] marukobune without stems are called marubune, meaning a round boat. These facts appear to suggest that in at least some early drawings, the bow was drawn accurately and represented correctly.

The oldest marukobune with a stem is dated to the last part of the 1860s, and found in a photo taken by Felix Beato (Felice Beato).[36] Marukobune with shin are also found in some 19th century drawings, supposedly painted by Giho Yamagata of Nagahama, between 1841 and 1847,[37] and in the landscape drawings of southern Lake Biwa by Hakuen Hirose in 1855.[38]

Among records from the Edo period,[39] according to one document,[40]

Chapter IV The Hull Structure and Evolution of Marukobune: A Hypothesis

Genjuro Kitamura and his family were running a shipping business in Maihara and owned boats. They refer to a marukobune with cargo capacity of 270 koku (40 t) as a shinkurobune (black stem boat). Another document has a description of the boats with black painted shin (stems)[41], and another indicates that shin were first painted black in the early 17th century, when Naotaka Ii was the feudal lord of the Hikone domain, to make them easily identifiable[42].

Two notable descriptions of marukobune construction, one with a stem and the other without a stem, are found in two documents. "Marukobune-sunpo-cho" (丸子船寸法帳) declares, "If the shin is long enough, heita (bow planking) can be supported." which seems to emphasize the importance of this timber. "Wakan-sen-yo-shu" (和漢船用集) on the other hand, reports, "The boat is long, narrow and deep, and side planks are joined above the bottom forming a curve, but it does not have tana. The upper side plank is called omogi, its bow section is made of vertical planks joined round but it does not have a stem." This description possibly indicates that the round bow marukobune in the old paintings is the marutabune or marukibune boat types also mentioned and shown in the drawings attached to the documents.

Thus the historical records indicate that the round-bow marukobune (without stems) existed at least before the middle of the 18th century, that both styles coexisted in the middle of the 18th century, and that only the marukobune with stem survived to the latter half of the 19th century.

Models of the two different styles of marukobune were tank tested to measure their wave-making resistance, as a joint research project by the author with N. Umeda, Professor of Engineering, Osaka University Graduate School, in November 2006 (Photo. 4).[43] The only difference between the two models was the bow shape (with and without a stem). The test results revealed that the wave-making resistance differs significantly with different bow shapes, and it was concluded that this would result in a substantial difference in the possible sailing speeds of full-sized boats. The resistance of full-size boats

(4) Another Element of the Bow, Heita.

Two models of marukobune.

Model of rounded stem

Ready for tank test.

Photo. 4 The two different marukobune models for tank test.

was calculated, and the boat speed estimated under real sailing conditions on Lake Biwa.

While the results showed that marukobune with round bows were more stable and had larger internal volume for cargo, overall stem-built boats exhibited better sailing performance in a wider range of wind speeds. The stem-built boats also showed better lateral resistance, another important factor in sailing performance. This supports the author's aforementioned hypothesis regarding the evolution of the bow shape. Given that the two types overlapped, the superior performance of the boat with a stem would be readily noticed. Therefore, one would expect to see the inferior marukobune with a round bow superseded over time by the marukobune with stem.

Chapter IV The Hull Structure and Evolution of Marukobune: A Hypothesis

Sailing on Lake Biwa required a deep knowledge of its unique water currents and wind conditions (Chapter. I-(1)). Sailing marukobune required making the most of these currents and the winds as driving forces, while minimizing inherent resistance. It may be that, facing a challenging sailing environment, local sailors opted for increased speed and maneuverability over stability and cargo capacity.

Change of Sailing Routes versus the Mission of Marukobune

The change in bow shape might be related to the decline of Lake Biwa's water transport. In 1672 the westward sailing route from the Sea of Japan coast to Osaka via Shimonoseki and the Seto Inland Sea opened. This decreased the amount of transport via Lake Biwa. During the lake's peak period, around the end of the 17th century, over 1,000 marukobune were active, according to historical records.[44] These boats had shipping licenses (funa-kabu or ura-kabu) assigned to their home ports (ura or minato). The licenses supposedly were first issued in about 1690 to ensure the collection of taxes on marukobune.[45] In some documents,[46] 966 licenses at a total of 58 ports along the coast of Lake Biwa were recorded. A few ports had large quantities of licenses.[47] There are descriptions such as "The license for 12 boats was issued by the shogunate, however it has become difficult to maintain the marukobune for cargo transport because of financial problems, inevitably hirata (flat bottomed boats) are used for transport."[48], and "Because of difficulty of late, now hiratabune are used."[49] These records show that the ports suffered from the opening of the westward shipping route and were unable to maintain marukobune. The trade from the northern part of Japan to Otsu via Lake Biwa critically declined, and the ports were severely impacted. To cope with this situation, a plan was laid to connect Tsuruga and Shiozu by canal. This new route between Tsuruga and Lake Biwa was never realized because of opposition from farmers and shipping agencies. So, a new market for water transport was sought as cargo shipping via Lake Biwa

(4) Another Element of the Bow, Heita.

declined.

One of the new missions of marukobune is illustrated in a painting by Giho Yamagata (Fig. 15-a). In this drawing the boat is described "a hayabune (speed boat) departs the port of Nagahama daily and arrives at Otsu." Hayabune was originally another term for a sekibune (Fig. 16) which was the primary warship used on Lake Biwa. Sekibune was meant to be a checkpoint boat used by pirates in the Medieval period, and it derived from the fact that they built checkpoints (seki) in various places and collected tolls from boats sailing through the checkpoints.[50] It was designed for speed, thus it was also called hayabune, and it was the primary boat of the military.

The hayabune drawn by Giho Yamagata was a passenger boat that sailed the route between Nagahama and Otsu. According to writings, it started regular service on May 26th, 1841 for residents in the domain of Hikone. The boat departed Nagahama at 6 p.m. and arrived at Otsu at 6 a.m. the following day. A diary included in "Hayabune-monjo" states, "Previously the hayabune was a small marukobune-type boat. However, the first hayabune was replaced by a ko-haya-zukuri type in April, 1868, and another hayabune was replaced in March 1869. Only two boats are ko-haya-zukuri."[51] There are some other accounts, such as "[hayabune is] used for an express need with rapid paddling."[52], and "A rule was established that a skilled skipper had to be assigned (to hayabune) and unskilled skippers were prohibited."[53].

Furthermore, an oshikiri-hayabune was permitted to enter service at the port of Maibara in 1807[54] and at the port of Mastubara and Nagahama in 1849[55]. Oshikiri means "Pushing and cutting (the tides)". The oshikirihayabune was further developed, evolving into the kuruma (wheels) hayabune, which had wooden paddle wheels on both sides of the bow (Fig. 17). A sailor rotated them by marching on a treadle attached to an axle. This mechanism was expected to allow the boat to sail in any direction, regardless of the wind direction and strength. When the kuruma-hayabune was first planned, its feasibility was questioned by fellow sailors, but it was

199

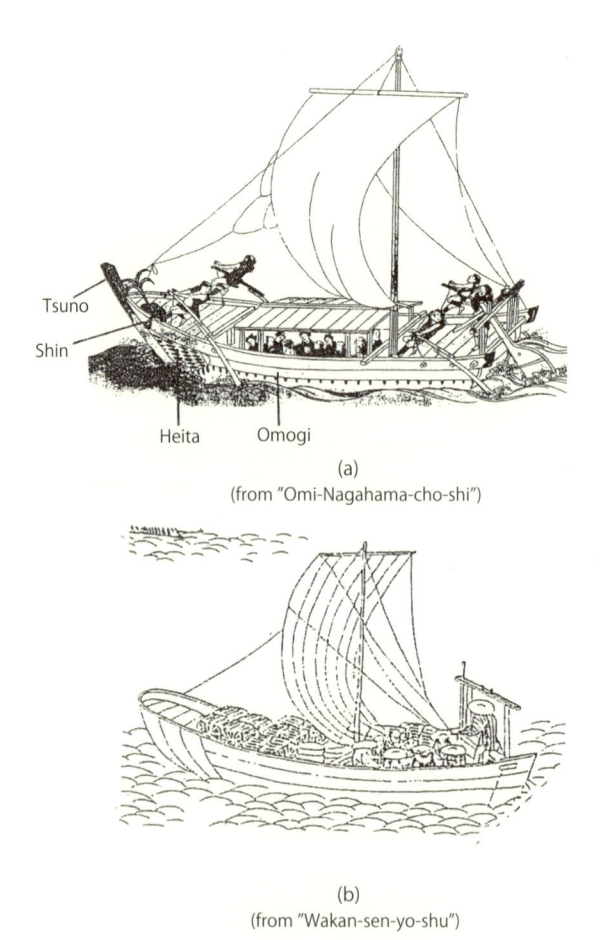

Chapter IV The Hull Structure and Evolution of Marukobune: A Hypothesis

Tsuno
Shin
Heita   Omogi
(a)
(from "Omi-Nagahama-cho-shi")

(b)
(from "Wakan-sen-yo-shu")
Fig. 15 Marukobune with shin(stem) (a) and without shin(b).

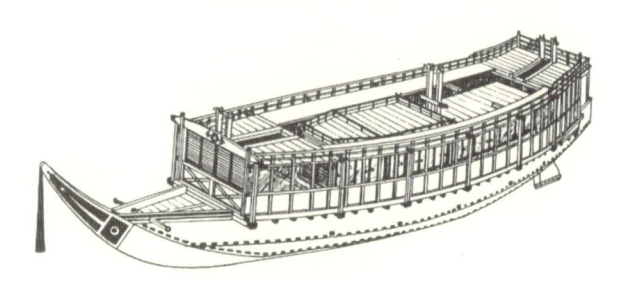

Fig. 16 Sekibune.

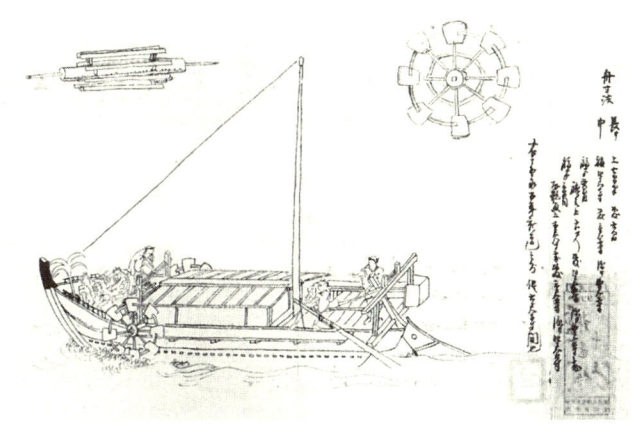

Fig. 17 Kuruma hayabune (boat with wheel).

reported that it worked well.[56]

Historical records show that hayabune was developed by modifying marukobune, then the wheels were added in an attempt to improve speed, and that these adaptations were directed towards use in regular passenger service. However, hayabune were not for cargo transportation, despite the fact that its routes were limited to the ports on the north shore of Lake Biwa and Otsu. Thus, the marukobune retired from the leading role of cargo transport, and played a new role as a passenger boat.

A passenger boat requires a higher level of safety and reliable, consistent operation. As a passenger carrier, it would have needed to keep to scheduled service, with fixed routes and departure times. Marukobune were sailing cargo boats. While they were capable of sailing the length of the lake in as little as 6 hours, if there was no wind, a boat might have to drift on the lake for 1, or even 2 weeks. It seems inevitable that marukobune would have evolved significantly to take on the role of passenger boats. As of today, however, no document has been found describing how marukobune was redesigned as hayabune, and exactly which elements were actually modified. We have to wait for further evidence.

Technological Influences – Hayabune and Bezaisen

It may be conceivable that marukobune were influenced by bezaisen,[57] the large sea-going coastal trading vessels of the Edo and early Meji periods. The route via Lake Biwa required cargo to be landed on the Sea of Japan coast first, transported overland to the lake, and then taken south across the lake to Otsu. From Otsu, the cargo had to be hauled overland again. The westward route is longer in distance, traveling around the southern end of Honshu and up the Inland Sea to Kansai, but no cargo handling, loading, or unloading is required en route. This allowed an expansion of cargo transportation. Considering this advantage, and in order to encourage the direct and efficient transport of goods,[58] in 1638 the shogunate lifted a ban on building kaisen (cargo boats) with cargo capacity over 500 koku. The bezaisen was developed as a modification of the futanaribune, which had been widely used for cargo transport in Seto Inland Sea, as well as from Kyushu in the west to Kanto in the east. Bezaisen were designed as cargo boats that could sail safely and easily in headwinds and crosswinds[59]. Its stem was the key design component that allowed these improvements in performance (Fig. 18). The stem of the futanaribune consisted of an upper and a lower construction. The upper part is box-shaped, and the lower part is miyoshizukuri (miyoshi construction) with a steep entrance angle. Whereas, the stem of the bezaisen is one piece of lumber that protrudes far above the sheer strake at a greater forward rake. This change, and the increase of cargo capacity of the bezaisen, was achieved within the existing techniques of wasen (Japanese boatbuilding) and entirely independent of foreign technologies (foreign travel had been banned since 1636). Beginning in the late 17th century and continuing into the 18th century, bezaisen of 1,000 koku (150 t) cargo capacity were built. Around the same period, straw mat sails were replaced with newly-developed, sturdy cotton sails, resulting in improvements in speed. The sail of 1,000 koku

(4) Another Element of the Bow, Heita.

Isebune

Futanaribune

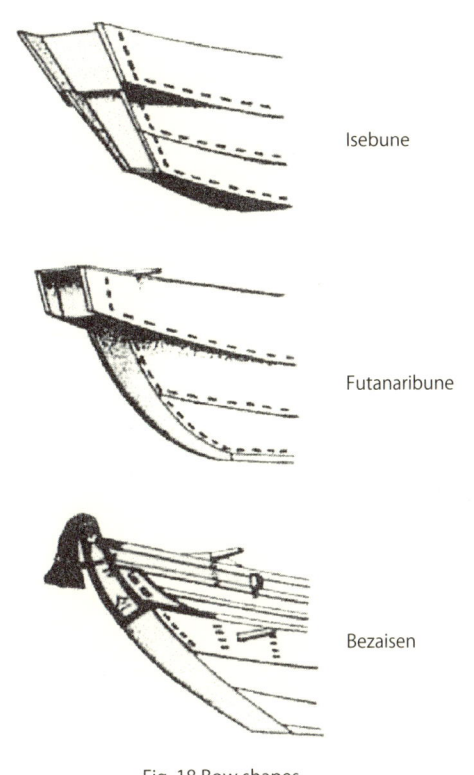

Bezaisen

Fig. 18 Bow shapes.

bezaisen is believed to have been composed of 21 to 25 vertical sail panels.[60]

The arrival of high performance bezaisen ushered the end of more than a few types of cargo boats. Futanaribune, which were the major large cargo boat in the latter part of the Medieval period to the Modern period,[61] isebune (widely used in the Ise region), hokkokubune (a cargo boat used in the northern coast of the Sea of Japan), and also probably hagasebune, to name a few of the boats that disappeared from use.

Among these boats the hokkokubune, drawn on the Enkaku-ji-ema (円覚寺絵馬)[62], has a round bow. Because of its round bow shape it was called an acorn boat (donguribune) in "Senko-yojutsu" (船行要術),[63] where

203

it says, "the bow was not designed to plough into high waves (of the Sea of Japan in winter)". The fact is that the use of the round-bow hokkokubune declined after the emergence of the bezaisen (specifically designed for speed and cargo capacity), which overlaps the decline of another round-bow boat, the marukobune of the Lake Biwa region. The author believes that the marukobune dropped the round bow and incorporated a sharp bow as result of the influence of the bezaisen.

The marukobune drawn by Giho Yamagata and the bezaisen demonstrate a few similarities in the stem (Fig. 15-a, Fig. 18). First, the stem timber protrudes far above the sheer strake. Secondly, copper sheet used for decoration was common to both. The stem of the bezaisen was a symbolic component and therefore it was made of camphor wood (kusunoki) for its attractive grain. The stem's upper portion, protruding above the sheer strake was wrapped with a copper sheet painted black, called nogi or mogi. In the case of the marukobune's stem, the tsura corresponds to nogi; it was also wrapped with copper sheet painted black, and the decorative sheathing was finished by driving in lines of square-headed nails called tsura-kugi.

Another similarity is found in the ceremony of the stem-raising, the shintate. This was the most important event in the entire marukobune building process (Chapter. II-(1)). After the bottom planks (shikiita) were joined together, the stem-raising ceremony was held on an auspicious day with the owner in attendance. Once the stem was securely fastened, the shipwright and the owner poured sake on both the stem and the transom, and they prayed for the safe completion of the boat. This corresponds to the frame-raising ceremony of a house, which is held when the ridge beam is put up.

There were two other ceremonies related to the marukobune building process, in addition to the stem-raising ceremony. One was during timber cutting, and the other was the launching ceremony. Boat building ceremonies were considered secret events by the builder, and therefore no detailed records exist. Consequently, the ceremonies of bezaisen builders are also not known. However, Ishii believes there was a similar ceremony for a warship of the same period, called kawarasueiwai, which means "stem mounting ceremony". After the bottom planks were mounted on the building jig, called the wagi, the stem and transom were set up on them, and the ceremony was held on an auspicious day[64], with a representative of the feudal government in attendance.

If the emergence of the bezaisen actually influenced the shape of the marukobune, the Omi merchants and the shipping agencies that worked for them might have contributed to it.[65] The Omi merchant played an important role in linking the cargo boats in the Sea of Japan coast to those on Lake Biwa. In the middle of the Edo period, as the agriculture-centric policy was eased and trade was permitted as a side business, merchants from Omi began to visit other regions. Later, some of them opened branch stores in these regions, keeping their main stores in Omi. In the late 16th century, some of the Omi merchants visited Hokkaido, developed a fishing and marine products industry, eventually trading those products with goods from Kyoto, Osaka and Edo (Tokyo).[66] They transported the goods mainly by hired boats, and these cargo boats (kitamaebune) were typically hokkokubune, which were then being used in the Sea of Japan.

The Omi merchants that stayed in the castle town of the Matsumae Domain in Hokkaido formed a partnership called Ryohama-gumi with other Omi merchants. They hired boats for their businesses and provided a stable supply of goods to the Matsumae Domain. These hired boats were called nidokosen. The shipping agencies also rented boats to Omi merchants located on the Sea of Japan coast in Hokuriku, in places like Ishikawa and Fukui. The Ukon family was one of these shipping agencies, (it branched off with one boat in 1680). It operated nidokosen for Omi merchants along the Sea of Japan coast between Matsumae and Tsuruga or Obama in the middle of the 18th century (from the Genbun period to the Horeki period). Later on,

Chapter IV The Hull Structure and Evolution of Marukobune: A Hypothesis

the Ukon family started their own trading business as well, called kai-tsumi-akinai meaning buy-load-trade. They owned only one bezaisen in 1796. It was wrecked in 1800 and they suffered a loss.[67]

The Omi merchants and the shipping agencies worked together, and they would have been well aware of the decline of the hokkokubune in the face of the technically superior bezaisen. One can only assume the boatbuilders of Lake Biwa were aware of the building techniques of the bezaisen, since Lake Biwa was not completely isolated from the coastal areas.

The hayabune and the bezaisen are both possible sources for the development of the alterations in stem shape of the marukobune. Regardless of the source, the evolution might have required innovations in boatbuilding tools as well. Finding an historical account which gives us an understanding of the tools of the period and their changes, and comparing them to the tools we know of today, will help to advance this study.

(4) Another Element of the Bow, Heita.

Bow Planking of Marukobune

Another element of the bow is heita (Preface-Fig. 2). It is the peculiar bow planking of marukobune, consisting of narrow planks arranged vertically from the stem backward forming a slightly convex curve. The bottom ends of the heita planks are mounted to the bottom planks. The heita are made of podocarp wood and the planks are edge-fastened. The seams of the planks are covered by copper plates called akaita, which are painted with black ink and rapeseed oil, and nailed on. Another layer of copper plates called datekasugai, cover the akaita. The datekasugai are spaced evenly and secured with iron nails.

A photograph of a marukobune taken at the end of the 19th century by Edward S. Morce (1838-1925)[68] (Fig. 19) shows marukobune with a stem. Judging by the relative size of the skipper, it is a small marukobune, but has features common to medium to large marukobune, namely the stem, the bow planking (heita), and omogi on the sides of the hull. However, it does not have a mechanism for mounting washboards. Neither is it equipped with a mast gallows, called kasagi. The mast is also not visible in the photograph. It is not clear whether it was stored in the hull, or the mast gallows was not needed for such a small boat, or if it is a type of marukobune powered only by oar. Medium and large marukobune were equipped with a sculling oar, but it was used only when docking and undocking, and it was not used for propulsion.

Although it is a small marukobune, it is notable that it has omogi and heita. They are components that require time and attention to detail by the builder. The author had assumed that these components might not be incorporated in small marukobune. Instead, she supposed that smaller marukobune would have been built using techniques common to other small traditional Japanese boats, incorporating thin and long timbers running from

Fig. 19 Marukobune from the photo taken by E. S. Morce.

stem the stern.　　However, the photo taken by Morse disproved the idea.[69]

Heita in Small Marukobune

The typical bow shape of the traditional Japanese boats is linear and sharp, and such a bow shape is created efficiently and naturally by plank construction.　Conversely, building a round hull using flat planks is labor intensive.　During the marukobune reconstruction project, the shipwright, Mr. Matsui, ensured the symmetry of the port and starboard heita by inspecting the bow repeatedly, sighting along the centerline, with saying, "Adjusting the shape is difficult."

Heita was presumably intended to improve the cargo capacity of boats, by increasing the beam of a hull forward (see section (1)).　In the case of large marukobune with cargo capacities of 400 koku, when the beam of the hull is significantly expanded to augment the cargo capacity, the bow needs to be widened accordingly.　In this situation, the heita structure consisting of planks would be an efficient way to create the desired curve and width.　However, this scenario is not applicable to small marukobune, which might not need the heita structure for this purpose.　Thus, the rationale for the use of heita should have been other than simply expanding capacity.

The oldest document describing heita in marukobune is "Marukobunebune-sunpo-cho" (1785), which says that the heita structure is well-supported if the stem is long enough, clearly emphasizing the relationship between the stem and heita. There is no mention of heita, however, in regard to the round bow marukobune in "Wakansen-yo-shu".[70] Therefore, the heita type of construction could be assumed to have been introduced at the same time as the stem. Alternatively, the bow construction described as "joining to form round" in "Wakansen-yo-shu" and the mounting process of heita we know today use common techniques, so heita-style bows in marukobune possibly originated in the round-joining technique.

Another tank test with model boats proved that a marukobune without a stem is more stable than a marukobune with a stem when meeting waves ahead of the beam.[71] The bow shape was altered to include a stem, for better speed. However, it presumably resulted in the marukobune sailing more poorly to windward in the variable wind conditions common to Lake Biwa. This negative feature of the new, sharper bow shape with a stem might have been mitigated by the round heita structure.

Notes
1 Nishimura 1938.
2 Matsumoto. N, 1978, p. 41.
3 Matsumoto. H, 1978, p. 444.
4 Miyamoto, 1981.
5 Ishizuka 1960, Sakurada 1958, Ishii 1983, Ishizuka's research was based on the opinion of Sakurada. See Adachi 1997, pp. 2-6 regarding the difference of views between Sakurada and Ishii.
6 Deguchi 2001, pp. 5-8.
7 Examples include boat models excavated at the Tononishi site and the Kamitakasago. (see the excavation reports in reference).
8 Worthington 1933.
9 Deguchi 1995, pp. 150-151.
10 ibid; 1995, pp. 295-299.

Chapter IV The Hull Structure and Evolution of Marukobune: A Hypothesis

11 Akanoiwan site 2004.
12 Yokota 2004, p. 22, line 10-16.
13 Found in the 7th excavation at the Shimonaga site, Iwasaki 1997.
14 See the excavation reports of Irienaiko site. Also Yokota 2004, p. 27, Fig. 5.
15 Yokota 2004, p. 23.
16 Deguchi 2001, pp. 155-193.
17 Kobayashi 1974, p.41, line 16-17.
18 Sumida 1944, p. 82, p. 182.
19 Ishii 1983, p. 47.
20 Ibid.
21 Ishizuka 1960, pp. 268-269, Deguchi 2001, pp. 167-174.
22 Senpaku-shihousho (『船舶仕様書』)".
23 Kobayashi 1974, pp. 26-43.
24 McGrail 1987, p. 44.
25 Matsumoto 1976 a, p.7 Referred to as the source: T. Esaka.
26 Matsumoto 1954, p. 251.
27 The comparison between 51 samples from across Japan (see Matsumoto 1952) and 11 samples from Shiga Prefecture (Otsu City Museum of History (ed.) 1993, pp. 124-134) indicated the average of the boats of Shiga Prefecture was 0.59 m and the average of other regions was 0.73 m.
28 An order to transport rice crops by a boat issued by Kurano-atai, a government official controlling the government's granary, to residents ruled by the Urabe family was described on a small wooden plate found at the Nishigawara-Miyanouchi site in Chuzu Town of Yasu County. (Excavation report of Nishigawara-Morinouchi site 1987, pp. 8-17). Such plates were supposed to have been put up as signs at major traffic points. It is evidence that the basis of the lake transport was established at around that time.
29 Such as the rite in Chikubu Island, Hiyoshisanno-sai festival, and Senko-sai festival of Takebe-taisha shrine. The festival of Chikubu Island is held annually from June 10th to 15th in Chikubu Island located off Biwa Town on the northern coast of Lake Biwa. It has a history of more than 1500 years. Chikubu-jima-sairei-zu (竹生島祭礼図), a painting of the Chikubu Island festival of the 16th century, illustrates Renge-e (蓮華会), a service at Jinguji temple in Tukubusuma shrine (都久夫須麻神社), and it pictures many boats gathering at the festival in detail. Hiyoshisanno-sai (日吉山王祭) festival is one of the three major festivals of Lake Biwa and it is held at Hiyoshi-taisha shrine in Sakamoto, Otsu City. It is convened annually for one and a half months starting from the first Sunday of March through April 15th. The primary religious service using boats is "Saru-no-shinji" (申の神事), a service of the Monkey of the twelve horary signs, on April 14th. The gozabune boat carrying a portable shrine (mikoshi) sails on the lake, and an offering of Awazu is dedicated to

the Lake. Senko-sai festival (船幸祭) is the annual festival of Takebe-taisha shrine, which originated from Yamato-takeru's expedition to the eastern Japan via a sea route. It is held annually on August 17th at the Seta River which begins on the south coast of Lake Biwa and is the one river flowing out of the lake. The boat is decorated at a smaller festival on the previous evening where a large portable shrine (mikoshi) is loaded on board, and sails down the Seta River to near Nango-arai-zeki, a dam at Nango.

30　Kyoto Prefectural Tango Folk Museum (ed.) 2004
31　Literature of the Heian Period and the Kamakura Period, including "Heikemonogatari" and "Heihanki. Ishii 1983, p. 146.
32　Ministry of agriculture, forestry and fisheries 1982. The author learned of this document and the numerical characteristics of ships with the assistance of Mr. Kenichi Kohashi of Shiga Prefecture Lake Biwa Museum.
33　Mohon-katada-keizu (『模本片田景図』) (1552), reprint of Katada scenary paintings, Wakan-sen-yo-shu(『和漢船用集』) ibid., and Omi-meishozu(『近江名所図』) (around 1558-1570, and 1814), drawings of Omi scenic places.
34　Hiyoshi-sanno-saireizu-byobu (『日吉山王祭礼図屏風』).
35　Ominokuni-katata-isome-ke-monjo (documents of Isome family in Katata, Omi)(『近江国堅田居初家文書』).
36　Felix Beato arrived in Japan in around spring of 1863, and opened a commercial photo studio in the alien settlement in Yokohama in 1865.
37　Nakagawa, S. 1988, a drawing in Vol. 2. Mr. Fumitada Hidehira of Nagahama Castle Historical Museum informed the author that the drawing is a work by Giho Yamagata.
38　Otsu City Museum of History (ed.) 1999, p. 3.
39　Kitamura-Genjuro-ke-bunsho (『北村源十郎家文書』) In Shiga University Archival Museum (ed.) 1999.
40　Funayakugin-nituki-Kitamura-Genjuro-kojogaki-an (船役銀ニ付北村源十郎口上書案), notes on shipping duties written by Mr. Genjuro Kitamura.
41　Shinkurobune-namae-yuishogaki-tsuke (真黒船名前由緒書付), one of the family documents refers the history of the shinkurobune. Date unknown. ibid., p. 20.
42　Kitamura-Genjuro-ke-yuishogaki (北村源十郎家由緒書), November 1803. ibid., p. 15.
43　Makino et al. 2006.
44　Kimura Tadayuki-ke monjo (Takayuki Kimura family's document) (木村忠之家文書) "Hyaku-hiratabune-yorozu-tomecho" (百艜船万留帳). See Otsu city office (ed.) 1982, vol. 4, p. 222.
45　ibid., p. 225.
46　Kanda-jinja-monjo(『神田神社文書』) and Kosui-ezu-narabini-uraura-funakabu-oboe(『湖水絵図ならびに浦々船株覚』).

47 Otsu with 150 licenses, Shiozu with 120, Imazu with 95, Kaitsu with 86, Funaki-minamihama and Yokoehama with 75 each, and Oura with 74. (ibid., p. 223).
48 Tani-Sumio-ke-bunsho (『谷寿夫家文書』), a family history document of the port of Sakamoto in 1751.
49 Kanda-jinja-bunsho(『神田神社文書』) (Same as above, p. 226).
50 Ishii 1983, p. 65.
51 Nakagawa, S. 1988, Vol. 2 (『長濱町誌』第2巻) p. 41, line 14-16.
52 ibid., line 1.
53 ibid., line 11-12.
54 Kitamura-Genjuro-ke-bunsho (『北村源十郎家文書』), ibid., p. 11.
55 ibid., p. 14.
56 1840, Kuruma-hayabune-hokki-ni-tuki-issatu-tuzuri (『車早船発起ニ付一札綴』) ibid., p. 11. It was not used widely and its actual performance is questionable.
57 For the comprehensive introduction of Bezaisen, see Masuyama et al., 2003, Brooks 2009.
58 Ishii 1983, p. 87.
59 ibid., pp. 90-92.
60 ibid., p. 89.
61 Futanaribune boats declined and in the 19th century they were used only for transporting lumber in Enshu, now the western part of Shizuoka Prefecture.
62 A votive picture of two boats in 17th century dedicated to Enkakuji Temple in Aomori Prefecture.
63 ibid., p. 191.
64 Ishii 1995, p. 148.
65 Omi merchants are also known as Goshu-shonin (Goshu merchants).
66 In 1588 Shinsuke Tazuke and Shichiroemon Takebe arrived at Ezo. 88% of the Omi merchants that visited Matsumae and Esashi were from Hachiman, Yanagawa and Satsuma, now Hikone City. (Sanraizu Publishing (ed.) 2001).
67 Ibid., 2001, p. 112.
68 Konishi & Oka (eds.), 2005.
69 Makino 2012.
70 ibid.
71 Joint research was conducted with N. Umeda, Professor of Osaka University Graduate School, and Y. Masuyama, Professor of Kanazawa Institute of Technology in 2007. To be published.

Summary

Folklore research conducted in the Lake Biwa region, especially the marukobune reconstruction project, is of great value in shedding new light on the history of traditional boats and the relationship between people and lake in pre-modern Japan. A review of the research enables us to state with considerable confidence that the middle of 20th century was an epochal period for traditional boats. The people's relationship to Lake Biwa, and consequently to water resources, underwent enormous changes. In this era, when the household use of lake water, flowing directly to villages and houses via canals and water channels, was replaced by the easy availability of tap water, the result was a separation between the people and the lake with its waterways.

The decline of marukobune in the middle of the 20th century was a result of the changes in transportation practices on Lake Biwa, and the fact that timber supplies became scarce in the early Showa period. In particular, the large timbers essential for omogi, the unique construction feature of these boats, became difficult to obtain. It would have been possible to make omogi by assembling multiple timbers, but instead this type of boat was abandoned outright. The demand for these boats had already declined, removing any incentive to adapt to dwindling materials.

The opening of the westward sailing route, the development of the railroad system, and the introduction of new boatbuilding materials, such as steel, had negative impacts on marukobune as a vital part of life in the region. However, if lake transportation had not declined so much, an alternative way of constructing omogi might have developed in the same way marukobune bow shape adapted to demands for more speed during the early Meiji period. If marukobune's hull structure were different, and did not require specialized timbers for omogi, they might have survived locally as a cargo boat. They might have endured at least as long as the simpler tabune did. However, omogi was the essential design component, pivotal in the evolution of increased breadth and cargo capacity.

Marukobune were well adapted to the lake environment and the surrounding shores, rivers and canals. However, these vessels could not adapt quickly enough to compete with land-based mass transportation in the modern era. At the same time they conceded small-scale transportation to tabune. This is an example of the modification of traditional boats being overshadowed by cultural and social evolution. In short, change was unable to keep up with evolution. By contrast, Lake Biwa's fishing boats are an example of the aggressive introduction of new technologies and materials, and boats are still used, albeit with a vastly changed appearance.

Modernization and its affects were detailed through an examination of the traditional boats of Lake Biwa. The natural and social conditions that created marukobune and steered its evolution were also uncovered, and possible scenarios were presented to explain how its role and structure were influenced by the changes in trade, culture and the natural environment of Lake Biwa.

The traditional culture uncovered by the researchers attracted local residents previously unaware of it. A new awareness of conservation and the natural environment probably helped stimulate this interest. For Japanese in particular, the gap between modern life and the past is very great. At the same time the project allowed many older people to share their memories, in turn providing vital information to the researchers.

The research activities around marukobune and the waterways of Lake Biwa awakened an interest in the wisdom of the past. One example of this involved senior high school students. Since a high school was located close to the workshop of the boatbuilder, Mr. Matsui, it was suggested that students visit him to learn about regional history. After several months, I was surprised to see that the students visited the boatshop often, and they became quite enthusiastic about talking with Mr. Matsui, trying to learn the traditional techniques of boatbuilding and local history. Soon they started to build a wooden model boat under the boatbuilder's guidance. They even began to tell other students and children what they had learned from Matsui. An elderly boatbuilder sharing his wisdom and knowledge with young students was a powerful symbol, and made all those involved recognize the significant changes in life style with respect to water between the past and present.

References

(A)

Adachi, H., 1997 「日本の船の発達史への一試論」(Nihon no fune no hattatsushi eno ichishiron), 『海事史研究』(Journal of the History of Maritime), Vol. 54, pp. 1-13. The Japan Society of the History of Maritime. (in Japanese)

Adachi, H., 1998 『日本の船—和船編』(Nihon no fune-Wasen), The Japanese Foundation for the Promotion of Maritime Science and the Museum of Maritime Science.(in Japanese)

(B)

Brooks, D., 2003 『佐渡のたらい舟〜職人の技法』(Taraibune(Tub boats) on Sado Island, Nautical History Research), Kodo Bunka Zaidan Publishing, Tokyo. (translated into Japanese)

Brooks, D., 2009 Bezaisen, Japan's Coastal Sailing Traders, In Bennett., J. (ed.) Sailing into the Past: Learning from Replica Ships. Seaforth publishing, South Yorkshire.

(D)

Deguchi, A., 1987 「刳り船の発達諸形態の分類と地域類型－日本とその隣接地域を中心として」(The Evolutional Typology and Geographical Distribution of the Dugout Canoe), 『国立民族学博物館研究報告』(Bulletin of The National Museum of Ethnology) Vol. 12-2, pp. 449-497. National Museum of Ethnology, Osaka. (in Japanese with English abstract)

Deguchi, A., 1995 『日本と周辺アジアの伝統的船舶—その文化地理学的研究』(Nihon to shuhen Ajia no dentoteki senpaku - sono bunka chirigakuteki kenkyu), Bunken Publishing, Tokyo. (in Japanese)

Deguchi, A., 1999 「丸子船復元—再生する人・モノ・技」(The Process of Maruko-Bune Boat Construction), In Yoda, M., Makino, K. (eds.), 1999 『よ

みがえる丸子船-琵琶湖最後の伝統的木造船復元展示記録』(Report on the construction of a marukobune boat, the traditional wooden boat formerly used for transport on Lake Biwa), Research Report of the Lake Biwa Museum Vol. 13, pp. 17-52, Lake Biwa Museum, Shiga. (in Japanese)

Deguchi, A., 2001 『丸木舟』(Marukibune), Hosei University Publishing, Tokyo. (in Japanese)

(E)

Ebise, S., 2000「琵琶湖の概況-琵琶湖の基本諸元と歴史的変遷-」(Basic Element of the Lake Biwa and its Historical Transformation), In Somiya, I.(ed.) 『琵琶湖-その環境と水質形成』(Lake Biwa - its environment and the water formation), pp. 1-7. Gihodo, Tokyo. (in Japanese)

(F)

Furukawa, A., & Ohnishi, Y. (eds.), 1992 『環境イメージ論-人間環境の重層的風景』(Images of Life-Environment), Kobundo, Tokyo. (in Japanese)

(H)

Hanada, K., 1993 「西田井遺跡」(Nishitai site), In Yasu Town Board of Education (ed.) 『野洲町埋蔵文化財調査集報2』(Yasu cyo maizobunkazaicyo-sashuho 2), pp. 79-82, Yasu Town Board of Education, Shiga. (in Japanese)

Hashimoto, T., 1984 『琵琶湖の民俗誌』(Biwako no minzoku shi), Bunka Publishing Bureau, Tokyo. (in Japanese)

Hashimoto, T., 1990 『ワタリスジ談義-琵琶湖周辺の気候と民俗』(Watarisuji - The Climate and Folklore in the Lake Biwa Region). In the Society of Environment Education Around the Lake Biwa Region (ed.) 『ビワコダス・湖国の風を探る 生活と科学の接点としての気象研究の試み』(BiwakoDAS: Exploring the Wind in Lake Biwa Country), the Lake Biwa Museum Research Report Vol. 14, pp. 93-101, Lake Biwa Museum, Shiga. (in Japanese)

Hayashi, H., 2003 「佐久良川流域-渡来人関係遺跡-」(The Sakuragawa

ryuiki – Toraijin kankei iseki). In Biwako ryuiki kenkyukai (ed.), 『琵琶湖流域を読む　下』(Biwako ryuiki o yomu ge), pp. 29-34, Sanrazsu insatsu, Shiga. (in Japanese)

(I)

Ishii, K., 1983　『図説和船史話』(Zusetsu wasen shiwa), Shiseido, Tokyo. (in Japanese)

Ishii, K., 1995　『和船I』(Wasen I), Hosei University Publishing, Tokyo. (in Japanese)

Ishizuka, T., 1960　『民俗資料による刳舟の研究』(Minzoku shiryo niyoru kuribune no kenkyu), Open-Air Museum of Old Japanese Farm Houses 12. (reprinted in 1996 as 『艪と刳舟』(Tatara to kuribune), Keiyusha, Tokyo). (in Japanese)

Iwasaki, S., 1997　「下長遺跡出土の木製品について」(shimonagaiseki shutsudo no mokuseihin nitsuite), Shiga ken bunkazai dayori (『滋賀県文化財だより』) Vol. 238, Shiga Prefecture Association for Cultural Heritage. (in Japanese)

(K)

Kada, Y., & A. Furukawa (eds.), 2000　『生活再現の応用展示学的研究－博物館のエスノグラフィーとして』(Applied Study of a Life-Scene Reconstruction Exhibition - Ethnography of the Lake Biwa Museum), Research Report of the Lake Biwa Museum Vol.16, Lake Biwa Museum, Shiga. (in Japanese with English preface)

Kanazawa, K., 1761　『和漢船用集』(Wakan senyo shu) (reprinted by Sumida, S. (ed.) as Kaidai wakan senyo shu (解題『和漢船用集』), Genmatsudo-shoten, Tokyo, 1944). (in Japanese)

Kawasaki, A., 1991　『日本丸木舟の研究』(Nihon marukibune no kenkyu), Hosei University Publishing, Tokyo. (in Japanese)

Kido, M., 1992　「水辺の集落の原風景」(Mizube no shuraku no genfukei), In

Watanabe, M. (ed.), 『湖の国の歴史を読む』(Mizuumi no kuni no rekishi o yomu), pp.139-174, Sinjinbutsu-oraisha, Tokyo. (in Japanese)

Kim, Z., 1997 「韓国の水中発掘古船」(Kankoku no suichu hakkutsu kosen), 『海事史研究』(Journal of the History of Maritime), Vol. 54, pp. 40-50. The Japan Society of the History of Maritime. (in Japanese)

Kimura, Y., 1987 『図説　滋賀県の歴史』(Zusetsu shiga ken no rekishi), Kawade Shobo Shinsha, Tokyo. (in Japanese)

Kimura, Y., 1992 「湖を渡った人と物の歴史」(Mizuumi o watatta hito to mono no rekishi), In Watanabe, M. (ed.),『湖の国の歴史を読む』(Mizuumi no kuni no rekishi o yomu), pp. 219-243, Shinjinbutsu-oraisha, Tokyo. (in Japanese)

Kimura, Y., 1995 「近江琵琶湖の湖上交通の変遷」(Omi biwako no kojokotsu no hensen) In Kimura, Y. (ed.), 『近江の歴史と文化』(Omi no rekishi to bunka), pp. 3-27, Shibunkaku, Kyoto. (in Japanese)

Kira, T. (ed.) 1995 Data Book of World Environments – A Survey of the State of World Lakes – Vol. 1-3. International Lake Environment Committee Foundation, United Nations Environment Programme, Kusatu.

Kitamura, S., Tsurumaki, M., Endo S., (eds.), 1983 「集水域の水文環境・水理環境」(Shusuiiki no suibun/suiri kankyo). In Biwako henshu iinkai (ed.), 『琵琶湖　その自然と社会』(Biwako sono shizen to shakai), pp. 53-61, Sanburaito shuppan, Kyoto. (in Japanese)

Kitamura, T., 1946 『近江経済史論攷』(Omi keizai shi ronko), Taigado, Kyoto. (in Japanese)

Kobayashi, S., 1974 『諏訪湖の漁具と漁法』(Suwako no gyogu to gyoho), Shimosuwa Museum, Nagano. (in Japanese)

Konishi, S., & H. Oka (eds.), 2005 『モースの見た日本　モースコレクション（写真編）』(Property Museum of Salem. E. S. Morse Collection/Photography) 4th edition, Shogakukan.

Kyoto Prefectural Tango Folk Museum. (ed.), 2004 『丹後の船大工』(Tango no funadaiku), Kyoto Prefectural Tango Folk Museum, Kyoto. (in Japanese)

(M)

Maehata, M., Akiyama, H., Matsuda, M., Doi, M., 2000 『琵琶湖の魚と漁具・漁法』(Biwako no sakana to gyogu/gyoho), The Lake Biwa Museum, Shiga (reprint). (in Japanese)

Makino, K., 1995 「丸子船の復元－琵琶湖最後の帆走木造船－」(Marukobune no fukugen-biwako saigo no hanso mokuzosen)『(仮称) 琵琶湖博物館開設準備室ニュース瓦BAN』特別号(The Lake Biwa Museum news letter, special edition), Lake Biwa Museum, Shiga. (in Japanese)

Makino, K., 1999a 「滋賀県統計資料にみる丸子船の隻数の変遷」(Historical Changes of the number of Maruko Boats found in the Shiga Prefecture Statistical Report), In Yoda, M., & Makino, K., (eds.), 『よみがえる丸子船－琵琶湖最後の伝統的木造船復元展示記録－』(Report on the construction of a marukobune boat, the traditional wooden boat formerly used for transport on Lake Biwa), Research Report of the Lake Biwa Museum Vol. 13, pp. 87-90, Lake Biwa Museum, Shiga. (in Japanese with English summary)

Makino, K., 1999b 「船大工松井三四郎のライフヒストリー－昭和以後の木造船の消長について」(The Rise and Fall of the Wooden Boats after the Showa Period), In Yoda, M., & Makino, K., (eds.), 『よみがえる丸子船－琵琶湖最後の伝統的木造船復元展示記録－』(Report on the construction of a marukobune boat, the traditional wooden boat formerly used for transport on Lake Biwa), Research Report of the Lake Biwa Museum Vol.13, pp. 13-16, Lake Biwa Museum, Shiga. (in Japanese with English summary).

Makino, K., 1999c Why Maruko boat has disappeared? In Kawanabe, H., Coulter, J., Roosevelt, A., (eds.), Ancient Lakes; Their cultural and biological diversity, Kenobi, Belgium.

Makino, K., 2001 「明治初期の木造船の分布と特徴」(Meiji shoki no mokuzosen no bunpu to tokucho), In Lake Biwa Museum (ed.) 『琵琶湖を語る50章－知っていますかこの琵琶湖—』(Do You Know about this Lake? – 50 Chapters Talking About Lake Biwa), pp. 257-262, Sanraizu insatsu, Shiga. (in Japanese)

Makino, K., 2003 「丸子船の横断面が語ること」(What the cross section of the marukobune boat tells.-A clue to understanding the structure of a traditional wooden boat of the Lake Biwa region), 『史学』(The Historical Science) 72-3, 4, pp. 189-204, The Mita Historical Society, Keio University, Tokyo. (in Japanese with English title)

Makino, K., 2005a 「丸子船の舳先の形状について」(Bow shape of the marukobune boat, traditional boat in the Lake Biwa region.『史学』(The Historical Science) 73-2, 3, pp. 35-49, The Mita Historical Society, Keio University, Tokyo. (in Japanese with English title)

Makino, K., 2005b 「丸子船の横断面に見られる和船の原型要素について」(Some primitive factors reflected on the cross section of the marukobune boat in the Lake Biwa region), 『史学』(The Historical Science) 73-4, pp. 109-129, The Mita Historical Society, Keio University, Tokyo. (in Japanese with English title)

Makino, K., 2007a 「湿地における艜船の利用」(The Usage of Tabune in the Wetland), In The Organizing Committee of the Symposium on Wetland Restoration & Department of Lake Biwa and the Environment, Shiga Prefecture (eds.) International Symposium on Wetland Restoration Proceedings, pp. 305-312, Shiga.

Makino, K., 2007b 「琵琶湖集水域、特にエコトーンにおける艜船の利用について」 (Utilization of Hiratabune, the traditional wooden boats for fishing and agriculture in the Lake Biwa region, especially in the eco-tone zone). 『史学』(The Historical Science) 75-2, 3, pp. 117-139, The Mita Historical Society, Keio University, Tokyo. (in Japanese with English title)

Makino, K., 2012 「モースが見た丸子船－丸子船のヘイタ構造－」 (Maruko boat found in a photograph taken by Edward Morse – The Heita structure of a Marko boat). 『史学』(The Historical Science) 81-1, 2, pp. 223-236, The Mita Historical Society, Keio University, Tokyo. (in Japanese with English title).

Masuyama, Y., et al. 2003 Numerical Simulation of Wearing Maneuver of "Naniwa-maru," Reconstruction of a Japanese Sailing Trader in Early 1800's,

Journal of Kansai Society of Naval Architects, Vol. 240, pp. 77-84, Osaka University, Osaka.

Matsumoto, N., 1978 『日本民族文化の起源』(Nihon minzoku no kigen) Vol. 1-3, Kodansha, Tokyo (in Japanese).

Matsumoto, H., 1978 「アウトリッガーカヌーに関する覚書」(Autoriga kanu ni kansuru oboegaki), In Yabuuchi, Y., (ed.) 『漁撈文化人類学の基本的文献資料とその補説的研究』(Gyoro bunka jinruigaku no kihonteki bunkenshiryo to sono hosokuteki kenkyu), Kazamashobo, pp. 423-451, Tokyo. (in Japanese)

Matsusaka City, Dept. of Cultural Property & Matsusaka City, Board of Education (eds.) 2003 『全国の船形埴輪』(Zenkoku no funagata haniwa), Matsusaka City. (in Japanese)

McGrail, S., 1987 Ancient Boats in N.W.Europe – the archaeology of water transport to AD 1500, Longman Series, Longman Inc, New York.

Ministry of Agriculture, Forestry and Fisheries (ed.), 1982 『漁船検査規則』(Ghosen kensa kisoku), Tokyo. (in Japanese)

Miyahata, M., 1978 「あきないと交通路」(Akinai to kotsuro), Shiga Prefecture, Board of Education (ed.) 『びわ湖の漁労生活』(Biwako no gyoro seikatsu), pp. 249-250, Shiga prefecture, Shiga. (in Japanese)

Miyamoto, T., 1981 『日本文化の形成』(Nihon bunka no keisei), Soshiete, Tokyo. (in Japanese)

Miyaji, A., 2003 「筏流しとカットリヤナ」(Ikadanagashi to kattoriyana), In Biwako ryuiki kenkyukai (ed.), 『琵琶湖流域を読む 上』(Biwako ryuiki wo yomu jo)), pp. 33-38, Sanraizu insatsu, Shiga. (in Japanese)

Mizuno, S., 1994 「山門領近江国木津荘に関する基礎的研究」(Fundamental Study on Kozu-no-sho in Ohmi Province Governed by Sanmon), In The Lake Biwa Historical Environment Study Group (ed.) 琵琶湖の歴史環境－その変動と生活－』(Historical Geo-ecology around Lake Biwa, it's change and life), Research Report of the Lake Biwa Museum Project Office No. 2 , pp. 33-52, Lake Biwa Museum, Shiga. (in Japanese with English contents)

Mizuno, M., 1965 「滋賀県近江八幡市元水茎遺跡」(Motosuikei Site, Omihachiman City of Shiga Prefecture), 『日本考古学年報』(ARCHAEOLOGIA JAPONICA - Annual Report of the Japanese Archaeological Association) Vol. 18, Japanese Archaeological Association, Tokyo. (in Japanese)

(N)

Naisuimen Gyoro Kenkyukai (ed.), 1999 『現存漁具記録調査報告』(Genzon gyogu kiroku chosa hokoku), Research Report of the Lake Biwa Museum No. 7, Lake Biwa Museum, Shiga. (in Japanese)

Nakagawa, M., 2003 「第一次調査区出土の丸木舟の保存処理」(Daiichi-jiku shutsudo no marukibune no hozonshori). In Cultural Properties Protection Division, Shiga Prefectural Board of Education & Shiga Prefecture Cultural Properties Protection Association (eds.), 『琵琶湖北東部の湖底・湖岸遺跡』2分冊(The Underwater Archaeological Sites in the North East Region of Lake Biwa. 2 volumes), Shiga Prefectural Board of Education, Archaeological Survey Report Associated with the Lake Biwa Development Project 7, pp. 144-146, Shiga. (in Japanese)

Nakagawa, S., 1988 『近江長濱町志』(Omi Nagahama cho shi), Taizando, Shiga. (in Japanese)

Nakai, H., 1997 『近江の城－城が語る湖国の戦国史』(Omino shiro - Shiro ga kataru kokoku no sengoku shi), Sanraizu insatsu, Shiga. (in Japanese)

Nishismura, S., 1938 『先史時代及び原史時代の水上運搬具』(Senshijidai oyobi genshijidai no suijo unpangu), 人類学先史学講座(Jinruigaku senshi koza) Vol.6, Yuzankaku, Tokyo. (in Japanese)

(O)

Otsu City Museum of History (ed.), 1993 『琵琶湖の船－丸木舟から蒸気船へ－』(Biwako no fune – marukibune kara jokisen e-) , Otsu City Museum of History, Shiga. (in Japanese with English foreword)

Otsu City Office (ed.), 1982 『新修大津市史』(Shinshu Otsu City History. Revised edition), Otsu City Office, Shiga. (in Japanese)

Ogasawara, Y., 2003 「渡来系氏族と古代の開発」(Toraikei shizoku to kodai no kaihatsu). In Biwako ryuiki kenkyukai (ed.), 『琵琶湖流域を読む　下』(Biwako ryuiki wo yomu ge), pp. 174-176, Sanraizu insatsu, Shiga. (in Japanese)

Okamoto, I., 1974 「びわ湖の水の循環」(Water Circulations in Lake Biwa). In Institute of Lake Science, Shiga University (ed.), 『琵琶湖　I　自然を探る』(Lake Biwa Vol. I. Sizen wo saguru), pp. 40-96, Sankyo kagaku sensho, Tokyo. (in Japanese)

(S)

Sahara, M., & Harunari, H., 1997 『原始絵画』(Primitive Paintings), Kodansha, Tokyo. (in Japanese)

Saijo, Y., Mitamura, O., 1995 『新編　湖沼調査法』(Shinpen kosyo chosaho), Kodansha Scientific, Tokyo. (in Japanese)

Sakurada, K., 1958 「現存漁船資料による日本の船の発達史への接近の試み」(Genzon gyosen shiryo niyoru nihon no fune no hattatsushi eno sekkin no kokoromi), 『日本の民具』(Nihon no mingu), Institute for the Study of Japanese Folk Culture (ed.), Kadokawa-shoten, Tokyo. (Reprinted in 1980 as The Tradition of Fishing Life, Boats and Fishing Nets, In 『桜田勝徳集 3　漁撈生活と船・網の伝承』(Sakurada katsunori shu 3, gyoro seikatsu to fune, ami no densho), pp.252-269, Meicho-shuppan, Tokyo.) (in Japanese)

Sakurai, E., 1995 「琵琶湖の交通」(Biwako no kotsu), In Amino, Y., & Ishii, S. (eds.), 『信仰と自由に生きる』(Shinko to ziyu ni ikiru), pp. 240-281, Shinjinbutsu-orai-sha, Tokyo. (in Japanese)

Sanraizu insatsu (ed.), 2001 『近江商人と北前船』(Omi shonin to Kitamae bune), Sanraizu insatsu, Shiga. (in Japanese)

Seguchi, S., Nakagawa, H., 2003 「尾上浜遺跡・尾上遺跡」(Onoehama Site/Onoe Site), In Shiga Prefectural Board of Education & Shiga Prefecture Cultural Properties Protection Association (eds.), 『琵琶湖北東部の湖底・湖岸遺跡』2分冊(Biwako hokutobu no kotei/kogan iseki. 2 bunsatsu), Shiga Prefectural Board of Education, Archaeological Survey Report Associated with the Lake Biwa Development Project 7, pp. 27-72, Shiga. (in Japanese)

Sekiguchi, T., 1985 『風の事典』(Kaze no jiten), Hara shobo, Tokyo. (in Japanese)

Shibata, M. (ed.), 1991 『滋賀県の地名』(Shiga ken no chimei), Heibonsha, Tokyo. (in Japanese)

Shiga Prefecture (ed.) 1979 『びわ湖の漁撈生活』(Biwako no gyoro seikatsu), Shiga prefecture, Shiga. (in Japanese)

Shiga Prefecture Board of Education (ed.) 1980 『びわ湖の専業漁撈』(Biwako no sengyo gyoro), Shiga prefecture, Shiga. (in Japanese).

Shiga Prefectural Fisheries Experiment Station (ed.) 1910 『琵琶湖漁具図説』(Biwako gyogu zusetsu), Shiga prefecture, Shiga. (in Japanese).

Shiga Prefecture, Planning Coordination Division, Planning Department, (ed.) 1990 『環びわ湖放射状ネットワークの形成に向けて－滋賀県総合交通ネットワーク構想』(Kan Biwako hoshajo nettowaku no keisei ni mukete- Shigaken sogo kotsu nettowaku koso), Shiga prefenture, Shiga. (in Japanese).

Shiga Prefecture, Planning Coordination Division, Planning Department, (ed.) 1994 『平成6年度滋賀県重要施策大綱』(Heisei 6nendo Shigaken juyo shisaku taiko), Shiga prefecture, Shiga. (in Japanese)

Shiga Prefecture, Planning Coordination Division, Planning Department, (ed.) 2002 『平成14年度滋賀県重要施策大綱』(Heisei 14nendo Shigaken juyo shisaku taiko), Shiga prefecture, Shiga. (in Japanese)

Shiga Prefecture, Department of Agriculture and Forestry (ed.), 1968 『第3次滋賀県農林振興計画』(Dai3ji Shigaken norin sinko keikaku), Shiga prefecture, Shiga. (in Japanese)

Shiga Prefecture, Agricultural Administration Division, Department of Agriculture and Fisheries, (ed.) 2003 『しがの農林水産業 平成15年』(Shiga no norinsuisan gyo, heisei 15nen), Shiga prefecture, Shiga. (in Japanese)

Shiga Prefecture (ed.), 1967 『滋賀県市町村沿革史第五巻（資料編一）』(Shigaken shichoson enkakushi dai 5kan (shiryo hen 1), Shiga prefecture, Shiga. (in

Shiga Prefecture (ed.), 1962 『滋賀県物産誌』(Shiga ken bussan shi), 17 volumes, Shiga prefecture, Shiga. (in Japanese)

Shiga Prefecture, General Affairs Section, The 1st Department (ed.), 1882- 『滋賀県統計書』(Shiga ken tokei sho), Shiga prefecture, Shiga. (in Japanese)

Shiga University Archival Museum, Faculty of Economics (ed.) 1999 『江戸時代の米原湊』(Edo jidai no maihara minato), Special exhibition catalogue, Shiga University Archival Museum, Faculty of Economics, Shiga. (in Japanese)

Society of Environment Education Around the Lake Biwa Region (ed.) 『ビワコダス・湖国の風を探る　生活と科学の接点としての気象研究の試み』(BiwakoDAS: Exploring the Wind in Lake Biwa Country), the Lake Biwa Museum Research Report Vol.14, Lake Biwa Museum, Shiga. (in Japanese with English summary)

Sugie, S., 1995 「中世湖上交通と八幡航路の展開」(Chusei kojo kotsu to hachiman koro no tenkai), In Kimura, S., (ed.) 『近江の歴史と文化』(Omi no rekishi to bunka), pp. 157-171, Shibunkaku, Kyoto. (in Japanese)

Sugitachi, S., 1993 『今堅田の船大工仲間』(Imakatata no funadaiku nakama), unpublished manuscript. (in Japanese)

(Y)

Yasumoto, C., 2003 『潮を開く舟サバニ－舟大工・新城康弘の世界－』(Shio o hiraku fune, Sabani. Funadaiku Yasuhiro Shinjo no sekai), Yaima Paperbacks, Nanzansha, Okinawa. (in Japanese)

Yokota, Y., 2004 「準構造船ノート」(Jun kozo sen noto), In Shiga Prefecture Board of Education (ed.), 『財団法人滋賀県文化財保護協会紀要』(Shiga ken bunka zai hogo kyokai kiyo) No. 17, pp. 21-28, Shiga. (in Japanese)

Yoshino, M., 1985 『風の世界』(Kaze no sekai), University of Tokyo Press, Tokyo. (in Japanese)

Yoda, M., Makino, K. (eds.), 1999 『よみがえる丸子船－琵琶湖最後の伝

統的木造船復元展示記録-』)Report on the construction of a marukobune boat, the traditional wooden boat formerly used for transport on Lake Biwa), Research Report of the Lake Biwa Museum Vol. 13, Shiga. (in Japanese with English summary)

Yoda, M., 1999 『信長　船づくりの誤算-湖上交通史の再検討』(Nobunaga funezukuri no gosan- kojo kotsu shi no saikento), Sanraizu insatsu, Shiga. (in Japanese)

Yoda, M. (ed.), 2003　『企画展示『湖の船』開催記録　琵琶湖最後の船大工・松井三四郎大いに語る』(Report of the Special Exhibition "Boats on the Lake"- The Traditional Boats Builder Matsui Sanshiro and his Lifework), Research Report of the Lake Biwa Museum No. 19, Shiga. (in Japanese with English title)

Yoshida, M., 1977　『塵劫記』(Jinkoki), Iwanami Shoten, Tokyo. (In Japanese originally written in the middle of 17th century.)

(W)

Worthington, E.B., 1933 Primitive Craft of the Central African Lakes, Mariner's Mirror Vol. 19-2. pp. 146-163, The Society for Nautical Research, London.

Watanabe, A., 2000 「琵琶湖集水域の農業・農村」(Biwako shusuiiki no nogyo/noson), In Somiya, I.(ed.) 『琵琶湖-その環境と水質形成』(Lake Biwa: its environment and the water formation), pp. 33-35, Gihodo, Tokyo. (in Japanese)

Excavation and Survey Reports.

Akanoiwan site

Shiga Prefecture Board of Education & Shiga Prefecture Association for Cultural Heritage (eds.) 1987　『湖岸堤天神川水門工事に伴う埋蔵文化財発掘調査概要報告書2　赤野井湾遺跡』(Kogantei tenjingawa suimon koji ni to-

References

monau maizo bunkazai hakkutsu chosa gaiyo hokokusho 2 Akanoiwan iseki), Shiga prefecture, Shiga. (in Japanese)

Shiga Prefecture Board of Education & Shiga Prefecture Association for Cultural Heritage (eds.) 2004 『赤野井湾遺跡現地説明会資料』(Akanoiwan iseki genchi setsumeikai shiryo), Shiga prefecture, Shiga. (in Japanese)

Amagonishi site

Shiga Prefecture Board of Education & Shiga Prefecture Association for Cultural Heritage (eds.) 1998 『尼子西遺跡－犬上郡甲良町尼子出屋敷－』(Amagonishi iseki-Inukami gun Kora cho Deyashiki-), Shiga prefecture, Shiga. (in Japanese)

Chomeiji site

Shiga Prefecture Board of Education & Shiga Prefecture Association for Cultural Heritage (eds.) 1984 『長命寺湖底遺跡発掘調査概要－近江八幡市－』(Chomeiji kotei iseki hakkutsu chosa gaiyo-Omihachiman shi-), Shiga prefecture, Shiga. (in Japanese)

Dainakanokominami site

Shiga Prefecture Board of Education (ed.) 1967 『大中の湖南遺跡調査概要 滋賀県文化財調査概要 第5集』(Dainakanokominami iseki chosa gaiyo, Shiga bunkazai chosa gaiyo 5), Shiga prefecture, Shiga. (in Japanese)

Hirokawa site

Shiga Prefecture Board of Education (ed.) 1979 『広川遺跡発掘調査報告書－古代郷倉跡 滋賀県高島郡今津町－』(Hirokawa iseki hakkutsu chosa hokokusho-Kodaigokuraato Shiga ken Takashima gun, Imazu cho-), Shiga prefecture, Shiga. (in Japanese)

Irienaiko site

Maibara Town Board of Education (ed.) 1987 『米原町埋蔵文化財調査報告書VI 入江内湖発掘調査報告書－米原町立小学校新設に伴う発掘調査－』(Maibara cho maizo bunkazai chosa hokokusho VI Irienaiko hakkutsu chosa hokokusho –Maibarachoritsushogakko shinsetsu ni tomonau hakkutsu chosa-), Maibara town, Shiga. (in Japanese)

Maibara Town Board of Education (ed.) 1988 『米原町埋蔵文化財調査報告書IX　入江内湖遺跡(行司町地区)発掘調査報告書-滋賀県立文化産業交流会館建設に伴う発掘調査-』(Maibara cho maizo bunkazai chosa houkokusho IX Irienaiko iseki (Gyoji Town region) hakkutsu chosa hokokusho–Shigakenritsubunkasangyokoryukaikan kensetsu ni tomonau hakkutsu chosa), Maibara town, Shiga. (in Japanese)

Kamitakasago site

Otsu City, Board of Education (ed.) 1992 『上高砂遺跡発掘調査報告書--一般国道161号(西大津バイパス)建設に伴う』(Kamitakasago iseki hakkutsu chosa hokokusho–Ippankokudo161 (Nishiotsu baipasu) kensetsuni tomonau). 大津市埋蔵文化財調査報告書 20(Otsushi maizo bunkazai chosa houkokusho 20), Otsu City, Shiga. (in Japanese).

Otsu City, Board of Education (ed.) 1992 『埋蔵文化財包蔵地分布調査報告書3』(Maizo bunkazai hozochi bunpu chosa hokokusho 3).大津市埋蔵文化財調査報告書 22(Otsushi maizo bunkazai chosa hokokusho 22), Otsu City, Shiga. (in Japanese)

Kitamachiya site

Gokasho Town Board of Education (ed.) 1992 『五個荘町文化財調査報告24-法源寺遺跡・堂田遺跡(第6次)・八田遺跡・北町屋遺跡(第6次)、堂田遺跡(第7次)』(Gokasho cho bunkazai chosa houkoku 24-Hogenji iseki/Doda iseki (dai 6ji)/Hatta iseki/Kitamachiya iseki(dai 6ji)/Doda iseki (dai 7ji), Gokasho town, Shiga. (in Japanese)

Kurohashi site

Shiga Prefecture Board of Education & Shiga Prefecture Association for Cultural Heritage (eds.) 1995 『黒橋・八甲遺跡-近江八幡市西庄町所在-』(Kurohashi/Hakko iseki- Omihachiman shi Nichinosho cho shozai-,), Shiga, (in Japanese)

Matsubaranaiko site

Shiga Prefecture Board of Education & Shiga Prefecture Association for Cultural Heritage (eds.) 1993 『松原内湖遺跡発掘調査報告書2-彦根市松原

町-』(Matsubaranaiko site Excavation Report I – Matsubara Town, Hikone City-), Shiga. (In Japanese)

Misono site

Shiga Prefecture Board of Education & Shiga Prefecture Association for Cultural Heritage (eds.) 1975 『美園遺跡発掘調査報告』(Misono Site Excavation Report), Shiga. (in Japanese)

Motosuikei site

Mizuno, M., 1965 「滋賀県近江八幡市元水茎遺跡」(Motosuikei Site, Omihachiman City of Shiga Prefecture), 『日本考古学年報』(ARCHAEOLOGIA JAPONICA - Annual Report of the Japanese Archaeological Association) Vol. 18, Japanese Archaeological Association, Tokyo. (in Japanese).

Shiga Prefecture Board of Education (ed.) 1966 『近江八幡市元水茎町遺跡調査概要』(Summary Excavation Report of Motosuikei site in Omihachiman City), Shiga. (in Japanese)

Myorakuji Site

Shiga Prefecture Board of Education & Shiga Prefecture Association for Cultural Heritage (eds.) 1993 『妙楽寺遺跡-彦根市日夏町-県営かんがい排水事業関連遺跡発掘調査報告書-1』(Myorakuji Site Excavation Report-Hinatsu Town, Hikone City-. Survey report during the prefectural irrigation and drainage project. Vol. 1), Shiga. (in Japanese)

Ninoaze site

Moriyama City Board of Education (ed.) 1997_ 『守山市文化財調査報告書第62冊 二ノ畦遺跡・酒寺遺跡発掘調査報告書』(Ninoaze Site and Sakadera Site Excavation Report. Moriyama City Archaeological Research Report. Vol. 62), Shiga. (in Japanese)

Nishigawara-Morinouchi site

Chuzu Town Board of Education & Chuzu Town Archaeological Research Committee (eds.) 1987 『中主町文化財調査報告書第9集 西河原森ノ内遺跡第1、2次発掘調査概要』(Summary of the 1st and 2nd Excavation of Nishigawara-Morinouchi Site, Chuzu Town Archaeological Research Report Vol. 9),

Shiga. (in Japanese)

Nishitai site

Hanada, K., 1993 『野洲町埋蔵文化財調査集報2』(Nishitai site. In Yasu Town Board of Education (ed.) Yasu Town Archaeological Research Report. Vol 2), pp.79-82, Yasu Town Board of Education, Shiga. (in Japanese)

Nojiokada site

Kusatsu Board of Education (ed.) 2000 『野路岡田遺跡現地説明会資料』(Nojiokada Site onsite briefing note), Shiga. (in Japanese)

Ogawara site

Shiga Prefecture Board of Education & Shiga Prefecture Association for Cultural Heritage (eds.) 2000 『小川原遺跡3‐犬上郡甲良町小川原所在－ほ場整備関係遺跡発掘調査報告書 XXIII-5』(Ogawara site 3 (in Ogawara, Kora Town, Inukami County) Excavation Report XXIII-5 during the farm improvement project), Shiga. (in Japanese)

Onoehama site

Seguchi, S., Nakagawa, H., 2003 「尾上浜遺跡・尾上遺跡」(Onoehama Site/Onoe Site), In Shiga Prefectural Board of Education & Shiga Prefecture Cultural Properties Protection Association (eds.), 『琵琶湖北東部の湖底・湖岸遺跡』(Underwater archaeological sites in the North East Region of Lake Biwa). 2 Volumes, Shiga Prefectural Board of Education, Archaeological Survey Report Associated with the Lake Biwa Development Project 7, pp. 27-72, Shiga. (in Japanese)

Sekinotsu site

Shiga Board of Education (ed.) 2004 『大津市関津遺跡現地説明会資料』(Sekinotsu Site onsite briefing note), Shiga. (in Japanese)

Shorakuji site

Notogawa Town Board of Education (ed.) 1996 『正楽寺遺跡 能登川町埋蔵文化財調査報告書第40集－縄文後期集落の調査』(Shorakuji site. Archaeological Research Report Vol. 40. The settlements in the late Jomon Period), Shiga. (in Japanese)

Tononishi site

Notogawa Town Board of Education (ed.) 1993 『斗西遺跡（第2次調査）能登川町埋蔵文化財調査報告書第27集』(Tononishi site (2nd research). Archaeological Research Report Vol. 27), Shiga. (in Japanese)

Uchino site

Shiga Prefecture Board of Education & Shiga Prefecture Association for Cultural Heritage (eds.) 2004 『ほ場整備関係遺跡調査報告書31-2内野遺跡・塚立古墳群』(Uchino Site/Tsukadatekofungun. Survey report during the farm improvement. Vol. 31-2), Shiga. (in Japanese)

Yamamoto site

Gokasho Board of Education (ed.) 1997 『五個荘町文化財調査報告33』(Gokasho Town Archaeological Research Report. Vol. 33), Gokasho Town Board of Education. Shiga. (in Japanese)

Yokoe site

Shiga Prefecture Board of Education & Shiga Prefecture Association for Cultural Heritage (eds.) 1986 『横江遺跡発掘調査報告書I, II－滋賀県住宅供給公社による横江住宅団地建設に伴う発掘調査報告書－』(Yokoe Site Excavation Report Vol. I & II. Survey Report during the construction of the Yokoe apartment complex by Shiga Prefecture Housing Supply Corporation), Shiga. (in Japanese)

Index

A
acculturation 5, 9
acorn boat 203
Ado River 37, 52, 56, 109, 124, 170, 172
adze 89, 182
Ajiro 52, 63
akaita 81, 92, 207
Akanoi 17, 47, 123, 124, 138, 144, 150, 151, 210, 227, 228
Akanoihama 47
algae-collecting boat 164
Amagonishi site 54, 228
Amano River 58, 164
amiuchibune 17, 23, 147, 149
Amur River 181
Anap Pond 19, 190, 191
Ane River 40, 164, 167
apprentice 69, 71, 106, 108
Asazuma 33, 55, 57, 58, 60, 64
Asazuma-tsukuma 33
Aso River 37
Asuka period 51
Atsumi Peninsula 180, 184
axe 42, 51, 58, 71, 89, 198
Ayame 18, 101, 154
Azuchi-Momoyama period 16, 58, 59

B
beam 23, 24, 25, 27, 28, 42, 51, 58, 64, 69, 146, 154,157, 161, 184, 185, 188, 192,194, 195, 204, 208, 209
beam expansion 185, 188
beka 179
bevel gauge 74, 89
bezaisen 202, 203, 204, 205, 206
bilge 23, 26, 84, 185, 189
blacksmiths 89, 119
black stem boat 196
boatbuilder 25, 72, 75, 76, 77, 81, 89, 90, 92, 95, 102, 108, 109, 110, 206, 214, 215
boatbuilding 9, 13, 26, 37, 44, 68, 69, 72, 74, 89, 106, 109, 110, 202, 206, 214, 215
boat building ceremony 204
boatmen 38, 51, 109
boat production 112
boatyard 6, 20, 71, 72, 73, 106, 108
bocho-type boats 19, 23, 180, 184, 186, 192
bokushodoki 23

borakaze 39
bottom plank 24, 25, 27, 28, 70, 76, 77, 108, 176, 178, 179, 182, 184, 185, 186, 189, 204, 205, 207
bow plank 68, 70, 102, 108, 179, 195, 196, 207
bow section 47, 78, 123, 182, 195, 196
bow shape 196, 197, 198, 203, 208, 209, 213
buy-load-trade 206

C
caldera lake 31
camphor tree 44, 190, 204
canal 27, 47, 72, 107, 119, 120, 124, 136, 146, 147, 153, 198, 213, 214
capacity 19, 24, 25, 27, 69, 76, 77, 97, 107, 113, 119, 122, 123, 126, 144, 176, 178, 179, 182, 184, 185, 186, 188, 190, 192, 196, 198, 202, 204, 208, 209, 214
cargo boat 9, 23, 24, 25, 27, 60, 112, 113, 118, 144, 146, 147, 151, 157, 164, 167, 187, 201, 202, 203, 205, 214
carpenter 89, 90, 95, 102, 109, 110
carpenters square 89
casting net 134

233

catamaran 176, 190, 192
cattle boat 153, 161
caulking 20, 21, 76, 78, 79, 81, 82, 93, 94, 95, 127
chalk line 74
checkpoint 26, 51, 55, 56, 63, 199
Chikatsu-omi 51
Chikubu Island 30, 126, 167, 210
China 16, 19, 36, 37, 42, 47, 51, 170, 181, 185, 190, 191
Chinai River 170
chisel 28, 75, 90, 91, 94, 95
Chomeiji 18, 42, 125, 126, 134, 138, 157, 159, 228
Chomeiji underwater site 42
chonna 89
Chosenjinkaido 155
connected boat 192
convex plane 92
copper plate 92, 127, 207
craftsman 36, 72, 89
crater lakes 31
cross section 7, 9, 19, 76, 81, 176, 177, 181, 185, 186, 188, 221
crosswind 202
cultural changes 5
currents 15, 39, 40, 41, 198

D

Dainakanoko 42, 52, 159, 228
Dainakanokominami site 52, 228
dambebune 23, 144
dammed lake 33
dashi-no-oyakata 109
datekasugai 81, 127, 207
dejio 40
dimension 25, 72, 107, 146, 157, 176, 184, 188, 192
dip net 134
dobune 179, 188, 189
donguribune 203
dotaku 46
dotsukikanna 92
dugout 15, 19, 42, 43, 44, 46, 62, 176, 177, 179, 180, 181, 182, 183, 187, 190, 191, 192, 216

E

Echi 18, 28, 36, 51, 56, 63, 120, 121, 143, 159, 161, 162, 170
Echi County 18, 121, 161, 162
Echi River 36, 120, 121, 159, 161
Echizen 56, 170
Echizentsuruga 170
ecotone 143
Edo period 16, 24, 26, 27, 33, 37, 61, 70, 83, 102, 124, 187, 188, 195, 205
eguribune 179
engine-powered boat 134
engine-powered marukobune 121, 123
enma 95, 144, 218
Enryakuji Temple 37, 56, 58
eri 23, 154
evolution 19, 176, 179, 183, 187, 197, 206, 214
expansion 27, 130, 176, 178, 179, 181, 182, 184, 185, 186, 188, 189, 202

F

farming 7, 9, 27, 42, 44, 128, 135, 139, 140, 143, 151, 153, 154, 155, 157, 159, 161, 164, 170, 172
festival 126, 138, 192, 210, 211
fishing boat 7, 17, 18, 19, 22, 23, 26, 84, 97, 112, 113, 117, 135, 140, 143, 144, 146, 147, 150, 154, 157, 158, 159, 164, 167, 170, 172, 173, 189, 192, 193, 194, 214
flat bottomed boat 112, 198
forecasting the wind 38

fork-shaped 19, 179, 182
fork-shaped bow 179
fubuki 23, 150
Fukamizo 172
Fukui 46, 124, 179, 205
funa-kabu 198
Funaki 34, 52, 56, 109, 157, 174, 212
funayuki 138
furikake 20, 23, 70, 72, 77, 78, 80, 102, 185, 189
Fushimi 59
futanaribune 202

G

gallows 20, 24, 81, 86, 207
Gamo 18, 36, 55, 138, 143, 155, 156
Gamo County 18, 55, 138, 155, 156
Giho Yamagata 195, 199, 204, 211
gill net fishing 159, 172
glacier lake 33
Godaisankaido 36, 155
Gokasho 54, 157, 229, 232
gunwale 70
Gyeongju 190

H

Hachiman 18, 34, 59, 60, 118, 119, 120, 157, 158, 212
Hachimanbori 18, 118, 119, 157, 158
Hachirogata 179
hagasebune 187, 203
Hamaotsu 122, 123, 125, 127, 138
hamehiki 92
hammer 75, 91, 93, 94, 95
handsaw 76, 95
Hannan 56
hanzori 92
Happukaido 36, 64, 155
Harie 126, 172
Harihata River 37
Hashikake System 96
hayabune 20, 25, 26, 199, 201, 206, 212
Hayate 39
headwind 202
Heiankyo 23, 35, 55
Heian period 23, 37, 52, 55, 63
Heijokyo 35
heita 3, 24, 68, 70, 78, 102, 195, 6, 207, 208, 209, 221
heita structure 208, 209
Hesaki 24
hiarashi 39
Hideyoshi Toyotomi 58
hiei-arashi 39
Hiei Mountains 37, 39, 56, 144
Higashiazai 18, 143, 166, 167
Higashiazai County 18, 166, 167
hikimawashi 91
Hikone 17, 25, 34, 42, 58, 60, 109, 120, 121, 124, 125, 127, 136, 137, 161, 164, 174, 196, 199, 212, 230
Hikone-San-Minato 34
Hino 36, 151, 155, 157
hinoki 81
Hino River 36, 151, 155
Hira 7, 9, 15, 24, 33, 37, 39, 170, 221
Hira Mountains 37, 170
hiratabune 7, 23, 24, 64, 65, 112, 174, 198, 211
Hirokawa site 55, 228
Hiyoshi 56, 63, 210, 211
hobashira 24
hogosen 176
Hokkaido 181, 205
Hokkoku 24, 56, 164, 167, 170
hokkokubune 24, 187, 203, 204, 205, 206
Hokkokukaido 56, 164
Hokkokuwakiokan 167
Hokuriku 24, 54, 57, 167, 205
Hokurikudo 24, 54, 57, 167
hollowed out boat 179
hollowed-out log 189
hollowed-out timber 188

235

Hongo 56
Honshu 202
hot-bulb engine
　121, 123, 126, 127
hottatebashiratate-
　mono 24
hull 3, 7, 26, 44, 51, 68,
　69, 74, 77, 78, 81, 84,
　92, 97, 102, 143, 144,
　151, 172, 175, 181, 184,
　186,188, 189, 207, 208,
　213
Hyakkokubune 24

I
Iba 39, 71, 161
ibaritori 71, 89
Iga 52, 155
igushi 24, 52
Ika 18, 19, 24, 119,
　124, 125, 126, 143,
　167, 168, 173, 222
Ika County
　18, 119, 124, 125, 126,
　167, 168
ikadabune 24
ikura 24, 27, 154, 155, 161
Ikuramotooshi 24
Imahama 17, 153
Imakatata 84, 144, 226
Imazu 18, 34, 55, 58, 60,
　101, 135, 170, 172, 173,
　212, 228
injiya 39
inkline 74, 90
inland water 190

International Lake
　Environment Com-
　mittee (ILEC) 30
Inukami 18, 36, 37, 54,
　143, 161, 163, 228, 231
Inukami County 18, 54,
　161, 163, 231
Inukami River 36, 37
Irienaiko 16, 47, 49, 50,
　62, 161, 210, 228, 229
Irienaiko site 16, 47, 49,
　50, 62, 210, 228
Ise 36, 64, 155, 203
isebune 203
Ishida River 56, 170
Ishidera 161
Ishikawa 167, 179, 205
Ishiyama 52
Iso 24, 26, 65, 164, 211
Isome-ke-monjo
　24, 26, 65
itazu 27, 72, 176

J
Japanese cedar 42, 50,
　70, 181, 182, 189
Japanese cypress 64,
　70, 81
Japanese sailing boat
　117
Japanese-style
　113, 117
Japanese-style boat
　113, 117
jig 26, 205
Jintsu River 179

jio 39, 40, 64, 231
Jishimai-kechige
　-chusinjo 24, 63
joining plank 74, 75, 189
Jomon period 15, 42, 43

K
kaisen 17, 24, 25, 116,
　202
Kaitsu(kaizu) 34, 60,
　125, 170, 172, 212
kai-tsumi-akinai 206
kaji 24, 25, 64
kajitoko 24
kajitokonoana 24
kajitsuka 24
kakiita 21, 24, 70, 86, 154
Kamakura 1, 2, 56, 58,
　64, 211
Kamakura period 58
Kami 39, 209, 229
kami-kaze 39
Kamomioya shrine 55
Kamo River 146, 170
kanaorekakko 179
kanazashi 72, 89
Kanda-jinja-monjo 24,
　211
kandotatsubiki 89
Kannonji temple 59
Kansai 202, 222
Kanto 64, 202
Kanzaki County 18, 39,
　159, 160
Karasuma Peninsula
　84, 101

kasagi 20, 24, 81, 86, 207
Kasturagawa 172
kasugai 24, 76, 81, 127, 207
katabune 17, 28, 147, 150, 179
katasajiki 24
Katata 17, 26, 33, 37, 56, 59, 60, 63, 64, 69, 84, 109, 110, 135, 144, 146, 211
Katata Hills 37
Katsuno 33, 55, 56, 170
Katsunotsu 55, 56, 170
kawabune 164, 176, 179
Kawado 136
Kawamichi 167
Kawanami 167
kawarasueiwai 205
Kawarasueiwai 24
kawashimo 40
kawaya 136, 174
kazashio 40
keibiki 74, 89
kenkatashiro 25
kensakibune 25
keshiki-mi 38
keshiki-wo-miru 38
Kido River 37
kigaeshi 89
kijishi 36
Kitafunaki 19, 172, 173
Kitamachiya site 54, 229
Kitamura-Genjuro -ke-monjo 25
Kitamura-Genjuro

-ke-yuishogaki 25
Kita River 37
kiwariho 25
kobiki 25, 89, 109
kobikinoko 89
kobiro 90
kochibune 179
Kofun period 16, 37, 46, 48, 49, 51, 179, 182, 190
Koga 18, 52, 143, 155, 227
Koga County 18, 155
Koga Mountains 52, 155
koguchitsuba 75
Kohayabune 25
kohayazukuri 199
Kohoku 42
koitoami (gill net) fishing 157
Kojiki 52
kokaisen 17, 25, 116
komo 21, 25, 86
komobuki 25
komooshimune 25
Konohama 18, 63, 123, 127, 134, 153, 154
Korean Peninsula 16, 42, 46, 47, 51, 180, 181, 185, 190
Kotosanzan 25
Koura-aratamegaki 25
kozosen 176
Kozu 55, 56, 58, 63, 222
kudarijio 40
kugijime 95
kumei 180

kumibune 19, 25, 173, 192
kuranoatai 51
kuribune 176, 218
kurihangoe 170
Kurita 17, 143, 144, 147, 148
Kurita County 17, 144, 147, 148
Kurohashi site 47, 229
Kurozu 36
kuruma-hayabune 25, 199
Kusatsu 57, 64, 103, 120, 122, 123, 127, 135, 137, 139, 147, 231
kusegane 74, 89
kusunoki 190, 204
Kutsuki 37, 170, 172
Kutsukidani 170
Kyoto 11, 23, 25, 27, 37, 52, 55, 56, 57, 58, 65, 70, 101, 123, 135, 144, 146, 170, 185, 205, 211, 219, 226
Kyushu 181, 202

L

lagoon 31
Lake Biwa 1, 2, 3, 5, 6, 7, 9, 10, 12, 15, 16, 17, 22, 23, 25, 27, 30, 31, 33, 34, 35, 36, 37, 40, 42, 43, 45, 46, 47, 50, 51, 52, 55, 56, 58, 59, 61, 63, 68, 69, 81, 84, 85, 89, 96, 97,

98, 100, 101, 102, 103,
105, 106, 109, 111, 112,
118, 120, 121, 122, 123,
126, 127, 128, 130, 131,
132, 138, 140, 142, 144,
146, 147, 151, 153, 159,
161, 164, 167, 170, 174,
182, 185, 190, 191, 192,
193, 194, 195, 197, 198,
199, 201, 202, 204, 205,
206, 209, 210, 211, 213,
214, 217, 218, 220, 221,
222, 223, 224, 225, 226,
227, 231
Lake Biwa Museum 2,
   10, 12, 22, 68, 84, 85, 96,
   97, 102, 103, 118, 121,
   128, 174, 211, 217, 218,
   220, 222, 223, 226, 227
lake environment 2,
   214
Lake Hamana 180, 184
Lake Suwa 180, 184,
   189
lake transportation 33,
   51, 52, 56, 59, 101, 103,
   170, 213
launching ceremony
   83, 204
local history 215
log 26, 27, 68, 77, 80, 109,
   172, 174, 176, 178, 189
logger 89, 109
lower side planking
   70, 102
lumber surveyor 109
lumber transportation

170
lumberyard 110

M

maebiki 89
Maihara(Maibara) 16,
   34, 60, 196, 199, 228,
   229
maki 77, 78, 81, 137, 157
makihada 81
makinawa 25, 81
Makita 39
mallet 71, 81, 90, 93,
   94, 95
Mano 37, 63
Manyoshu 52, 62
marking gauge 72, 89
marubune 7, 17, 23, 65,
   116, 195
marukibune 179, 180,
   196, 218, 223
marukobune 1, 2, 3, 5,
   6, 7, 8, 9, 10, 11, 12, 15,
   16, 17, 19, 20, 21, 25, 39,
   61, 67, 68, 69, 70, 74, 76,
   77, 78, 81, 83, 84, 85, 86,
   88, 93, 96, 97, 98, 99,
   101, 102, 106, 107, 108,
   112, 113, 116, 117, 118,
   119, 120, 121, 122, 123,
   124, 125, 126, 127, 164,
   167, 175, 180, 182, 183,
   184, 185, 186, 187, 188,
   189, 190, 192, 195, 196,
   197, 198, 199, 200, 201,
   202, 204, 205, 206, 207,

208, 209, 213, 214, 217,
220, 221, 227
marukobune communi-
   cation desk 97
marukobune recon-
   struction project 7,
   10, 68, 208, 213
marukobune
   -sunpocho 25
Marukobune Tankenta
   3, 96, 97, 98, 101, 102
Marukobune
   Tankentai 96
maruko-type
   construction 112
marunomi 90
maruta 179, 180, 184,
   189, 196
marutabune 180, 184,
   196
mast 20, 69, 70, 81, 84,
   86, 106, 108, 134, 184,
   207
mast gallow 20, 81,
   86, 207
material culture 10
matsu 25
Matsubara 15, 34, 42,
   43, 47, 60, 121, 161, 229,
   230
Matsubaranaiko 15, 42,
   43, 47, 161, 229, 230
Matsubaranaiko site
   15, 42, 43, 229, 230
matsuemon weaving
   16, 83
Matsumae 205, 212

Matsumae Domain 205
Medieval period 16, 33, 36, 37, 57, 192, 199, 203
Meiji period 17, 23, 114, 125, 140, 141, 188, 213
metate 71
mikoshi 192, 210, 211
Mikumotsu 52
mikuriya 25, 52, 55, 63
Minakuchi Hill 155
minami 39, 40, 52, 119, 144, 147, 151, 167, 172, 212, 228
Minamifunaki 144, 172
Minamihama 40, 167
minamijio 40
Minamikaze 39
Minamitsuda 119
minato 33, 198, 226
Mitsuya 18, 164
miyoshi construction 202
miyoshizukuri 202
mizaraita 25
model boat 12, 16, 47, 49, 51, 97, 102, 209, 215
modernization 5, 12, 106, 129, 130, 131, 132
mogi 204
Moriyama 55, 57, 58, 64, 101, 122, 123, 124, 127, 134, 135, 137, 138, 153, 230
Moriyama River 153
morotabune 180
Motosuikei site 42, 230

Mt. Gozaisho 36
Mt. Hiei 37, 56
Mt. Ibuki 164
Mt. Iga 52
Mt. Isaki 120
Mt. Koga 52
Mt. Mikami 153
Mt. Ryozen 164
Mt. Takashima 52
Mt. Watamuki 36
multipurpose boat 172
Muromachi period 56
Muromachi periods 56
Myorakuji site 58

N

Nagahama 34, 40, 60, 119, 121, 124, 164, 195, 199, 211, 223
Nagaokakyo 35
nakajiki 25, 76
Nakanosho 157
Nakasendo 26, 36, 37, 60, 151, 155, 164
nakashio 40
Nara period 36, 51, 52, 62, 185
narrow saw 91
natural environment 5, 10, 174, 214
navigation(navigate) 30, 157, 192
nidokosen 26, 205
nigawara 192
Nihonshoki 52
Niigata 179

Niihama 135
Ninoaze 55, 230
nishi 39
Nishiazai 18, 83, 119, 124, 125, 126, 142, 167, 169
Nishiazai County 18, 167, 169
Nishigawara-Morinouchi site 51, 63, 210, 230
Nishinosho 157
Nishitai site 58, 217, 231
niwa 39, 51, 221, 222
noborijio 40
Nobunaga Oda 58
nogi 204
nokogiri 20, 76, 82
Notogawa 18, 39, 159, 161, 231, 232
nuikugi 26, 74

O

oar 26, 42, 47, 50, 62, 134, 135, 207
Obama 56, 61, 205
oban 26, 28, 138
obiro 90
Obusa 157
Ofunato 179
Oga Peninsula 179
Ogoto River 37
oibana 26, 161
oire 94
Oishi 35
Oki Island 40, 64, 120,

239

124, 143, 144, 157
okijio 40
Okinawa 21, 181, 226
Okinoshima 18, 56, 157, 158
Okishima 143, 144
Okushima 56
omeshibune 26
Omi 23, 26, 34, 36, 37, 42, 47, 63, 64, 65, 103, 118, 119, 120, 124, 125, 126, 134, 136, 137, 138, 140, 155, 157, 205, 206, 211, 212, 219, 222, 223, 224, 226, 228, 229, 230
Omihachiman 42, 47, 118, 119, 120, 125, 126, 134, 136, 137, 138, 157, 222, 228, 229, 230
Omi-meishozu 26, 211
Omi merchant 26, 157, 205, 206, 212
Ominokuni-Katata-Isome-ke-monjo 26
Omi-roku 26, 65
Omiya River 37
Omi-yochi-shiryaku 26, 65
Omizo 34, 124
omogi 3, 20, 26, 68, 70, 77, 78, 80, 97, 102, 108, 176, 185, 187, 188, 189, 196, 207, 213, 214
omogi construction 176
omogizukuri 26, 176
omoki 188, 189

Onoe 42, 167, 224, 231
Onoehama site 42, 231
Osaka 12, 55, 56, 59, 61, 62, 64, 196, 198, 205, 212, 216, 222
oshikiri-hayabune 26, 199
Otani 37
Otsu 15, 16, 33, 34, 36, 39, 40, 55, 56, 58, 59, 60, 84, 103, 109, 110, 119, 120, 121, 122, 123, 124, 125, 126, 127, 134, 135, 139, 144, 146, 150, 151, 170, 172, 174, 198, 199, 201, 202, 210, 211, 212, 223, 229
Otsu-no-miya 55
Oura 33, 34, 119, 123, 124, 167, 170, 212
Oura River 167, 170
outrigger 176, 190
Oyabu 121, 164
oyakata 109, 172

P

pine 25, 26, 44, 64, 181
plane 91, 92
plank construction 176, 208
plank drawing 72
pleasure boat 28, 112, 138
podocarp 25, 44, 68, 70, 71, 77, 185, 207
pole rest 150, 159, 161,

172
port 34, 36, 37, 47, 52, 55, 57, 60, 63, 76, 121, 123, 124, 125, 126, 164, 199, 208, 212
portable shrine 192, 210, 211

R

rabbet plane 92
raft 36, 172, 176, 185, 190
raft-assembly 172
raft-type boat 24, 190
railroad 9, 61, 118, 213
railroad system 213
repair work 108
rice wine 71
ripsaw 91
river 33, 35, 36, 37, 39, 40, 47, 52, 55, 56, 58, 60, 62, 109, 121, 122, 123, 124, 136, 137, 144, 146, 154, 155, 159, 164, 167, 170, 172, 174, 181, 211
river boat 164
ro 26
rope bitt 195
round boat 195
round hull 208
round-joining technique 209
rubrail 68, 77
ryoba 91
Ryohama-gumi 26, 205
ryosen 64, 113
Ryukyu Islands 42

Ryukyumatsu 26

S
sabani 180, 181
sade 134
sail 21, 83, 84, 97, 98, 102, 117, 120, 123, 144, 150, 157, 199, 202, 203
sailboat 112, 124
sailor 52, 84, 96, 125, 127, 198, 199
Sai River 37
saizuchi 94
Sakamoto 33, 37, 56, 57, 58, 59, 63, 64, 144, 210, 212
Sakata 18, 143, 164, 165
Sakata County 18, 164, 165
sake 56, 71, 77, 123, 204
Sakhalin 181
saki 39
sakiboso 91
sakiyari 81
Sakura basin 36
sanmon 56
Sanriku 179
Sanshiro Matsui 6, 7, 12, 20, 69, 106, 174
San-ura 34
saozashi 26, 150, 159, 161, 172
sasabune 179
sashigane 72, 89
sashiita 26, 185, 186
Satsuma 161, 212

saw 76, 78, 89, 90, 91, 95, 119, 120, 124, 137, 176, 224
sawmill 89, 110
sawyer 89
seam 20, 74, 76, 81, 82, 95, 207
Sea of Japan 9, 24, 46, 51, 55, 61, 180, 187, 188, 198, 202, 203, 204, 205
seki 61, 63, 123, 198, 199, 218, 224, 228, 229
sekibune 19, 26, 199, 200
Sekinotsu 16, 35, 36, 60, 61, 231
Sekinotsu site 16, 60, 231
semi 16, 19, 23, 26, 27, 44, 46, 47, 50, 97, 176, 178, 179, 180, 181, 182, 184, 185, 186, 187, 188, 189, 191, 192
semi-dugout boat 44
semi-planked boat 16, 19, 23, 27, 46, 47, 50, 176, 178, 179, 181, 182, 184, 185, 186, 187, 188, 189, 191, 192
Senkoyojutsu 26
Seri 36, 37, 161, 222
Seri River 36, 37
Setahashimoto 35
Seta River 34, 35, 36, 52, 60, 132, 144, 147, 211
Seto Inland Sea 61, 198, 202

seven checkpoints 56, 63
sewing nail 74
sewn boat 26, 176
sheer strake 21, 27, 70, 87, 102, 202, 204
Shichirihangoe 170
Shiga 10, 11, 15, 16, 17, 20, 22, 23, 26, 37, 64, 101, 102, 103, 113, 123, 128, 130, 140, 142, 143, 144, 145, 146, 147, 155, 170, 174, 190, 210, 211, 217, 218, 220, 221, 222, 223, 224, 225, 226, 227, 228, 229, 230, 231, 232
Shiga County 17, 144, 145
Shigaken-bussanshi 26
Shigaken-toukeisho 26
Shiga Prefecture 10, 11, 22, 23, 26, 37, 101, 102, 103, 113, 128, 130, 140, 170, 174, 210, 211, 218, 220, 221, 222, 223, 224, 225, 226, 227, 228, 229, 230, 231, 232
Shiga Prefecture Product Report 26, 140, 170
Shiga Prefecture Statistical Report 113, 140, 170, 220
Shigaraki 147, 155
Shigaraki Mountain

241

147, 155
shijimi (clam) fishing 157
shijimikakibune 17, 26, 147, 149
shiki 3, 19, 20, 23, 26, 27, 38, 63, 64, 70, 76, 77, 79, 176, 177, 179, 181, 182, 183, 184, 185, 186, 189, 190, 199, 204, 228
shiki-expanded 3, 23, 27, 176, 181, 182, 185, 186, 190
shikiita 204
Shimogasa 122, 151
Shimonaga 19, 47, 50, 178, 210
Shimonaga site 19, 47, 50, 178, 210
Shimonoseki 61, 198
Shimoogawa 172
Shimosakamoto 120
Shimotoyoura 52, 138, 157
Shimoyogo 167
shin 19, 27, 77, 102, 164, 195, 196, 200,
Shina 33, 57, 58, 63, 64, 126
Shinasahi 126
Shinkai 4th site 50
shinkurobune 27, 196, 211
Shinkurobune-namae-yuishogaki-tsuke 27, 211
shintate 204

Shinto shrine 58
shio 23, 39, 40, 47, 52, 54, 139, 167, 229
Shiozu 33, 41, 55, 56, 60, 118, 119, 124, 125, 170, 198, 212
Shiozukaido 170
shipping license 198
shipwright 6, 7, 10, 12, 16, 20, 69, 71, 75, 76, 77, 84, 89, 98, 106, 107, 108, 112, 174, 188, 195, 204, 208
shogunate 24, 198, 202
shoreline 17, 22, 27, 33, 34, 62, 130, 131, 132, 133, 153, 157, 167
shoreline compexity 27
Showa period 103, 114, 117, 118, 134, 135, 138, 213, 220
side plank 24, 26, 27, 28, 44, 50, 70, 72, 102, 144, 176, 182, 185, 186, 187, 188, 189, 196
side planking 26, 28, 70, 72, 102, 176, 182, 185, 187, 188, 189
sightseeing boat 102, 112, 113, 125, 126, 147
skin boat 176
skipper 125, 199, 207
small-scale transportation 214
social environment 10
sokoshio 40

Soma River 36, 52
soridai 92
sorikobune 180, 184
Sosuibune 17, 27, 146, 147
specialization 109
speed boat 199
staple 24, 76
steamboat 113, 116, 117, 164, 167, 170
stem 7, 19, 20, 27, 51, 77, 79, 96, 101, 102, 103, 109, 132, 164, 185, 191, 195, 196, 197, 200, 202, 204, 205, 206, 207, 208, 209, 213
stem-built boat 197
stem mounting ceremony 205
stem-raising 27, 77, 204
stem-raising ceremony 204
stern 7, 35, 47, 51, 57, 58, 70, 77, 81, 90, 95, 113, 126, 129, 147, 155, 161, 167, 172, 179, 181, 191, 208, 211, 212
stern sheer planking 70
su 27, 154,
Sugaura 33, 170
sugutsuba 75
Suikei 134
sumitsubo 74, 90
suriawase 76
surinoko 20, 76, 82
Suzuka Mountain 36,

242

155, 159, 161
Syonakanoko 159

T
tabune 3, 7, 9, 15, 17, 18, 21, 22, 23, 24, 27, 28, 65, 126, 128, 129, 130, 134, 135, 137, 138, 139, 143, 144, 147, 150, 151, 153, 154, 157, 158, 159, 161, 164, 167, 172, 173, 214, 179, 180, 184, 196, 198, 211, 213, 214, 221
Taga 157
tagane 95
Taisho period 114, 117, 118, 140
Takashima 18, 37, 52, 55, 109, 123, 124, 125, 126, 135, 142, 143, 170, 171, 228
Takashima County 18, 109, 170, 171
Takatoki 167
Takatoki River 167
Takeita 27
tamaritsuba 75
Tamba 36, 37
tana 19, 27, 35, 36, 52, 70, 102, 147, 174, 176, 177, 179, 181, 182, 183, 185, 186, 187, 188, 189, 196, 202, 203, 212, 219, 227
tana-Expanded (expansion) 27, 179,

182
tanaita 176
tanaitazukuri 27, 176
Tanakami 35, 36, 52, 147
Tanakami Mountains 35, 147
Tango 180, 192, 211, 219
Tango Peninsula 180
Tani-Sumio-ke-monjo 27
tank test 21, 196, 197, 209
tataki 94
tatebiki 91
tateita 179, 182, 195
tatsumi-kaze 39
technology 5, 181, 194
Tectonic lake 15, 27, 33
Tenjin 37
tenkozori 92
tobinoo 27, 70
Todaiji Temple 27, 52, 63
todate 27
Tohoku 5, 181
Tokaido 27, 36, 54, 57, 58, 121, 155
Tokara Islands 180, 181
Tokoeki 37
tomari 33
tombi 27, 109, 110
tomo 9, 12, 27, 28, 70, 103, 120, 146, 174, 179, 180, 192, 227, 228, 229
tomobuto 179, 192
tomodo 180
tomoikura 27

tomoita 27, 70
Tononishi site 47, 209, 232
top side planking 185, 187
tourism 10, 30, 61, 101
Toyama 179
Tozando 37, 54, 55, 57, 58
traditional boat 5, 6, 10, 11, 17, 22, 68, 89, 97, 101, 102, 103, 106, 111, 129, 213, 214, 221
traditional Japanese wooden boat 176
transition 3, 9, 61, 110, 143, 195
transom 70, 150, 179, 204, 205
transportation 7, 15, 30, 33, 36, 37, 47, 51, 52, 55, 56, 58, 59, 60, 61, 101, 103, 118, 119, 125, 128, 129, 140, 144, 146, 147, 153, 161, 164, 167, 170, 172, 187, 191, 201, 202, 213, 214
transverse expansion 27, 176, 184, 186
tsubanomi 75
Tsuchiyama 36, 155
tsukinomi 90
tsuna-kukuri 28, 195
tsura 28, 195, 204
tsura-kugi 28, 204
tsuribune 17, 28, 147, 149

Tsuruga 55, 56, 61, 170, 198, 205
twin boat 192

U
Uchino site 55, 232
ue 42
Uji River 52, 62, 63
Ukon family 205, 206
Umegahara 164
umi-kasegi 39
ura 33
ushibune 17, 28, 153, 154, 161
Uso River 36, 161

V
vertical expansion 27, 176, 179, 181, 182, 185, 186
vertical plank 195, 196
volume curve 28
volunteer 96, 98
V-shaped foredeck 26, 161

W
wagi 205
Wakan-sen-yo-shu 28, 196, 211
Wakasa 36, 170, 179
Wakasa Bay 179
waki-jiki 28, 76
Wani 33, 37, 63, 123, 124

wasen 28, 176, 202, 216, 218
washboard 157, 185, 207
water level 22, 71, 130, 131, 132
Water transportation (transport) 3, 30, 42, 46, 47, 56, 58, 59, 61, 153, 161, 164, 198, 222
weather forecasting signs 38
western-style 95, 113
westward sailing route 16, 61, 198, 202, 213
wind 15, 25, 37, 38, 39, 40, 41, 62, 81, 83, 84, 103, 121, 122, 125, 197, 198, 199, 201, 202, 209, 213
wind condition 25, 198, 209
wind speed 197

Y
ya 71, 89
Yabase 33, 56, 57, 58, 63, 64, 151
Yagawa 52
yakatabune 17, 28, 147, 150
Yamada 17, 33, 56, 57, 58, 63, 64, 120, 123, 127, 135, 143, 150, 170
Yamagata 179, 195, 199, 204, 211

Yamamoto site 54, 232
Yamanakagoe 57
yamanokami 71
yamashi 109
Yamashiro 155
Yamato 28, 51, 155, 191, 211
Yamato Imperial Court 51, 191
yana 42, 44, 63, 222
Yanamune 37
Yana River 37
Yasaka 57, 121, 164
Yasu 17, 36, 51, 52, 55, 58, 122, 134, 136, 138, 143, 144, 151, 152, 154, 155, 210, 217, 226, 231
Yasu County 17, 51, 151, 152, 210
Yasu River 36, 52, 55, 122, 155
yatoku 28, 81
yattoko 94
Yayoi period 16, 23, 42, 46, 179
yogane 93
Yogo 167
Yogo River 167
Yokaichi 157
yoki 89
yokobiki 89
Yokoehama 172, 212
Yokoe site 58, 232
Yokoyama Mountain 164
yokuzuchi 81
yosejio 40

yotsudeami 42
Yotsugawa 172
yubuki 39
yukishimaki 39
yusen 28

Z
Zeze 61, 134, 135
Zeze domain 61

《著者略歴》

牧野　久実（まきの　くみ）

神戸市出身。慶應義塾大学文学部史学科卒業、同大学院文学研究科民族学考古学専攻修士課程修了、同博士課程中退、テルアビブ大学考古学研究所留学。
国立民族学博物館外来研究員、（仮称）滋賀県立琵琶湖博物館開設準備室、滋賀県立琵琶湖博物館専門学芸員を経て、現在、鎌倉女子大学教育学部教育学科教授。
博士（史学）。専門は民族学、考古学。

《著書》

『琵琶湖の伝統的木造船の変容―丸子船を中心に―』雄山閣（単著）東京 2008 238pp.
『イスラエル考古学の魅力』ミルトス（単著）東京 2007 235pp.
『聖書の世界の考古学』A. Mazar著　リュトン　東京 2004（共訳者：杉本智俊）414pp.
『古代湖の考古学』クバプロ　東京 1999（共編者：松井 章）191pp.

2013年2月28日　初版発行　　　　　　　　　　　　　《検印省略》

（英訳版）琵琶湖の伝統的木造船の変容―丸子船を中心に―
"Marukobune", the traditi

onal sailing boats in the Lake Biwa region, Japan.

著　者	牧野　久実
発行者	宮田哲男
発行所	株式会社　雄山閣

　　　　〒102-0071　東京都千代田区富士見2-6-9
　　　　ＴＥＬ　03-3262-3231（代）／ＦＡＸ　03-3262-6938
　　　　ＵＲＬ　http://www.yuzankaku.co.jp
　　　　e-mail　info@yuzankaku.co.jp
　　　　振替　00130-5-1685

印　刷　ティーケー出版印刷
製　本　協栄製本

Ⓒ Kumi Makino 2013 Printed in Japan　　　　　　　ISBN978-4-639-02262-6 C3021
法律で定められた場合を除き、本書からの無断のコピーを禁じます。